Islam through Objects

BLOOMSBURY STUDIES IN MATERIAL RELIGION

Bloomsbury Studies in Material Religion is the first book series dedicated exclusively to studies in material religion. Within the field of lived religion, the series is concerned with the material things with which people do religion, and how these things—objects, buildings, landscapes—relate to people, their bodies, clothes, food, actions, thoughts and emotions. The series engages and advances theories in "sensuous" and "experiential" religion, as well as informing museum practices and influencing wider cultural understandings with relation to religious objects and performances. Books in the series are at the cutting edge of debates as well as developments in fields including religious studies, anthropology, museum studies, art history, and material culture studies.

Bloomsbury Studies in Material Religion

Christianity and Belonging in Shimla, North India, Jonathan Miles-Watson
Christianity and the Limits of Materiality, edited by Minna Opas and Anna Haapalainen
Figurations and Sensations of the Unseen in Judaism, Christianity and Islam, edited by Birgit Meyer and Terje Stordalen
Food, Festival and Religion, Francesca Ciancimino Howell
Material Devotion in a South Indian Poetic World, Leah Elizabeth Comeau
Qur'anic Matters, Natalia K. Suit
The Religious Heritage Complex, edited by Cyril Isnart and Nathalie Cerezales
Museums of World Religions, Charles D. Orzech

BLOOMSBURY STUDIES IN MATERIAL RELIGION

Islam through Objects

EDITED BY ANNA BIGELOW

BLOOMSBURY ACADEMIC
LONDON • NEW YORK • OXFORD • NEW DELHI • SYDNEY

BLOOMSBURY ACADEMIC
Bloomsbury Publishing Plc
50 Bedford Square, London, WC1B 3DP, UK
1385 Broadway, New York, NY 10018, USA
29 Earlsfort Terrace, Dublin 2, Ireland

BLOOMSBURY, BLOOMSBURY ACADEMIC and the Diana logo are trademarks of Bloomsbury Publishing Plc

First published in Great Britain 2021

Cover design: Ben Anslow
Cover image: Tijani *tasbih* © C. Ryan Perkins (2020)

A catalogue record for this book is available from the British Library.

Library of Congress Cataloging-in-Publication Data
Names: Bigelow, Anna, editor.
Title: Islam through objects / edited by Anna Bigelow.
Description: 1. | New York : Bloomsbury Academic, 2021. | Includes bibliographical references and index.
Identifiers: LCCN 2021000714 (print) | LCCN 2021000715 (ebook) | ISBN 9781350138308 (paperback) | ISBN 9781350132818 (hardback) | ISBN 9781350132825 (pdf) | ISBN 9781350132832 (epub)
Subjects: LCSH: Islamic civilization. | Material culture—Religious aspects—Islam. | Material culture—Islamic countries.
Classification: LCC DS36.855 .I78 2021 (print) | LCC DS36.855 (ebook) | DDC 306.6/97--dc23
LC record available at https://lccn.loc.gov/2021000714
LC ebook record available at https://lccn.loc.gov/2021000715

ISBN: HB: 978-1-3501-3281-8
PB: 978-1-3501-3830-8
ePDF: 978-1-3501-3282-5
eBook: 978-1-3501-3283-2

Series: Bloomsbury Studies in Material Religion

Typeset by RefineCatch Limited, Bungay, Suffolk
Printed and bound in India

To find out more about our authors and books visit www.bloomsbury.com and sign up for our newsletters

CONTENTS

List of Figures and Plates vii
Acknowledgments xiii

Introduction: Thinking with Islamic Things
Anna Bigelow 1

PART ONE Tracing Images 15

1 Clothes of Righteousness: The MGT Uniform in the Twentieth Century *Kayla Renée Wheeler* 17

2 The Masonic Muhammad: Modern Franco-Iranian Visual Encounters in Prophetic Iconography *Christiane Gruber* 31

3 Repetition and Relics: Tracing the Lives of Muhammad's Sandal *Richard McGregor* 49

PART TWO Identifying Objects 65

4 "The Greatest and Only Flag Known:" The Lapel Pin in American Islam *Michael Muhammad Knight* 67

5 *Tasbih* in West African Islamic History: Spirituality, Aesthetic, Politics, and Identity *Ousman Murzik Kobo* 81

6 Caps, Heads, and Hearts *Scott Kugle* 95

PART THREE Objects in Practice 109

7 What Comes to Light When a Lamp is Lit in Bektashi Tradition *Mark Soileau* 111

8 The Agency of the Material *Taviz* (Amulet) in a South Indian Healing Room *Joyce Burkhalter Flueckiger* 127

9 The Life of a Tablet *Aomar Boum* 143

PART FOUR Circulatory Systems 159

10 Coins and Fish: Sovereignty, Economy, and Religion in the Islamicate Indian Ocean *Roxani Eleni Margariti* 161

11 The Aljibe del Rey in Granada *D. Fairchild Ruggles* 173

12 Zamzam Water: Environmentality and Decolonizing Material Islam *Anna M. Gade* 189

Notes on Contributors 205
Notes 209
Bibliography 219
Index 241

FIGURES AND PLATES

Cover: Tijani *tasbih*. Photo by C. Ryan Perkins

Figures

1.1 Ethel Sharrieff, Chicago, Illinois, 1963 by Gordon Parks. Courtesy of and copyright The Gordon Parks Foundation. 16
1.2 Temple No. 2 Clothing Store advertisement in *Muhammad Speaks* from August 1966 (photo by author). 26
2.1 The Prophet Muhammad in his youth, poster on paper, painting signed by Fath ʻAli, printed by Matbuʻat-i Shemrani, Tehran, Iran, *c.*1940–60. Collection of Elizabeth Puin (J-2). 33
2.2 Opening page of the ʻAli Khan Vali photographic album, which includes icons of the Young Muhammad (at top), ʻAli, Hasan, and Husayn, Tehran, Iran, 1879–1900. Harvard University, Fine Arts Library, Special Collections, AKP111. 34
2.3 Icon depicting the Prophet Muhammad (at top), *ahl al-bayt* (middle), and Nasir al-Din and members of the Qajar elite, 1304/1889. Bunyad Museum, Tehran. 37
2.4 *Agá* (Turkish Gentleman), in Frederick Calvert, *Eastern Costume*, Engraved from the Collection of Lord Baltimore, after designs by Francis Smith, (London: 1768). The Edwin Binney Third Collection of Orientalist Prints, Fine Arts Library, Harvard University, AKP287.235. 40
2.5 Depiction of Favart's comedy entitled *Soliman II ou les trois Sultanes*, illustration made by Sainfal, engraved by Mauduit, and published by Boulard, Paris, 1825. Bibliothèque nationale de France, Estampes et photographie, PET FOL-EF-266. 41
2.6 Ottoman standards and banners, in Antoine Laurent Castellan, *Moeurs, usages, costumes des Othomans, et abrégé de leur histoire*, Paris: Nepveu, 1812, vol. 4, plate E, between pages 234 and 235. Edwin Binney

	Third Collection of Orientalist Prints, Special Collections, Fine Arts Library, Harvard University, AKP287.235.	42
3.1	Tracing of the Prophet's Sandal from al-Maqqari, *Fath al-Muta'al*. Al-Azhar University Library, manuscripts section (Al-Shawam, *raqam khass* 5450).	50
3.2	Tracing of the Prophet's Sandal from al-Habbal's tracing in al-Jamal, *Al-Minah al-Ilahiyya bi-sharh Dala'il al-khayrat*. Ann Arbor, University of Michigan, Special Collections Library (Isl. Ms. 526).	56
3.3	Tracing of the Prophet's Sandal from al-Maqqari, *Fath al-Muta'al*. Staatsbibliothek zu Berlin -Preußischer Kulturbesitz (Hs. Or. 10653).	57
3.4	Tracing of the Prophet's Sandal from al-Maqqari, *Fath al-Muta'al*. Al-Azhar University Library, manuscripts section (Al-Shawam, *raqam khass* 5883).	58
3.5	Tracing of the Prophet's Sandal from al-Maqqari, *Fath al-Muta'al*. Al-Azhar University Library, manuscripts section (Al-Shawam, *raqam khass* 5883).	59
3.6	Tracing of the Prophet's Sandal from al-Maqqari, *Fath al-Muta'al*. Al-Azhar University Library, manuscripts section (Al-Shawam, *raqam khass* 5450).	60
3.7	Tracing of the Prophet's Sandal from al-Maqqari, *Fath al-Muta'al*. Al-Azhar University Library, manuscripts section (Al-Shawam, *raqam khass* 5450).	61
3.8	Tracing of the Prophet's Sandal from al-Maqqari, *Fath al-Muta'al*. Al-Azhar University Library, manuscripts section (Al-Maghariba, *raqam khass* 6299).	63
4.1	Nation of Islam lapel pin. Collection of Michael Muhammad Knight (photo by Anna Bigelow).	73
4.2	Allah, the former Clarence 13X, lapel pin. Collection of Michael Muhammad Knight (photo by Anna Bigelow).	78
5.1	Praying with *tasbih*. Photo by author.	92
6.1	The author's Sufi teacher, Pir Rasheed Kaleemi, wears a white four-cornered *kulah* while praying over the tomb of Amir Hasan Sijzi in Khuldabad, Maharashtra, in 2008 (photo by author).	104
6.2	Man in meditation while listening to Qawwali songs at the Dargah of Nizam al-Din Awliya in Delhi, wearing a conical *kulah* (photo by Adeel Amjad Ghaznavi).	106
6.3	A boy prays over the cloth-covered tomb of Pir Rasheed Kaleemi (died 2013) in Hyderabad, with a baseball hat turned backwards so that he can prostrate toward the tomb (photo by Mohammed Mubeen).	106
7.1	Taht-ı Muhammed, Hacıbektaş, Turkey (photo by author).	112
7.2	Taht-ı Muhammed, Manisa, Turkey (photo by author).	121

8.1 *Taviz* canisters (photo by author). 128
8.2 Child's *taviz* wrapped in cotton cloth, 2018 (photo by author). 132
8.3 Lateefa writing *falita* and sheet of *abjad ka phal* calculations, 2018 (photo by author). 134
8.4 Akber and Lateefa at healing table, 2007 (photo by author). 136
8.5 Fish shaped *taviz* (photo by author). 137
9.1 The author in conversation with the Shaykh of the local Qur'anic school, al-Baraka village, Tata Province (photo by author). 145
9.2 An informant and a descendant of a generation of slaves from Senegal, Akka (photo by author). 148
9.3 Zawiya M'Ghimima (photo by author). 150
9.4 Imam of the local mosque of Tagadirt, Akka (photo by author). 156
10.1 Dirham with the two swimming-fish motif, struck in Aden in the name of sultan 'Ali al-Mujahid, 736AH/1335–1336CE. New York, American Numismatic Society, 1998.22.39. 164
10.2 Dirham with single fish, struck in Aden in the name of al-Afdal al-'Abbas, 770AH/1368–1369CE. New York, American Numismatic Society, 1998.22.59. 164
10.3 Dirham with two swimming-fish motif, struck in Aden in the name of al-Ashraf, 791AH/1389CE. Note the difference with al-Mujahid's issues, Fig. 10.1. Copenhagen, The David Collection, DK C268. Photography by Pernille Klemp. 165
10.4 Exceptional dirham struck in Zabid featuring wreath of tiny fish. Collection of the author. Photography courtesy of Steven Album Rare Coins. 165
11.1 Aljibe del Rey (photo by author). 174
11.2 Model (from the Alhambra) showing site topography and rivers (photo by author). 177
11.3 The Acequia de Aynadamar (photo by Javier Martin, public domain). 177
11.4 Map of Granada, drawn by Ambrosio de Vico, engraved in 1795 by Felix Prieto (public domain). 178
11.5 Aqueduct connecting the Generalife to the Alhambra (image credit: AdriPozuelo, public domain). 180
11.6 San José minaret and aljibe opening (on the lower left) (photo by author). 183
11.7 Courtyard in the Carmen del Ajibe del Rey (photo by Constantinos Raptis). 185
11.8 Aljibe del Rey, cistern interior (photo credit: Constantinos Raptis). 186

11.9 Aqueduct linking the Carmen del Aljibe del Rey (on the right) to the Dar al-Horra (the rear wall of which is on the left) (image by author). 186
11.10 Interior face of the Aljibe del Rey (photo by author). 187
12.1 Vial of *zamzam* water. Collection of the author (photo by C. Ryan Perkins). 190

Plates

1 Ultrasuede and feather outfit (center) designed by Carmen Muhammad in 2017 on display from the Contemporary Muslim Fashions exhibit at the Cooper Hewitt Smithsonian Design Museum, New York City (photo by author).
2 Iranian postcard of the "Young Muhammad," purchased in Tehran by author in 2001.
3 The Prophet Muhammad in his youth, oil painting on canvas (*parda*), Iran, *c.*1900–1950. Private collection, Flint, Michigan.
4 "Great Men" Carpet, Kirman, 1900–1930. World Cultures Museum, Amsterdam, 6407–1.
5 "Great Men" Carpet, Kirman, 1918. Private collection, Michigan.
6 Detail of Plate 5 showing the Prophet Muhammad labeled with the number 18, "Great Men" Carpet, Kirman, 1918. Private collection, Michigan.
7 "Great Men" Carpet, Kirman, *c.*1900–1920, workshop of Milani Kirmani. From Sakhai 1997, 78.
8 "Tableau des Principaux Grands Hommes," printed by Maison Basset, Paris, *c.*1850–80. Musée National de l'Education, Rouen, France.
9 Detail of "Tableau des Principaux Grands Hommes," printed by Maison Basset, Paris, *c.*1850–80. Musée National de l'Education, Rouen, France.
10 Tracing of the Prophet's Sandal from *Hadhihi sifa timthal na'l al-Nabi* copied by Ahmad ibn Muhammad al-Qadiri. The National Library of Israel (Ms. Yah. Ar. 353).
11 Tracing of the Prophet's Sandal from al-Maqqari, *Fath al-Muta'al*. Staatsbibliothek zu Berlin -Preußischer Kulturbesitz (Hs. Or. 10653).
12 Tracing of the Prophet's Sandal from al-Maqqari, *Fath al-Muta'al*. Al-Azhar University Library, manuscripts section (Al-Maghariba, *raqam khass* 6299).
13 Tracing of the Prophet's Sandal from al-Maqqari, *Fath al-Muta'al*. Al-Azhar University Library, manuscripts section (Al-Maghariba, *raqam khass* 6299).

14 A sample of *tasbih* (*misbah*) (photo by C. Ryan Perkins).
15 A *tasbih* showing the extra bead added to deceive the French (photo by C. Ryan Perkins).
16 Followers of Shaykh Abdullai Maikano wearing their *tasbih*. This style of wear is comparable to the Hamawi followers of Shaykh Boubacar, although there is no connection between the two Tijaniyya groups (photo by author).
17 Chishti cap given to the author at initiation in Hyderabad (photo by author).
18 An elder Khadim (hereditary custodian) of the Dargah of Nizam al-Din Awliya in Delhi, wearing a white *kulah* cap wound with an ochre orange turban cloth, presides over the Qawwali performance at the Urs of Amir Khusro in 2018 (photo by Isaac Foster Mirza).
19 Members of the Chishti Order, followers of the prominent modern Sufi leader, Khwaja Hasan Sani Nizami (died 2015), wear a rounded *kulah* of marigold yellow, as they listen to Qawwali at the Khanqah of Nizam al-Din Awliya, located behind the tomb of Mughal Emperor Humayun, where Bahadur Shah Zafar sought refuge from British conquest (photo by Isaac Foster Mirza).
20 Young men listening to Qawwali during the Urs of Amir Khusro in Delhi sport a variety of caps that are sewn, embroidered or crocheted, including one (front center) with 786 written with sequins and one (back center) with a handkerchief tied as a cap (photo by Isaac Foster Mirza).
21 Men walk in procession to the major Chishti Dargah in the Deccan, that of Banda Nawaz Gisu Daraz at Gulbarga, carrying baskets of flowers on their heads (photo by author).
22 Amma blessing patient with *dua* (prayer), 1991 (photo by author).
23 *Taviz* tied to Hindu woman's wedding pendant (*tali*) (photo by author).
24 Qur'anic tablet exhibited at Abdellah Guennoun Cultural Building in Casablanca in July 2019 (photo courtesy of Nouria Riyadi).
25 Quranic school of al-Baraka village (photo by author).
26 A collection of unused tablets in Akka (photo by author).
27 Tray depicting full zodiac, made in Mamluk Egypt for the Rasulid sultan al-Mu'ayyad Da'ūd b. Yūsuf (696AH/1296CE–721AH/1321CE. New York, Metropolitan Museum of Art, 91.1.605.

28 The Patio de la Acequia, Generalife Palace, Granada (photo by author).

29 The Alhambra and Generalife, with snow-capped mountains in the distance (photo by author).

30 Diagram of the Acequia de Aynadamar's water flow (image credit: Archivo Histórico de la Facultad de Teología).

31 Map showing the route and source of the Acequia de Axares, Acequia Romayla, and Acequia Real (image credit: Dennis & Ruggles, after Garcia-Pulido).

32 Water diverter in Timimun oasis, Algeria (photo credit: Godong / Bridgeman Images).

33 Elevation schematic of Meccan aquifer (image by author with acknowledgment to Dongeng Geologi).

ACKNOWLEDGMENTS

Islam through Objects was greatly facilitated by a workshop from December 6–8, 2019 at Stanford University sponsored by the Abbasi Program in Islamic Studies with funding from the Department of Religious Studies, the Center for South Asia, the Office of the Dean of the Humanities, the Department of Anthropology, and the Department of Art History. We are so grateful for the support and the hospitality. In organizing this event, Zack al-Witri (Associate Director of the Abbasi Program) and Colin Hamill (Abbasi Program Coordinator) were professional and meticulous. The workshop was also fortunate to have two respondents to provide critical feedback and additional camaraderie – David Morgan and Kambiz GhaneaBassiri. Through the process of editing and compiling the manuscript many people have offered advice, pushback, insights, scrutiny, and support – Zack al-Witri, Aomar Boum, Kambiz GhaneaBassiri, Christy Gruber, Thomas Blom Hansen, Colin Hamill, jem Jebbia, Scott Kugle, Lynn Meskell, C. Ryan Perkins, Rob Rozehnal, and Omid Safi. Jem also worked on the index and further editing with an excellent eye for detail.

We are especially grateful to our reviewers who went through every page of the book and gave us thoughtful and encouraging feedback. At Bloomsbury, we thank the editorial team of the series on Material Religion – Birgit Meyer, David Morgan, Crispin Paine, S. Brent Plate, Katja Rakow, and especially Amy Whitehead – for trusting in the volume. In particular, Whitehead reviewed the entire volume giving comments on every chapter, which was invaluable. Our editor Lalle Pursglove was enthusiastic about the project from the beginning and has been a wonderful interlocutor. We also thank the entire Bloomsbury team including Lily McMahon, Camilla Erskine, Sophie Beardsworth, Merv Honeywood at RefineCatch, and the designers for all of their hard work in bringing this compilation to fruition.

Introduction: Thinking with Islamic Things

Anna Bigelow

> *Is there an inanimate object* (jamad) *which does not possess rational speech* (nutq)*, a plant which has not realized the magnification of its Creator, an animal which does not attest through its state, or a human being not connected to his Lord? That would be impossible.*
>
> Ibn 'Arabi, *Futuhat Al Makkiyya*[1]

What makes an object Islamic? For Ibn 'Arabi (d. 1240), one of the most subtle, if also idiosyncratic, thinkers of his own or any time, the first answer is that everything is Islamic, endowed by the creator God with an innate awareness of its divine createdness (*fitra*). The whole manifest universe is a sign (*aya*) of God's creative power and all things—sentient and insentient—exist in a state of praise and worship by their very nature. Ibn 'Arabi also suggests that all objects possess a form of speech, drawing on the Qur'an for evidence:

> Hence every possible thing in existence must glorify God with a tongue that is not understood and a dialect that not everyone comprehends. But the people of unveiling hear it, and the faithful accept it in faith and worship, for God says, "There is nothing that does not glorify Him in praise, but you do not understand their glorification. Surely He is Clement, Concealing" (17:44)
>
> ibid.: 246

This highly suggestive passage claims that all things possess forms of communication, but not all humans are attuned to their frequencies.

Though Ibn ʻArabi's is just one of many voices that make up Muslim engagements with the material world, some of his concepts and queries anticipate directions that the study of material religion is taking centuries later. Each of the Islamic objects engaged in this collection offers its own theory of materiality in ways both specific to their Islamic contexts and general in terms of culturally embedded materialities. As we will see in the following chapters, the sandal tracing of Ibn ʻAsakir, the lapel pins of the Nation of Islam, the Bektashi lamp, the carpets of Kirman and Tabriz, the tilted cap of Amir Khusro, a vial of *zamzam* water, the garments of Ethel Sharieff, the king's well in Granada, Shaykh Salma's Tijani prayer beads, Rasulid fish coins, Amma's amulets, and Bakki's wooden Qur'an tablet are all expressions of Muslim materiality and enable their own interpretive interventions. In widening the scope of material religion and Islamic studies, the goal of this volume is to refine our senses and our explicit and implicit theoretical models and open up what constitutes the material world and what constitutes Islamic materiality. In so doing, we bring a range of disciplinary models and methodologies to the project of understanding Islam through objects.

Objects as orientations

Each chapter takes an object's-eye view—beginning from a thing, an item, an artifact, a material production or reproduction—as a point of entrance into a particular world of Islam. In so doing this volume provides not one but many answers to how object-oriented analyses help us recognize the complex webs of making, use, meaning, and value that intersect through certain things, places, and times. The Islamic things engaged by the authors in this volume "are allowed to dictate the terms of their own analysis," to varying degrees, but in all cases the objects themselves are seen as shaping the worlds in which they are located (Henare, Holbraad, and Wastell 2006: 4). Rather than approaching religious objects solely or primarily as expressions of theologies, the present volume collects genealogies of particular objects to illuminate diverse Islamic subcultures. Embracing the power of the particular, each contribution is the story of an object that shapes and is shaped by the world it inhabits on multiple levels, from the personal to the political, the social to the spiritual, the commodified to the aestheticized. These Islamic objects are not necessarily, or ever only, materialized theologies. Rather, taken together, they demonstrate how Islamic objects help us to understand material religion in general and how Islamic epistemes help us understand the things that permeate and activate our worlds.

This project considers the ways in which objects can be understood as being Muslim or Islamic, and how various orientations within Islam inhabit material cultures in specific ways. Many studies have established that Islam's reputation for iconophobia and a categorical antipathy to most forms of material mediation is overblown (Elias 2012; Flood 2019; Gruber 2019; Gruber and Haugbolle 2014; Meyer and Stordalen 2019). But more work remains to be done to situate somatic and object-oriented approaches within Islamic Studies, and this volume is part of that effort. Art and architectural historians in the field have long explored objects and spaces, but they tend to involve more formal analysis and privilege elite and monumental works and original usage or purpose, leaving room for socially and politically embedded studies of Islamic objects of all varieties and provenance (Flood 2006: 146). In a similar way, Islamic Studies has tended to weigh textual studies and classical formations more heavily in the balance of scholarship and attention, approaches that will ideally be complemented by expansion into the material cultures that permeate the full range of Muslim life. Multi-sited interdisciplinarity is required for this endeavor.

The chapters in this volume do not reject texts and theologies as critical components in the study of Islamic materialities. Rather, they investigate how the production, circulation, and deployment of things comprise key elements of complex assemblages that resist any simple equivalence between an Islamic concept or principle and a material manifestation. The objects considered here intersect between religions, economies, environments, and politics shaped by multiple formations of theological authenticity. Thus, these objects are productive sites in many ways. Some reveal histories that slither through shifting cosmopolitan milieux, as in the case of Christiane Gruber's study of the figure of the Masonic Muhammad that unfolds like a detective story. Others work across religious boundaries as vectors of distributive agency, providing healing and protection, as in Joyce Flueckiger's study of amulets in India. Some mark belonging in particular communities or groups, such as the Chishti Sufi cap discussed by Scott Kugle. By comparison, the fourteenth-century Rasulid fish coins examined by Roxani Margariti cross social, political, and religious boundaries, enabling questions of use, meaning, and sovereignty. Each of these items communicates identity within and between cultural networks, as well as produce disciplined subjects through proper deployment and ideal comportment engendered by their material properties. All of these objects are more than direct expressions of theological principles, but none exist in worlds uninformed by multiple ways of imagining the relationship between the divine and material planes. Indeed, in their passages between mundane worlds, the circulation of objects such as the Rasulid coins are, what Nile Green calls, "leaks in the hull of historical models characterized by the drawing of impermeable cultural boundaries." (Green 2006: 66)

Authorizing discourses: texts and talks

The interplay of human perception and material properties is partly, though by no means exclusively, informed by religious norms and expectations as expressed in the many Islamic texts that address the nature and purpose of the material world. In both the Qur'an and Hadith (records of Muhammad's speech and actions) the phenomenal world is often rendered as an arena for contemplation and a proving ground in which human effort is exerted to respond properly to the revelation's ethical and spiritual guidance. The Qur'an's audience is repeatedly enjoined to observe the world around—its harmony and order, its bounty and beauty, its wonders and familiarities—and to recognize therein evidence not only of God's existence but of God's very nature.

> Consider the sun and its radiant brightness, and the moon as it reflects the sun! Consider the day as it reveals the world, and the night as it veils it darkly! Consider the sky and its wondrous make, and the earth and all its expanse! Consider the human self, and how it is formed in accordance with what it is meant to be, and how it is imbued with moral failings as well as with consciousness of God!
>
> 91:1–8[2]

The unifying principle of *tawhid* (divine unity) is conceptualized as manifest through created, phenomenal, material, and immaterial things. As participants in this creation, humans must endeavor to engage deeply and appropriately with the world while maintaining an abiding awareness of its fleeting temporality. Though not all of creation is aesthetically or morally appealing, the Qur'an reminds humanity that beauty is not only part of the divine plan and evidence of divine sovereignty, but it also presents, at least in part, an opportunity for moral self-cultivation. "Behold, We have willed that all beauty (*zinat*) on earth be a means by which We put men to a test, [showing] which of them are best in conduct; and verily, [in time] We shall reduce all that is on it to barren dust!" (18:7–8) How one responds to appealing things and environments is an opportunity to practice good conduct (*akhlaq*) and beautiful behavior (*adab*), and to manifest one's perception and insight through proper responses to the beautiful. Though beauty may be ephemeral, in a frequently cited hadith from the Sahih Muslim, a canonical Sunni collection, the Prophet says that "God is beautiful (*jamil*) and loves beauty (*al jamal*). Arrogance means ridiculing and rejecting the Truth and despising people."[3] In context, the statement is a subtle teaching on the difference between arrogance and worldliness, and the legitimate appreciation of beauty as a divine attribute and as part of a divine creation.

The notion of human interactions with the material world as proving grounds for morality, ethics, and upright living, is also sustained in Islamic cultures in which the most authoritative discourses are not, or not only, the Qur'an and Hadith. The written and oral teachings of charismatic leaders and exemplars populate every place and time in which Islam has found a home. For example, one of the defining characteristics of the USA based

Nation of Islam (NOI) movement is the emphasis on proper bodily comportment as spiritual and material entrainment. In both Michael Muhammad Knight and Kayla Renée Wheeler's contributions we see outward signs of belonging—lapel pins and uniform clothing—as both markers and makers of ideal conduct and self-discipline, even as these teachings are in constant negotiation in the practice of the members. This is made clear in the words of Elijah Muhammad, the NOI founder, as quoted by Wheeler, wherein he enjoins cleanliness, minimalism, and self-respect as part of becoming "fit members of any decent society of nations." (Chapter One: 23) The women who designed, made, wore, and modified the uniform in Wheeler's chapter, and the NOI and Five Percent wearers of the lapel pins in Knight's, are all engaged with the interpretive tradition of their communities through sartorial and adornment practices. The cap denoting discipleship in Kugle's discussion of the symbolic, historic, and personal significance of the Chishti custom of investiture, is also primarily activated by the relationship of Sufi master and *murid* (seeker-student). Produced, shaped, and worn by generations of Chishti disciples, the cap marks belonging and striving through an affective connection to the teacher and the tradition. The cap's beauty lies not merely in its aesthetic properties but also in its metonymic qualities associated with the master. Richard McGregor highlights the iterative power of repetition and reproduction in his chapter on tracings of Muhammad's sandal, demonstrating that piety and efficacy operate through multiple registers.

The objects that populate Muslim lives may or may not be beautiful by every aesthetic judgment, though some argue, as Oludamini Ogunnaike does, that "In fact, beauty is a criterion of the authentically Islamic. There is nothing Islamic that is not beautiful." (Ogunnaike 2017) Ogunnaike asserts that art is a medium through which divine unity (*tawhid*) is made perceivable to the imaginal faculties with which humans are endowed by God. "It is through imagination (*khayal*) that the Islamic arts render the invisible divine visible, and it is through imagination that we can perceive the mysteries of transcendent divine unity immanent in these sensory forms." (ibid.) Indeed one of the most productive tensions in Islamic theology is that between immanence (*tashbih*) and transcendence (*tanzih*) and, as Ogunnaike suggests, human imagination can be cultivated to perceive the transcendent through the immanent. Ultimately, "All of the Islamic arts exist to support the supreme art: the purification of the soul, the cultivation of character, and the remembrance of God." (ibid.) In this view the arts fulfill a mediational role between immanence and transcendence, between this world (*dunya*) and ultimate reality (*din* or *haqiqa*). Rather than incommensurable poles, these modalities interpenetrate and interdepend, providing humanity with guidance. Islamic objects, in this frame, are mediational: giving form to the formless, giving expression to hidden truths. For Ogunnaike, objects in their multiplicity ideally function as signs of God's unity. In a distinct way, this is true of the Bektashi lamps illuminated by Mark Soileau in Chapter Seven of this volume. Though these lamps are not exemplars of high art and intricate craft, the lamp is a dense coalescence of Bektashi teaching, ritual practice, and marking of ritual time and space. Innumerable and indistinguishable in their form, they are materially essential for the Bektashi spiritual gathering—making God, the master, and the disciples conceptually and physically present in and through their revealing light.

In his study of Islamic art and aesthetics, *Aisha's Cushion*, Jamal Elias asserts that "the religious image's primary place is not one defined by beauty or an aesthetic admiration for the skill of its creator, but by its efficacy as a representation, which is to say, the effectiveness with which it allows the observer to access what is perceived through the image." (2012: 20) Elias contends that site-based images and objects of worship can be understood as metaphors or symbol systems that "function through a process of indirection and can only really be made sense of through the observation of their implicative techniques." (21) In pushing the field beyond stale tropes of Islamic iconophobia, Elias argues that studying the implicative techniques of Islamic arts—including ritual, performance, and commerce—allows us to see the interplay of bodies and material objects as both commodities and as containers of spiritual value and power. In expanding from, though not abandoning, aesthetics and questions of beauty, a much wider material world opens up, enabling multiple relational frames. Elias also invokes "corpothetics", a term coined by Christopher Pinney in the context of Hindu visual culture, that goes beyond the aesthetic, the transactional, and the commodified, to include the wider sensory repertoires involved in the productive, consumptive, and performative aspects of visual regimes (2004: 194). This enables closer observation of the ways in which embodied, material practices are indices of object efficacy and are productive of certain dispositions and sentiments. This is particularly evident in Flueckiger's chapter where the efficacy of the amulets written by a Muslim woman healer for her multireligious clientele is predicated not on discursive comprehension, but proper execution and authority. The corpothetics of the Islamic subcultures examined in this volume provide insight into how Muslims navigate the competing social, political, and devotional regimes available to them. Though primarily mediational, objects for Elias also partake in the social construction of value and in shaping the field of ethical action populated by things.

This is certainly also true of Shahab Ahmed's treatment of Islamic materiality in his tome *What is Islam? The Importance of Being Islamic*, a work that above all argues for a capacious, exploratory, "coherently contradictory" definition of Islam over and against legalist, textualist, and prescriptive models. Ahmed addressed material and artistic formations throughout the book, mostly in terms of arts, crafts, garments, and especially poetry produced by and for elite patrons. Through these examples he asserted that "objects of everyday life are objects to which the user stands in a relationship of quotidian intimacy." (Ahmed 2016: 415) For Ahmed, the very everydayness of meaningful objects also speaks to a transcendence made available through the object's role in producing an "art of consciousness" that witnesses to higher values. By extension we could suggest that non-elite, ephemeral, and mass-produced objects are also participants in an art of consciousness whose "daily use is the altering and orienting of consciousness towards an ongoing state of the meaningfulness of everyday life as hermeneutical engagement with Revelation as Pre-Text, Text, and Con-Text (416)."[4] The alterations and orientations engendered by objects and bodies can be understood as having hermeneutical capacities, not merely as expressions of belief, but also as orienting agents of the creative process that is Muslim becoming. This is particularly important if one insists that the arts of consciousness are engaged by all Muslims in diverse ways, regardless of gender, race, ethnicity, ability, sexuality, class, or age. Theorizing "what Islam is" does not belong only to the text-producing and legal-minded. On the contrary, as the chapters in this volume reveal, the selection of a garment or adornment, the consideration of an image or an object, the adaptations to built and natural environments, and the manipulation of materials of devotion or daily need, offer theories and interpretations of Islam as well. These objects embody notions of appropriate practice, enculturated norms, personal choices, markers of identity, and internalized values. For example, in the case of Bakki, the protagonist of Aomar Boum's chapter on the wooden tablets used for Qur'anic learning, the tablet became an extension of his own body. This illustrates the capacity of material objects not just to mark, but also to produce a fundamental identity shift, as Bakki's status as a former slave would typically have excluded him from such training, but by learning how to prepare and care for, use and preserve the tablet, he was himself transformed in his own eyes and that of his community. In this frame, Islamic things can be understood as vectors through which the art of consciousness unfolds.

What matters? Power and presence

At this juncture we must also recognize the erasures that occur when only certain forms of materiality are regarded as having aesthetic or social value or as being truly Islamic. As Omar Kasmani points out "this work on visualities and materialities is being imagined in a climate where what is framed as "Muslim" is often pronouncedly pious, overwhelmingly masculine, if not simply aggressive or traditional." (Kasmani and Maneval 2016: 48) To that list we might add assumptions of Arab heteronormativity and a legacy of Orientalist and colonial determinations concerning the legitimate fields of inquiry into Islam. Kasmani's edited volume *Muslim Matter* is an effort

> . . . to reflect, if not represent, the complexity of lived experiences in dialogue: places where prayer goes hand-in-hand with ideas of amusement

> and where simple pleasures offset the harshness of conflict-ridden environments; or persons that straddle social expectations amidst non-normatively lived genders and sexualities; also communities which are in conversation with non-Muslim majorities; and occasions where the human-ness of the subject takes precedence over its Muslim-ness.
>
> Kasmani 49

Framed in this way, the study of Muslim material culture is a profoundly humanistic enterprise that engages a critical mode of politics. Expanding the field of what constitutes Islamic material culture is also a central purpose of the essays in this collection as they consider objects that are beautiful as well as those that are unremarkable, functional as well as decorative. What makes these objects "Islamic" is not necessarily their expression of any theological principle, but rather their embeddedness in particular Islamic cultures and the conceptual affordances they provide as ways of grasping complex epistemic webs.

This reminds us that the interpretive possibilities available to a given person or community with regards to the objects within its orbit are neither accidental nor absent of politics. As Gruber and Haugbolle express it in their introduction to the 2013 volume *Visual Culture in the Modern Middle East*, "forms of viewing become constitutive for subjectivities and social structures . . . At the same time, and perhaps in a self-fulfilling prophecy, visual representations create and reinforce those same systems." (xviii) The mutual imbrication of objects and their contexts points further to the possibility that objects are not merely passive recipients of the subject's interpretive abilities and limitations. This represents a shift in the field of material religion. Whereas Colleen McDannell argued in her foundational 1995 work *Material Christianity* that "Material culture in itself has no intrinsic meaning of its own. Objects or landscapes are understood and gain significance when their "human" elements can be deciphered." (3–4), now we see a clear shift to account for the power of things. As Talal Asad put it, "the power of things—whether animate or inanimate—is their ability to act within a network of enabling conditions." (Asad 2006: 213) This begs the questions: how might we understand the way things act and how do we recognize the networks of enabling conditions?

Certainly, these material objects help us to grasp the labor involved in navigating multiple authorizing regimes; they are the product of work, whether naturally occurring or of human manufacture. Things are embedded in local economies, politics, and authority structures, but these objects could also be understood to possess what Jane Bennett would call "thing-power" as they produce effects and affects in their orbits. "Thing-power" in Bennett's terms is "the curious ability of inanimate things to animate, to act, to produce effects dramatic and subtle" (2010: 6).[5]

From this perspective, things, whether naturally occurring or manufactured through various agencies, have observable effects and affects as they resonate beyond their physical limits in producing and manifesting feelings, concepts, changes, and affirmations. They are also made up of elements that are distinct, belonging to multiple orders such as inorganic and organic, biological and mechanical assemblages. This echoes one of Sally Promey's key points concerning the relational dimension of material religion. She writes, "This study of sensory and material cultures has thus been constituted as a *relational* enterprise with respect to people and things . . . It also suggests useful reconfigurations of material agency itself as relational and contingent, as a matter of people and things in specific encounters and contexts." (Promey 2014: 15) Seeing things in relation to people, rather than solely as inanimate objects of human subjects, suggests that the study of things is not dissimilar to the study of human individuals or social structures. The fourteenth-century Granadan well, *Aljibe del Rey*, explored here by D. Fairchild Ruggles, is precisely such a relational enterprise. As her essay demonstrates, the human and non-human, natural and manufactured, fluid and fixed assemblage of the well intersects with its builders, benefactors, and beneficiaries in ways that both manifest and maintain social hierarchies.

For Bennett, understanding things as partaking of thing-power means to understand them as vital matter. The implications of vital matter are significant for this historic epoch often called the Anthropocene, explained by Anna Gade as "the geologic era in which humanity indelibly alters the planetary record." (Gade 2019: 2) Bennett sees vital matter as a critical intervention in a world where the existence of all things is being troubled, in no small part due to the environmental degradation driven by the imperatives of late-stage neo-liberal capitalism. In her assessment:

> Vital materialists will thus try to linger in those moments during which they find themselves fascinated by objects, taking them as clues to the material vitality that they share with them. This sense of a strange and incomplete commonality with the out-side may induce vital materialists to treat nonhumans—animals, plants, earth, even artifacts and commodities—more carefully, more strategically, more ecologically.
>
> Bennett 2010: 17–18

The permeability of things and the permeability of bodies opens both up to a recognition that human existence is infused with non-human things, and vice-versa. Humans and things are assemblages comprised of physical matter, sensory experiences, and spiritual sensibilities situated within sympathetic alliances of political, economic, and social structures. This intertwined existence emerges profoundly in Gade's chapter, which considers Mecca's *zamzam* water—a spring with a prophetic origin story, emerging from beneath the heel of the prophet Isma'il when, as a child, he kicked the earth while his mother Hagar searched for life-giving water. The water from this aquifer today exemplifies a convergence of water management and purification technologies, changing local and global environmental conditions, the pilgrimage industry in Saudi Arabia, and constant demands as a faithful public seeks its spiritual blessings. This convergence evokes Bennett's suggestion that if humans recognized their shared material vitality with all that is, the resulting sense of sympathetic alliance with animate and inanimate things could have transformational potential.

Perhaps more pertinently, it brings us to another of Ibn 'Arabi's insights into the nature of things in this world, that humanity must recognize the "reality, truth, rightness, and properness of things, and, on the basis of this recognition, to give them their *haqq*, that is, what is appropriate for them and rightfully due to them." (Chittick 2005: 81–82) For Ibn 'Arabi, all things (sentient and insentient) have *haqq* and it is the ethical duty of humanity to honor this and act accordingly "with the demands that these realities make upon us. We cannot dissociate object from subject and then claim that the object has no divine rights, that it lays no obligations on the subject who knows it." (ibid.: 99) This is taken up in the context of the Mevlevi Sufi order, in which things generally perceived as inanimate "are actually alive . . . because everything carries a spirit. Everything provides a service. It is a debt for the served to reward and respect those who serve." (Can 2005: 226) And so the dervishes will "step only gently on the ground when they walk" and kiss the glass, spoon, and table that facilitated their nourishment.[6] Respect and reverence should characterize every interaction with all things, whether perceivably sentient or not.

This line of inquiry suggests that to grasp the many possibilities facilitated by Islamic things requires attention not just to the theologies, demographics, economies, and social networks productive of things, but also to the possibilities engendered by the mediation of power that is both extrinsic and intrinsic to them. As Promey points out, citing W.J.T Mitchell, "Scholars 'need to show how things that people make, make people'—and, [Promey] would add, how the things toward which we orient ourselves shape our perceptions of the environments we inhabit and the possibilities available to us." (2014: 8) This observation picks up from Mitchell's compelling question "what do pictures want?" that asks how we might endeavor to respond through the particularities of the objects studied in this volume (Mitchell 2005). The question resonates with the Qur'an's query "Am I not your Lord?" (7:172), which Carl Ernst characterizes as the fundamental articulation of Islamic ethical being (Ernst 2003: 110). As an expression of human *fitra* (innate nature), every person is asked to recognize themselves in response to the divine charge to live in consciousness of God. The answer to the Qur'an's question is then found in the unfolding of the human life. In both interrogations, humans are required to conceive of themselves as part of a web of existence, and not as the only (or even the most important) strand of that web. In the posthuman Anthropocene, this dislocation is a critical intervention and gives "to each that has a *haqq* its *haqq*." Gade builds on this idea in her discussion of *zamzam* water as productive material through which to decolonize the study of material religion and the environmental humanities by recognizing that how we imagine or understand things (such as water) "may alter the *real* horizons of ontology, extraction, and transaction." (Chapter 12: 21)

Sensing sensibilities

Another consideration is offered by scholars advocating attention to a more robust religious sensorium in which material culture plays an essential role. David Morgan, for example, points out that materiality occasions the "infinitely varied means by which human beings feel their way into their worlds, feel themselves, feel the past, anticipate the future, feel together." (2010: 71) Here feelings are attuned not just to other humans or to doctrines and belief, but to a more capacious world of things both animate and inanimate. It also suggests the possibility of an improvisational or speculative mode of sensation; an experiment in being that is suggestive of Shahab Ahmed's notion of an "exploratory Islam." Yet importantly, Morgan also points out that societies invest a great deal in promoting shared feeling amongst their members and alerts us to the prominent role of material objects in producing kindred sensibilities (58). The senses are not outside the realm of bio-power (or thing-power) and operate with shifting constraints and freedoms afforded and conditioned by their contexts. Thus, while, as Gruber and Haugbolle point out, material objects exist within "holistic systems of creative expression that, more often than not, encompass a panoply of sensory experiences," (2013: xi) there are often limits to those possible experiences. Indeed, one of the challenges to understanding objects embedded in religious worlds is the interplay of individual sensibilities with an entraining system or systems. Charles Hirschkind studies this as the production of an ethically responsive sensorium in the context of normative models of moral personhood that are presented (in part) through a particular material formation: Egyptian cassette sermons (Hirschkind 2006). Hirschkind's interlocutors strove to respond appropriately—appropriateness being a vector of power—to the stimulation of the self by a particular type of reformist Islam in the late twentieth century. Though primarily accessed through audition, the resulting sensorium could inform every interaction of the internal with the external world and vice versa. This view of the self as an assemblage, acting within and acted upon by the material world it encounters, suggests the ways in which material objects are both made by and make the human subject, a phenomenon that unfolds in several cases in this volume.

While Hirschkind explores this process in relation to what he termed the "Islamic Revival" (*al sahwa al islamiyya*) in late twentieth-century Egypt, a similar dynamic is observable in my own research fields among Muslims engaged with the popular shrine-based cultures of Islam (Bigelow 2010; 2012; 2019). The cultivation of moral personhood that takes place in shrines is embodied, materialized, and disciplinary, and sometimes also improvisational. Each shrine has its own etiquettes, authorities, and constituencies. What is offered, taken, purchased, distributed, or ingested is sometimes determined by the authoritative regimes of the sites and sometimes responsive to exigency or individual imagining. The various purposes imagined and enacted by the participants are understood by some to be achievable only if the proper things, behaviors, and attitudes cohere. For others, as in the case of Amma's *taviz*, discussed by Flueckiger in this volume, the efficacy of the ritual is contingent primarily upon correct execution and not on intention, preparation, or self-discipline.

Whether for the benefit of the self or others, the engagements at shrines produce a moral assemblage. Emplaced material objects, and the people who engage them, facilitate or inhibit transactions between religious actors and their conceptions of the divine and how divine power is productively engaged. Attention to the material culture of a religion allows what Morgan calls the "felt life of belief" to emerge from the sometimes abstract debates over doctrine that often overshadow the pragmatics of everyday and embodied religion (2010: 56). The ability of persons and things to mediate divine power or to facilitate intercessory benefits is a richly debated subject in Islamic legal and theological traditions. The hermeneutic potential of mediational practices is key to understanding those debates. For denizens of the shrines I study, things—grave coverings, flowers, scents, foods, amulets, strings, ashes, padlocks, money—are essential and ubiquitous. They generate blessings, offer healing, transmit power, circulate comfort, and elicit various affective responses. For some, their existence is so quotidian as to be uninteresting. Others, particularly those aware of critiques, are invested in defensive polemics using textual and or experiential evidence of the legitimacy and efficacy of their devotions.

The acceptability of things—certain kinds of things or things in general—is contested among various schools of Islamic thought. An amulet that one Muslim treasures as a connection to a spiritual guide, may be regarded as innovative and idolatrous by another. Even prayer beads that may seem so ubiquitous as to be unquestioned in most cultures (Muslim or not), are for some schools of thought both innovative (*bid'a*) and smacking of idolatry (*shirk*). This is a point raised by Ousman Murzik Kobo in this volume, describing debates in Burkina Faso between proponents of prayer beads and those so critical of the use of *tasbih* (prayer beads) that they would toss them out of mosques with their toes (Chapter 5: 91). Though they reject their use, such gestures clearly also point to the potency of the *tasbih* to either corrupt or enhance one's prayers. Kobo further demonstrates how the *tasbih* both represent the bearer's identity and help to shape it through cultivated practice. Considering the acceptability of objects, Leor Halevi argues that the inextricability of things from religion claimed by some scholars of material religion is overstated. Instead he attunes us to how the Salafis he studies do in fact extricate things from religion using their preferred tools of law and theology (2016: 106–7). While acknowledging the inherent materiality of the cosmos, Halevi points out that the particular assemblages of material culture are deliberately formed, carefully selected, and vigilantly policed. In his book *Modern Things on Trial*, Halevi examines how new inventions were deemed *halal* or *haram* (or in between) during the period of the great reformist thinker Rashid Rida in the late nineteenth and early twentieth centuries (2019). His study demonstrates the productive power of things—toilet paper, gramophones, telegraphs, paper money—to demand legalistic, textualist, disciplinary labor from the world they come to define.

Material Islamic studies

Ultimately, the chapters in this volume have many ways of considering what Islamic objects are and what we can learn from them. Some authors engage explicitly with theories of materiality and others take a more implicit approach, demonstrating that theorizing takes multiple forms and ideally emerges from the object in focus rather than imposes upon it. These studies make it clear that the somatic and object-oriented aspects of the culture of Islamic things are as significant in understanding the formations of Islam as the doctrines, texts, and ethics that also intersect in the production and interpretation of those things. The everydayness and habitual quality of the objects in this volume make this a useful venue to observe the production of ethical ideals through interpretive engagements comprehended through bodies and objects.

Each chapter in Part One: Tracing Images takes a particular visual image as a starting point and traces its history through multiple iterations, interpretations, and replications, revealing complex stories that take twists and turns through times, places, and publics—Ethel Sharieff's uniform and unflinching gaze, Muhammad's place in a pantheon of great men, and the Prophet's sandal tracing. Part Two: Identifying Objects brings the role of objects in marking and making individual and collective identities to the fore—lapel pins, prayer beads, and a Sufi cap. Part Three: Objects in Practice turns to the use and manipulation of objects in the context of religious practice—ritual gatherings, spiritual healings, and Qur'anic learning. Part Four: Circulatory Systems explores objects that resist fixing in place, as we see numismatics, hydrology, and the environmental humanities challenge the category of material religion itself. Individually, each chapter tells a story in which material objects animate and illuminate particular Islamic worlds. Collectively, they complicate perceptions of Islam as a monolithic and iconophobic religion, and offer new ways forward in the study of material religion and Islam.

PART ONE

Tracing Images

FIGURE 1.1 *Ethel Sharrieff, Chicago, Illinois, 1963 by Gordon Parks. Courtesy of and copyright The Gordon Parks Foundation.*

CHAPTER ONE

Clothes of Righteousness: The MGT Uniform in the Twentieth Century

Kayla Renée Wheeler

Standing in the center of a group of women dressed head to toe in crisp white garments is a short stout Black woman. She stares defiantly into the frame, the only woman in full focus (Figure 1.1). Her eyebrows are neatly plucked, her skin is flawless, and every article of clothing—from the paisley ascot to the dangling earrings—are immaculate. She exudes grace, beauty, and poise. Photographer Gordon Parks placed her strategically at the center of the frame, blurring the bodies of the women standing behind her, who wear matching outfits (Mitchell 2002: 29). The group's uniform pyramid formation communicates the strength and organizational power of the Muslim Girl's Training and General Civilization Classes (MGT-GCC), the Nation of Islam's women's auxiliary. Ethnic studies scholar Sylvia Chan-Malik describes the image as conveying the organization's "sense of anger and insurgency that drives NOI Muslim women's labor as wives and mothers" (2018: 101).

The woman at the center of the photograph is Ethel Muhammad Sharrieff, who was the Honorable Elijah Muhammad and Mother Clara Muhammad's eldest daughter and was the final architect of the Nation of Islam's public image of women in the organization in the form of the Muslim Girls Training (MGT) uniform. As the Supreme Captain of the Muslim Girls Training and General Civilization Classes (MGT-GCC), Sharrieff used her position to run the organization's clothing factory and store in Chicago and to finalize the MGT uniform, which consists of a blouse that covers the collar bones and elbows, loose-fitting skirts and pants that cover the ankles, and a matching scarf. As I argue throughout this chapter, modest dress in the Nation of Islam (NOI), especially the MGT uniform, played an important role in communicating its commitment to Black self-determination and Black pride.

The picture was taken for *Life* magazine and published on May 31,1963 as part of a larger fourteen-page photo essay on the Nation of Islam called, "Black Muslims," which was a result of three months of embedded research in the community in which Parks visited mosques and rallies in New York City, Chicago, and Los Angeles (Mitchell 2002: 27). The photo essay was the second biggest mainstream coverage of the Nation of Islam, following Mike Wallace and Louis Lomax's 1959 documentary "The Hate that Hate Produced," which introduced Malcolm X and Elijah Muhammad to white America and helped fuel growing anti-Black Muslim sentiment in the United States.

Despite the Nation of Islam's complicated relationship with the mainstream media, the photo essay proved to be beneficial to the organization. *Life* reached two million readers, compared to the Nation of Islam's journal, *Muhammad Speaks* that reached around 100,000 readers per week (Chan-Malik 2018: 99). For the Nation of Islam leadership, the Parks' photo essay provided them with the opportunity to share their message of community building and self-determination, as well as their emphasis on Black women's natural beauty, with a larger and more diverse audience. The photograph of Ethel Muhammad Sharrieff is one of four pictures of Black Muslim women in the Nation of Islam featured in the essay; the others were taken of women sewing, at the University of Islam, and attending the funeral of a member who was killed by the police. However, only Parks' image of Ethel Muhammad Sharrieff has remained popular within the Black American community among both Muslims and non-Muslims alike for the past fifty years. As a Black woman who grew up in Cleveland in the 1990s, the ubiquitous image was a source of awe and inspiration: the women were graceful, strong, proud and most importantly, dark skinned. They looked like what I hoped to embody one day. The emphasis on Black unity and Black beauty depicted in the photograph has made it a timeless image. At the center of the image is the MGT uniform, which I argue was central to creating a new collective identity for Black Muslims and helping the Nation of Islam become an economic stronghold.

In this chapter, I will use Gordon Parks' photograph to tell a broader sartorial history of the MGT uniform, as created by Mother Clara Muhammad and finalized by Sister Ethel Muhammad Sharrieff, and other expressions of NOI sartorial modesty relying primarily on writings produced by NOI members. By doing so, I will show how Black women's every day embodied practices were central to building and maintaining the Nation of Islam. As S. Brent Plate writes, "Religious traditions themselves originate and survive through bodily engagements with material elements of the world" (2015: 3). While this chapter looks at an Islamic object, I have chosen not to engage with the Qur'an to explain its meaning or purpose. The field of religious studies tends to privilege textualism, which is androcentric and reflects Protestantism's lasting influence on the field. In the case of the Nation of Islam, solely focusing on the Qur'an to describe a Muslim practice ignores the creative ways the organization has engaged with the Bible and other religious texts. By engaging with material religion theory, I am able to privilege the voices that are often marginalized in the field and provide new insights to a popular topic—Muslim women's dress practices—by focusing on the identities produced by the MGT and other iterations of modest dress in the Nation of Islam.

After a brief overview of the Nation of Islam, which was founded in July 1930, I will discuss the early developments of its understanding of sartorial modesty, which can be observed in the Muslim Girls Training and General Civilization Classes and editorials in *Muhammad Speaks*, the organization's official journal. Next, I will highlight Sister Ethel Muhammad Sharrieff's role in creating and circulating the image of the ideal Black Muslim woman through finalizing the MGT uniform and building the Nation of Islam's clothing factory and accompanying store. Finally, I will explore how the MGT uniform has lived on under Minister Louis Farrakhan's new iteration of the Nation of Islam. I situate my work in conversation with Dawn-Marie Gibson and Jamillah Karim (2014), Judith Weisenfeld (2017), and Ula Taylor (2017) who have all explored the role of Black women in building and sustaining the Nation of Islam.

History of the Nation of Islam

The Nation of Islam was founded in Detroit, Michigan in 1930 by W.D. Fard Muhammad who claimed to be from Mecca. He told his listeners that the King of Saudi Arabia had sent him to the United States to teach Black people about their forgotten past. According to Fard Muhammad, Black people were members of the Lost Tribe of Shabazz who had ruled the world before being oppressed by white people. During the transatlantic slave trade, Black people, whose true race was Asiatic Blacks, had lost their language (Arabic), religion (Islam), and cultural values. Fard Muhammad had been sent to the United States to help restore his listeners to their original position in society. Most of his early members were people who lived on the margins of society and had been disproportionately impacted by the Great Depression, including women, southern migrants and Caribbean immigrants, poor people, and the incarcerated. They were drawn to his message of self-empowerment and nation building. For many, it was a familiar message. The Nation of Islam emerged following Marcus Garvey's deportation to Jamaica in 1927 and the arrest and subsequent death of Noble Drew Ali in 1929, who was the leader of the Moorish Science Temple of America.

Fard Muhammad and his followers saw themselves as carrying on Marcus Garvey's commitment to Black self-determination and Black pride. In fact, many early NOI members had been Garveyites. Marcus Garvey founded the Universal Negro Improvement Association (UNIA) in Jamaica in 1914, before bringing it to the United States in 1916. Garvey believed that the only way Black people in the Americas could truly flourish was by repatriating to the African continent, specifically Liberia. As historian Nicholas Patsides (2007: 282) notes, this was a more attractive message to his Caribbean followers in New York City, who had a shared history of modern transnational migration and less established ties in the United States, compared to southern migrants. Conversely, Fard Muhammad and his successors sought to build a strong Black Muslim nation within the borders of the United States. Despite diverging beliefs concerning where Black diasporans should resettle, both the NOI and UNIA encouraged entrepreneurship, pooling resources, and supporting Black-owned businesses.

Originally founded in Newark, New Jersey in 1913, Noble Drew Ali moved the Moorish Science Temple of America (MSTA) to Chicago in 1923 and spread his message to other large midwestern cities, including Detroit. The MSTA taught its members that they were Moorish-Americans, not Negroes or Ethiopians, whose original religion was Islam and original language was Arabic. Ali encouraged his members to be productive, patriotic citizens. Conversely, the NOI rejected American nationalism. Many Nation male members refused to register for the draft or serve in the military, and as an organization the NOI did not actively fight for voting rights. What the two organizations shared was a belief that Islam was central to reconnecting Black people to their true ancestral past and liberating them from their financial constraints. It is likely that many early Nation of Islam members had heard of the MSTA and had perhaps been members because of its large membership in the Midwest. All three organizations shared a commitment to embracing new religio-racial identities that retraced their histories beyond the transatlantic slave trade and global white supremacy (Weisenfeld 2017: 5). The organizations also used clothing to construct new identities for their members and, as I will show throughout the remainder of this chapter, the NOI drew partial inspiration from its predecessors.

Early sartorial practices in the Nation of Islam

Modest dress in the NOI performed three primary interconnected functions: to reclaim a lost Black femininity, to distinguish members from other religious groups, and to cultivate an ethical self. Fard Muhammad encouraged his female members to wear extravagant clothing to show how financially successful the NOI and its members were, even during the Depression (Taylor 1998: 181). There was much sartorial diversity among NOI women, including fancy coats, ornate dresses, satin gowns, and turbans with crescent pins. Fard Muhammad encouraged his female followers to wear red, green, or white, which he stated were the colors of Islam (Sahib 1951: 137). These sartorial practices were like those of women in the Moorish Science Temple of America and the Ahmadiyya movement, who drew inspiration from the imagined "Islamic East." This sartorial diversity was important for the organization, as women were on the frontlines of fishing, or recruitment, in the Nation of Islam under Fard Muhammad.

Following Fard Muhammad's disappearance in 1934, one of his closest followers, Elijah Muhammad took over the Nation of Islam and moved its headquarters to Chicago, Illinois. As the second leader of the Nation of Islam, Elijah Muhammad institutionalized new gender ideologies concerning women's dress and movement in public spaces, emphasizing sartorial modesty and domesticity. Under Elijah Muhammad, hemlines got lower and the clothing became less ostentatious. Whereas women in the NOI under Fard Muhammad had been encouraged to actively recruit new members, although he limited their public leadership roles, Elijah Muhammad restricted women's fishing efforts and emphasized private leadership roles. Post-World War Two cultural shifts likely influenced Muhammad's gender ideology.

Central to the NOI under all its leaders was recovering a femininity and masculinity that had been denied to Black people in the Americas, beginning with the transatlantic slave trade. As Patricia Hill Collins (1990: 70) argues, the US has maintained the image of the Black woman as "Other" to justify intersecting race, gender, and class oppression. The Nation of Islam sought to invert the racial hierarchy that placed Black people, and specifically Black women, at the bottom and white people at the top. In doing so, white women were cast as ugly, savage, and unfeminine. On the other hand, Black women, especially those who joined the Nation of Islam, were viewed as naturally beautiful, pure, and civilized. Black women and girls learned how to embrace their original positions as "Mothers of Civilization" through attending Muslim Girls Training and General Civilization Classes (MGT-GCC) every week. According to Dawn-Marie Gibson and Jamillah Karim (2014: 25), the MGT-GCC served three purposes: fostering community; teaching members the domestic arts including cooking and sewing; and disciplining members who failed to meet the organization's moral codes.

The Nation's views on Black womanhood are clearly laid out in the Muslim Girls Training Notebook, which was given to every new female member during their orientation. The notebook provided a brief organizational history, rules and roles within the temple, and an overview of the "possessions of civilized women." Modest dress was central to creating a civilized woman. This was expressed most notably through wearing the MGT uniform. Through imitation of and correction by older sisters, new members learned how to dress properly during MGT-GCC meetings, MGT-GCC leaders conducted weigh-ins to ensure members did not exceed the maximum 120 pounds, and inspected women's uniforms. Those found to be overweight or wearing dirty, wrinkled, or ill-fitting uniforms could be suspended from the temple and banned from participating in all NOI functions for up to six months (Taylor 2017: 166). However, the regulation of women's bodies varied across temples and was often dependent on a member's relationship with the Royal Family or other members of the Nation's senior leadership team.

Mother Clara Muhammad, the first leader of the MGT-GCC, created the original MGT uniform, which was based on her own aesthetic preferences (Taylor 2017: 68). Unlike other NOI women who favored satin capes and gowns, Mother Clara often opted for long flowing color-blocked outfits that obscured her figure, paired with a matching scarf that left her face exposed. Mother Clara, as the wife of the organization's leader and at times the de facto leader, was a role model for all women in the Nation. Much like members of the Black Baptist church movement that Evelyn Higginbotham Brooks (1994) studied, for Mother Clara, dress functioned as a form of politics of respectability. She chose plain clothing that communicated her embrace of cleanliness, bodily discipline, and economic thrift. These were all attributes of civilized people, a far cry from the white supremacist tropes of Black people. As an organization, the Nation under Elijah Muhammad continued to use white, green, and red as their official colors, which were considered the colors of Islam. However, white was the most popular choice of color for women because it symbolizes purity (Muslim Girl's Training 2013: 13). The emphasis on the color white was a way to visually challenge stereotypes of Black women's sexual deviancy that marked them as hypersexual. This stereotype had been constructed by white enslavers to justify the sexual abuse that enslaved Black women endured.

The modest dress allowed women to reimagine Black women as the ideal woman. Modest dress was a physical reminder to Black Muslim women of their original values and beliefs. Margary Hassain wrote, "We wear this proper head-piece in the proper manner, and you see an immediate effect take place in the sister wearing it. In keeping with this cap of wisdom, we unconsciously snap to attention. We are full of pride and purpose. Foolishness of mind and sluggishness of body flees from us" ("The Woman in Islam" n.d.). Like the Egyptian women who participated in the mosque movement that Saba Mahmood studied (2005), modest dress, specifically the MGT uniform, helped women in the Nation of Islam cultivate an ethical self. Their dress helped to discipline their bodies, create physical gendered boundaries, and produce a demure, soft-spoken, and graceful demeanor. The MGT uniform should not be read as a passive object. In addition to disciplining the wearer's body, the MGT uniform reshaped geographical space—public city streets were transformed into sacred NOI spaces—and it communicated to viewers how the wearer should be treated. The uniform played an important role in recruitment initiatives, known as fishing. In her interviews with former Nation of Islam members, anthropologist Jamillah Karim (2006) found that many women were attracted to the organization because of its emphasis on modest dress and unified identity. Black women saw dress as a means of preventing sexual harassment, gaining respect from Black men, and communicating their commitment to building an independent Black nation. Modest dress was important to a person's spiritual and social reform, and was also imagined as way to produce healthy and productive citizens.

While NOI members were encouraged to embrace a new modest aesthetic, Elijah Muhammad denounced materialism and conspicuous consumption, advocating for thrift instead. In *Message to the Blackman in America* (1965: 192) he wrote:

> And our women should clean up. You do not have to have a dozen dresses. Just keep the one you have cleaned and press. Until we enforce cleanliness among the people of our Nation and get them into the spirit of self-respect and the spirit of making themselves the equal of other civilized nations of the earth we will never be recognized as being fit members of any decent society of nations.

Elijah Muhammad suggested that people cut down on their clothing spending by one-third (ibid.: 196). He told his members to not have any more clothes than necessary. All additional money was to be sent to headquarters or locally pooled to support NOI members and NOI initiatives, such as buying land. Although members of the Nation of Islam were expected to cut down on unnecessary expenses, women were still required to be neat, clean, and well-dressed at all times. This played an important role in visually communicating the organization's social and financial success to non-members. As an historian of African-American religious history, Judith Weisenfeld (2017: 126) writes, "the experience of being "well dressed" and clean helped to discipline members into their new identities and contributed to the process of forming a new collective." According to the Nation of Islam teachings, every ethnic group had their own unique dress; central to the Nation's dress was modesty and cleanliness, which was fully realized in the MGT uniform. This new collective identity rooted in sartorial modesty was co-constructed with clothing, Black women's bodies, and viewers.

Women members in the Nation saw immodest dress not only as a personal failure, but also as a symptom of society's moral decay, which had large sweeping consequences for its citizens. For instance, Margary Hassain linked the rise of immodest dress to the stock market crash in the 1920s. In a "Women in Islam" column for *Muhammad Speaks*, Hassain (1969b: 22) wrote: "Now America is being stripped of her monetary power and national prestige. She is pounded by the forces of nature. Walking hand-in-hand with the "recession" moral depravity and monetary collapse. The American woman has all but stripped herself of clothing." By dressing modestly, women in the Nation of Islam were returning to their natural state, helping civilize society at large, and promoting Black self-determination.

The Nation of Islam took an anti-fashion stance, arguing that mainstream fashion was for white women and led Black women to abandon their natural selves. Hassain wrote in another *Muhammad Speaks* column:

> For the first time we can be ourselves and we do not have to wear the helter-skelter clothing which are the so-called styles of the white man. . . . If the white man's style dictates dressed up, our Black women, ranging in ages from the cradle to the grave pull their dresses up. They no longer stop to think whether their form is attractive or misshapen or not. Let alone think of the decency aspect . . . This civilization of the white man is leading the woman more and more into beastlike life . . .
>
> 1969a: 30

According to the Nation of Islam, mainstream fashion was produced by men to sexualize women. Through imitating white women's dress practices, Black women had also imitated their values and behaviors. It made Black women pay too much attention to their physical features and could easily lead to low self-esteem for those who did not fit the mainstream fashion industry's narrow view of feminine beauty: light skinned, thin, straight long hair. Embracing the latest fashion trends turned Black women into animal-like zombies, who had forgotten their place in the social hierarchy. As such, it was important to develop and promote a unique NOI aesthetic for women: the MGT uniform. Outside of Clara Muhammad, perhaps no other woman played a more important role in creating the MGT uniform—thus helping solidify the Nation's collective identity and financially sustain the organization—than Ethel Muhammad Sharrieff.

Sister Ethel

Sister Ethel Muhammad Sharrieff was Elijah Muhammad and Clara Muhammad's eldest daughter. She was the first woman in the Nation of Islam to be given the title, "Sister Instructress" by Elijah Muhammad, taking over the role of orientating and disciplining women members from her mother (Hakim and Muhammad 2003). She served as the National Captain of the Muslim Girls Training and General Civilization Class, reporting directly to her father. In her position, Sister Ethel was responsible for creating and implementing the MGT-GCC curriculum (Amatullah-Rahman 1999: 86). Like her mother, Sister Ethel became one of the most visible faces of the Nation of Islam within the organization. She served as a role model for all female members. Sister Ethel also played an important role in shaping the non-Muslim public's view of the Nation of Islam. In addition to being featured in *Life* magazine in 1963, she and her family were featured in *The Messenger* in 1959 as an example of the ideal wife. In *The Messenger*, Sister Ethel was photographed in a dress that she designed and sewed, hosting a dinner party, teaching her daughters how to properly make a bed, and cooking. In these photographs, she is not wearing a hijab or the MGT uniform, which members were only expected to wear during official temple events and classes. While she proved to be an aspirational figure for women in the Nation of Islam, her lasting influence came in the form of the finalized MGT uniform and the businesses she created.

Sister Ethel produced the final version of the MGT uniform in 1967, which, like the original version, took inspiration from the Black Cross Nurses, the women's auxiliary for the UNIA (Gibson and Karim 2014: 51). The finalized MGT uniform consisted of a high-collar mid-thigh length tunic, loose fitting pants or skirts that stopped at the ankles, and a headscarf that left the wearer's earlobes and neck exposed to allow them to wear jewelry. Sister Ethel extended the length of the MGT skirt by two inches. The MGT uniform came in multiple colors including pink, yellow, lavender, and lime (ibid.: 122). Women were expected to wear the beige uniform during the Saturday MGT-GCC classes and white uniforms for official NOI events (Amatullah-Rahman 1999: 86). Lieutenants and captains in the MGT often wore fezzes and capes during official functions (Gibson and Karim 2014: 122). The Vanguard, an elite group of women between the ages of 16 to 30, who were tasked with protecting the community in the event that Muslim men were unavailable, wore pink uniforms with maroon piping (Amatullah-Rahman 1999: 86). The color coding reveals how structured the organization was. It is important to note that the uniform's final version under Elijah Muhammad's national leadership took place after the Immigration Reform Act was passed in 1965, which resulted in more immigration from Muslim-majority countries. This was likely a response to the increased presence of Arab and South Asian Muslims who had different understandings of sartorial modesty.

Sister Ethel also used her influence to convince her father to relax the organization's dress restrictions for everyday wear, allowing women to go without head coverings and jackets while in public (Taylor 2017: 125). Outside of official NOI functions and the MGT-GCC classes, women in the Nation were expected to cover their legs down to their ankles, arms down to their elbows, and cleavage. Married women were expected to cover their heads, which varied in style from fezzes to berets to scarves. In addition to running the MGT-GCC, Sister Ethel founded several businesses, the most notable being the Nation's clothing factory and store. Sister Ethel began the NOI factory in her basement, before moving it to its final location, on 79th Street in Chicago where it was called the Temple No. 2 Clothing Factory. The clothes were sold at a nearby store, also on 79th Street (Figure 1.2).

The Nation of Islam sought to create a unified Black-run nation within the borders of the United States. As such, the organization encouraged its members to build their own businesses and to patronize NOI and Black-owned business in their local communities. The Nation clothing factories and clothing stores proved to be one of the organization's most lucrative

FIGURE 1.2 *Temple No. 2 Clothing Store advertisement in* Muhammad Speaks *from August 1966 (photo by author).*

ventures. In addition to the selling MGT uniform, the store also sold jewelry, shoes, and modest everyday wear, which was purchased by both Muslims and non-Muslims. Women members were encouraged to buy their MGT uniform directly from the Temple No. 2 Clothing Factory as a means of keeping wealth within the Black Muslim community. They were expected to own two MGT uniforms to ensure they always had a clean one available. The uniforms produced in the Nation's factory and sold in their accompanying store ranged in price from $25.75 to $39.95 (Taylor 2017: 166). For the Nation's members, many of whom were poor or working class, these prices made the official uniform unattainable for many. This led many women to create knockoffs of the uniform for themselves and their families. The most talented seamstresses were able to sell their uniform to other members at a lower price than the official uniform. The NOI encouraged its members' ingenuity by hosting bazaars where they could showcase and sell their creations and by selling advertising space in the *Muhammad Speaks*. Sister Ethel also helped other Muslim women build small clothing stores and factories across the United States (Hakim and Muhammad 2003). While the

MGT uniform has remained one of the most visible symbols of the Nation of Islam, next to bow ties and bean pies, its place within the Nation of Islam has continued to evolve over time.

New beginnings of the MGT uniform

Following his father's death in February 1975, Imam W.D. Mohammed was appointed Chief Minister of the Nation of Islam. Imam Mohammed quickly made changes to the organization's structure, as well as its political and theological outlooks. He expanded upon his father's internationalist views, connecting the organization with other Muslims across the United States and the world. The multiple name changes between 1976 and 1985 are reflective of the organization's new orientation. Imam Mohammed resisted what he called "black supremacy," where Bilalians—the name for Asiatic Blacks—were superior to white people, who were viewed as inherently evil (Muhammad 1979).

Due to prior organizational financial mismanagement, Imam Mohammed also sold off many of the Nation's businesses and properties, including farmland, the *Muhammad Speaks* printing plant, the Temple No. 2 Clothing Factory, and restaurants in New York and Chicago, to pay off tax debt (Gibson 2012: 80–81). Imam Mohammed also issued new guidelines for women's dress and movement within public space, while retaining the organization's emphasis on gender segregation and commitment to thrift as a means of racial uplift. This led to more regional diversity in terms of defining sartorial modesty. Like his father, Imam Mohammed (1979) viewed women who spent their money on expensive clothes as producing the stereotypes—lazy, irresponsible, and immodest—that Bilalians were trying to challenge. According to Imam Mohammed, materialism and mass consumerism could lead to jealousy and competition, which is one of the primary causes of theft. While women were required to cover their heads while praying and inside mosques, Imam Mohammed otherwise loosened clothing restrictions. Additionally, women members were no longer required to wear the MGT uniform in the mosque or during official events. Instead, Imam Mohammed encouraged NOI women to create their own styles that reflected their intersecting identities as Black American and Muslim.

The MGT uniform would reemerge in the 1980s after Minister Louis Farrakhan, who, under Elijah Muhammad, had taken over Malcolm X's position as the Nation of Islam's national spokesperson and minister of Temple No. 7 in Harlem, broke off from Imam Mohammed's organization. Minister Farrakhan saw himself as continuing Elijah Muhammad's legacy, reinstating many of the theological beliefs that Imam Mohammed had changed. However, he made several changes to Muhammad's gender ideology, which have allowed for women within the NOI to take more visible leadership positions and to enter the fashion industry in greater numbers. Farrakhan reestablished the MGT-GCC, but attendance is not mandatory and female members are not required to wear the MGT uniform (Farrakhan 1989: 139). Additionally, female members' dress is no longer inspected during mosque visits. While many women celebrated the loosening of the dress code, others missed having a uniform that set them apart from their peers. These women experimented with fabrics, colors, and cuts to provide an updated version of the MGT uniform. For instance, Carmen Muhammad, the founder of Al-Nisa Designs, uses buttons, pockets, and bright colors like fuchsia to provide a modern take on the classic look.

Like Elijah Muhammad and Imam Mohammed, Louis Farrakhan sees modest dress as a means of protecting Black Muslim women from sexual violence. In a speech delivered at Morgan State University, Farrakhan stated, "You will not get the man you want showing yourself in a manner that is disrespectful." He continued, "To me a man is hard pressed to walk the street keeping his eyes where they should be. He sees the movement up here and goes right to the point. Then he go buy a Playboy magazine, then he go and buy a Hustler magazine, and before you know it rape is on the increase" (Farrakhan 1989: 137). These comments are reminiscent to those of Elijah Muhammad who believed that wearing short and tight clothes could attract unwanted attention from men. Farrakhan puts the onus on Black women to protect themselves, since men are both naturally attracted to women and mentally weak. This ignores the structural oppression Black women experience because of their intersecting identities.

In addition to preventing women from being objectified, Farrakhan also imagines sartorial modesty as a means of collapsing class differences. He wrote, "A dress code is a protection for you in that you gain the peace of mind from knowing that others have to conform to a code as well as yourself" (1993: 60). By rejecting materialism, they also reject competition that pushes girls and women to always look better than their peers. Yet, this ignores the diversity of dress practices among women in the Nation who continue to wear the MGT uniform daily or just for official events. For instance, at the Justice for Else rally in 2015, which commemorated the twentieth anniversary of the Million Man March, highlighted the diversity of MGT uniform styles—cotton, satin, silk fabrics in chocolate brown, peach, and sky blue—allowing women in the Nation to express their individuality while still communicating a united front to non-Muslims. Women in the Nation use clothing to talk back to male leaders and provide their own understanding of sartorial modesty while promoting a collective gendered and raced identity.

Conclusion

While Sister Ethel Muhammad followed her brother, Imam Mohammed, as he made changes to the organization, she remained close to Louis Farrakhan (Bush 2002). In both organizations, Sister Ethel continued to be a role model for righteous Black women who are committed to cleanliness, proper grooming, and modest bodily comportment. She showed Black Muslim women how to be dutiful wives, loving mothers, and successful community leaders. Sister Ethel balanced her domestic duties with running multiple successful businesses that allowed her to use the sewing and tailoring skills that she learned through the Muslim Girls Training and General Civilization Classes. Her legacy lives on in Gordon Parks' iconic photograph for *Life* magazine as an example of Black women's embodied resistance against white supremacy and the potential for a united Black nation through the MGT uniform. Since the 1930s, the Nation of Islam has used Black women's clothed bodies to rewrite their ancestral past, to upend the racial hierarchy in the United States that places Black people at the bottom, and to help build a semi-economically independent nation within a nation. Using material religion studies to explain Black women's everyday practices makes it possible to see the multiple audiences that Black Muslim women speak to when they dress their bodies, and the world-making they engage in when they step outside of the homes and enter an often hostile world.

CHAPTER TWO

The Masonic Muhammad: Modern Franco-Iranian Visual Encounters in Prophetic Iconography

*Christiane Gruber**

We're all like detectives in life. There's something at the end of the trail that we're all looking for.

David Lynch (American Filmmaker, B.1946)

Whence the "Young Muhammad"?

While pre-modern Persian images most often represent Muhammad as a bearded and mature adult embarked on his prophetic career, a notable corpus of images depicting a young Muhammad emerged in Iran over the course of the second half of the twentieth century (Plate 2). In these many postcards, posters, banners, and even carpets, Muhammad is shown as an adolescent boy smiling as he tilts his head slightly to the right. Thanks to a Persian inscription located at the bottom of some of these images, it is clear that artists and viewers considered these "Young Muhammad" images to be exact replicas of a Byzantine icon supposedly held in a European museum. Per the inscription, the icon is said to have been painted by the monk Bahira when he recognized the signs of prophecy when the adolescent Muhammad visited Busra in Syria during a caravan trip with his uncle Abu

Talib. Besides glorifying Muhammad's beauty and youth, these visuals of Muhammad, recognized and foreseen as a prophet already during his teenage years, proved highly popular in Iran during the 1980s and 1990s (Gruber 2016).

In more recent years, the original pictorial source of the Iranian image has come to light thanks to the scholarship of Pierre and Micheline Centlivres, who have demonstrated that these types of "Young Muhammad" images were based on an Orientalist photograph taken in 1905–6 by the photographers Lehnert and Landrock while they were stationed in North Africa (Centlivres and Centlivres-Demont 2005; Grabar and Natif 2003). Produced as postcards with captions reading either "Young Arab" (*Jeune Arabe*) or "Mohamed," such visuals reached Iranian artists through the mass media already by *c.*1950. Once in Iran, the French caption "Mohamed" was then interpreted as indicating the Prophet himself rather than a young Arab boy bearing a highly common Arabic name. This "strange encounter" between Orientalist photography and Iranian religious arts thus yielded the most popular image of the young Prophet, which circulated in a variety of media within Iran until 2006, at which time the Iranian government attempted to curb its manufacture and distribution in the aftermath of the *Jyllands-Posten* Muhammad cartoon controversy (Klausen 2009).

While this pictorial corpus of "Young Muhammad" images is well studied by now, another body of Iranian representations of the young Prophet remains largely unknown and unstudied. This second body of Iranian prophetic depictions show Muhammad as a young man standing upright and holding a banner. One poster, printed in Tehran around 1940–60, is now held in the collection of Elizabeth Puin, who notes in her catalogue of Islamic posters that this particular depiction of the Prophet is rare and quite possibly derived from an otherwise unidentified Western pictorial source (Puin 2008: vol. 2, 526–8, and vol. 3, 902, cat, no. J-2) (Figure 2.1). Puin appears correct in her assessment: images of a young and unbearded Prophet holding a banner, standing with pointed toe, with sword girdled to his waistband, and sporting a turban whose top appears as if a truncated fez, decorated with a plumette, certainly suggest a non-Islamic visual prototype, a question to which we shall return later.

This Persian iconographic rendition of the Prophet, however, is not as unusual as one might suppose. Undertaking further research in international libraries, museums, and other private and public repositories uncovers a plenitude of related materials. For instance, an oil painting on canvas depicts the Prophet in a similar manner (Plate 3). At over one meter in height, this large-scale painting most likely dates to the first half of the twentieth century, and its owner notes that it used to hang in a teahouse in Kashan before it was acquired in the 1970s, at which time it was taken out of Iran and made its way to the American Midwest (author's interview, 2015).

While dating to the Pahlavi period, this image emulates both the style and function of Qajar paintings executed on canvas known as *pardas* (literally,

FIGURE 2.1 *The Prophet Muhammad in his youth, poster on paper, painting signed by Fath 'Ali, printed by Matbu'at-i Shemrani, Tehran, Iran, c.1940–60. Collection of Elizabeth Puin (J-2).*

"cloth"). These types of figural depictions on canvas were displayed in coffeehouses, where they were used for public storytelling performances known as *parda-khwani,* or picture-recitation (Chelkowski 1989; Seyf 1989). Many of these canvas paintings depict war scenes from the *Shahnama* (Book of Kings) as well as the Battle of Karbala, enabling both reciter and audience members to regal in epic feats or mourn the death of early Shi'i martyrs. With regards to the image of Muhammad, it is also possible that this *parda* painting and others like it may have been used by Iranians for the communal recounting and glorification of the Prophet's valiant deeds, in particular his many accomplishments on the battlefield. This martial reading of an otherwise immobile Muhammad is supported by the gold inscription added to the Prophet's banner, which provides the famous Qur'anic verse declaring that: "Victory is from God and triumph is near" (61:13). Although lauded epigraphically as a warrior-leader, Muhammad does not sport attire suitable for a "rough-and-tumble" occasion. To the contrary, with his debonair red fez studded with jewels and a crescent moon, his bouffant trousers whose seams flutter out into billowy brown ribbons, and his dainty and well-laced shoes, the Prophet appears dressed for a French ballet-de-court rather than for the Hijazi battlefield.

Besides posters and paintings, this refined and rather Europeanizing pictorial rendition of the Prophet can also be found mounted to the opening page of a Qajar-period photographic album (Figure 2.2). This enormous album of over 1,400 photographs recording various individuals and sites in Iran, was compiled by the late Qajar diplomat and governor ʿAli Khan Vali (1845–1902) between 1879–1900. As many Persian manuscripts, books, and miscellanies that bear Shiʿi content or inflection, this work launches with a visual eulogy of the Prophet Muhammad, Imam ʿAli, and the *ahl al-bayt*. Immediately after this pictorial frontispiece in praise of the Prophet and members of his household appears a lengthy encomium to Nasir al-Din Shah (r. 1848–96), under whom ʿAli Khan Vali had served and with whom he traveled to the Shiʿi shrines in Ottoman-governed Iraq. Combining a lengthy laudatory text and two photographs of the Qajar ruler

FIGURE 2.2 *Opening page of the ʿAli Khan Vali photographic album, which includes icons of the Young Muhammad (at top), ʿAli, Hasan, and Husayn, Tehran, Iran, 1879–1900. Harvard University, Fine Arts Library, Special Collections, AKP111.*

in both standing and seated poses, the second page completes the album's front matter in praise of both religion and state, a combination that reflects its Qajar Persian-Shi'i context of production (Khosronejad 2018).

Returning to the album's opening page (Figure 2.2), the quasi-heraldic collage of devotional images remains largely freestanding and independent of an exegetical apparatus. Only one short textual insertion, comprising two lines of Persian text, surmounts the image of the Prophet at the top of the folio. Handwritten by 'Ali Khan Vali, the note explains that this blessed icon (*shama'il-i mubarak*) of Muhammad, the so-called "Seal of the Prophets" (*Khatim al-Nabiyyin*), was made before his prophetic appointment while he was on a commercial trip in Syria (*Sham*). While there, Muhammad was depicted by a monk (*rahib*) in his monastery (*dayr*). 'Ali Khan Vali then goes on to tell us that a photograph of this (painting on) canvas (*parda*) was taken during the "royal trips" to Europe (*farangistan*).

As is the case for the better-known "Young Muhammad" visuals (Plate 2), a textual inscription here specifies that the image is in fact a pictorial record of a painting that the monk Bahira made of the adolescent Muhammad while he visited Busra prior to his receiving Qur'anic revelations as an adult. Moreover, in this caption 'Ali Khan Vali notes that this pictorial record in fact comprises a photograph that was taken of the original painting, which at the time was held somewhere in *farangistan* and viewed during the so-called "royal trips". This is no doubt a reference to the multiple tours of Europe undertaken by Nasir al-Din Shah (in 1873, 1878, and 1899), who, like 'Ali Khan Vali, kept travelogues and was a keen practitioner of photography.[1]

As these various pictorial depictions and textual explanations suggest, this otherwise unstudied corpus of images representing a young Muhammad holding a banner dates from the late nineteenth century to no later than 1950. Through both iconographic details and attendant explications, these depictions point to a non-Islamic source, although this source has remained elusive to date. Nevertheless, Iranian artists and patrons evidently thought the visual prototype to be a Byzantine-period icon of Muhammad painted during his adolescence, which was subsequently transferred to and preserved in a European museum. As a result, Iranian cultural entrepreneurs, learned patrons, and popular owners and viewers thought to have before their eyes reproductions of an authentic painterly record of the Prophet made during his lifetime, preserved in a European museum and then subsequently multiplied through the reprographic and photographic arts.

While one can imagine a Muslim devotee's drive to own his or her copy of this kind of *vera icona*, what is less clear, however, is why the early twentieth century witnessed such an upsurge in the production of this image of a youthful Muhammad in particular. The search for other clues to uncover the image's source and its possible meanings thus presses on. If one is to follow the data wherever it may it lead us, quite surprisingly we find ourselves forced to exit the book and painterly arts in order to investigate an entirely different domain of production: namely, Persian pictorial carpets.

Interwoven paths: Muhammad among the great men of the world

By the dawn of the twentieth century, the Iranian carpet industry bloomed, catering to both a domestic elite and foreign clientele. Although geometric and vegetal motifs still held sway, Iranian carpet designers and manufacturers largely based in the cities of Tabriz and Kirman began to incorporate figural representations within the textile arts by drawing upon a wide array of European and Persian sources (Gustafson n.d.; Ittig 1985; Wilber 1979–80; Tanavoli 1994; Ahani et al. 2017). Among them exist more than two dozen rugs generally referred to as "Great Men" carpets, which were produced in Kirman during the first few decades of the twentieth century (Bailey 1982; Wilber 1979–80: 193). One large example, now held in the World Cultures Museum in Amsterdam (*Onverwachte* 2012: 158), measures almost four meters in height and includes more than fifty identified individuals in the center field and within roundels in the outer frame (Plate 4). At the bottom stand some of the famous men of world history, including Peter the Great, Louis XIV, Christopher Columbus, Harun al-Rashid, and Chengiz Khan. Above them can also be found great thinkers and leaders stretching back through early Islamic history (e.g., 'Umar), Graeco-Roman times (e.g., Socrates and Alexander the Great), and, in the upper right corner, the beginnings of monotheism under Moses (carrying the Ten Commandments) and Solomon (whose crown distinguishes him as an archetypical king). Moving up the rug's composition, the background is stippled by a white structure resembling a Greek Temple constructed of fluted columns and a pediment, while the topmost horizontal frame includes portrait medallions depicting the famous poets of the Persian tradition. This carpet rendering of "fifty-odd members of an exclusive men's club" (Bailey 1982: 14) displays the early twentieth-century Iranian fascination with world history and European thought, while folding the entirety of the composition within a quintessentially Persian cultural framework and artistic medium.

Today, the largest and most elaborate of the so-called "Great Men" carpets is held in the Carpet Museum in Tehran (Dadgar 2001a, 2001b: 130–1). Measuring over five meters in height and boasting more than 180 figures, this carpet is likely the most expensive and elaborate of all extant pictorial rugs. Besides the leaders and thinkers of old, including more than 100 Persian kings, at its bottom the carpet includes a number of members of the royal family, including Ahmad Shah Qajar (r. 1909–25), who was placed on the throne at only thirteen years of age by the parliament (*majlis*) after his father Muhammad 'Ali Shah was deposed. In this elephantine carpet, the last ruling member of the Qajar dynasty and members of the Qajar elite insert themselves within an already crowded scene, no doubt to emphasize the glory, authority, and legitimacy of the ruling household at a moment when the constitutional movement was putting a decisive end to Qajar rule within Iran.[2]

This strategy of visually connecting the Qajar ruling class with the "great men" of world history occurred not only in carpets but in paintings as well. For example, one icon made in 1304/1889 follows the same general pattern, albeit with some noteworthy alterations (Figure 2.3). At the bottom of the icon appear Nasir al-Din Shah and members of the Qajar elite, surmounted by 'Ali, Hasan, and Husayn, above whom a luminous, banner-wielding "Young Muhammad" stands in apotheosis (Khosronejad 2018: 74, 96). The icon proves technically experimental because the (modern) Qajar portrait photographs appear to have been pasted in and painted over, while the putti and cherubs, some painted in a bluish grisaille, owe much to (older) European painterly styles.[3] Registers of Persian poetry girdle this creative mix of media and styles; the verses praise God, the Prophet Muhammad, the *ahl al-bayt*, and Nasir al-Din Shah, who "gained only fruition from his faith's blessing"

FIGURE 2.3 *Icon depicting the Prophet Muhammad (at top),* ahl al-bayt *(middle), and Nasir al-Din and members of the Qajar elite, 1304/1889. Bunyad Museum, Tehran.*

(Khosronejad 2018: 75). Just as in the prologue to 'Ali Khan Vali's photographic album, contemporary carpets and icons depict the Qajars as if inheritors and custodians of the Islamic faith in a Persian-Shi'i geo-religious milieu.

Beyond pictorially crafting a Muslim-Shi'i-Qajar lineage, plenty of other "Great Men" carpets do not include depictions of the Qajar family. These non-royal rugs are smaller in size and appear to have catered to early twentieth-century wealthy and well-educated patrons, including Iranians who quite possibly took part in the constitutional movement and eventually served as members of the *majlis*. Many of these well-to-do "Great Men" carpets include about fifty figures that are numbered and whose names are provided in cartouches that function as a concordance within the surrounding frame of the carpets. Most germane for this study, these other carpets prominently depict the Prophet Muhammad in the topmost position (Plates 5–6). There, knotted in threads of wool and cotton, he stands—youthful, unbearded, with a banner in hand, and a plumette-topped turban, below a pediment bearing the Persian-language laudation: "Long live the great (*buzurgan*) and illustrious (*mashahir*) men of the world!" As *primus inter pares*, Muhammad indeed stands in excellent company, including Solomon, Moses, 'Umar, and other famous leaders of world history.

Most often the Prophet appears at the very top of the figural composition, as can be seen in the carpet dated 1918 (Plate 5). Here, as in other carpets, Muhammad is flanked by the same four individuals: namely Solomon, Moses, 'Umar, and Harun al-Rashid. Additionally, in these pictorial carpets, these so-called "great and illustrious" men are always numbered with the exact same digits. For instance, Moses is always number 1; Solomon, number 2; Muhammad, number 18; 'Umar, number 19; and Harun al-Rashid, number 22. By closely examining these minute details, it thus becomes clear that the same numerical system of identification is in use within the majority of these carpets. This evidence in turn points to a single, shared pictorial source that deploys the same concordance system that interlinks figures, numbers, names. Hence, the question begs to be posed yet again: what is the original pictorial source of the "Young Muhammad" holding a banner, which in this case is fitted within a tableau of the "great and illustrious" men of the world produced as pictorial carpets during the first two decades of the twentieth century?

Applying a laser-sharp eye to these carpets reveals major clues. Indeed, one Kirmani carpet, which was sold at auction and is now in private hands, holds the key to the entire puzzle (Plate 7). It includes the same groupings of "great men" and numerical concordance (Sakhai 1997: 78). However, at its top now appears Jesus Christ—whose name in Arabic letters ('Isa) has been inserted—among the top five protagonists, including the young Muhammad holding a banner. The addition of Christ hints at a European Christian audience or patron for this carpet, suggesting that it was produced for export to Europe rather than domestic Iranian consumption. This hypothesis is further strengthened by the inclusion of inscriptions written in French, including the note at the top that reads "*Fabrique* (workshop) *de Milani*

Kermani" as well as the names of the great men inscribed in French (e.g., Moïse, Napoléon, César, etc.). Last but certainly not least, the pediment praising the "great and illustrious men of the world" in Persian includes an epigraphic inscription in capital letters reading: "*TABLEAU DES PRINCIPAUX GRANDS HOMMES*" (Depiction of the Principal Great Men). This detail once again suggests a Francophone audience. Above all, however, it provides the final giveaway for the pictorial source of images of the banner-wielding "Young Muhammad" that were produced in various media within Iran at the turn of the twentieth century.

In an intriguing international twist, these "Great Men" carpets comprise a Persian textile adaptation of an earlier French image, made *c.*1850–80, bearing a title written in similarly uppercase letters, reading more fully: "*TABLEAU DES PRINCIPAUX GRANDS HOMMES qui sont illustrés dans toutes les parties du Monde par leurs belles actions, leur génie, ou leur courage*" (Depiction of the principal great men who made themselves illustrious in all parts of the world through their beautiful deeds, their genius, or their courage) (Plate 8). Below the image's identification appears the recognizable trope of the Greek pediment, which in this case bears the plaudit: "*Gloire immortelle aux hommes illustres*" (Immortal glory to the illustrious men). From the title of the image to the glorification of the world's great and illustrious men, rendered in French and Persian equivalents, the overlaps in the textual contents between the Persian rug and the French print are undeniable.

The French print was produced during the second half of the nineteenth century for use in elementary school courses on world history as well as for other French socio-cultural spheres, most especially masonic lodges, such as the Grand Orient in Paris, in which the notion of a global fraternity was often stressed through the "great man" or *grand homme* rhetoric and images, both of which became a hallmark of the Third Republic. Its many educational and ritual uses aside, the French print also foreshadows the Persian carpets by a few decades in its depiction of about fifty individuals as well as the numerical concordance of identification, which in this instance is located in the lower horizontal frame.

Among the world's eminent characters standing in the upper right are familiar faces and numbers (that is, 1, 2, 18, 19, and 22). Proceeding from left to right stand Moses holding the Ten Commandments, Solomon with his king's crown, the young Muhammad holding a banner made of yak or horse hair, 'Umar wrapped in a large brown cloak, and Harun al-Rashid sitting cross-legged and smoking the hookah (Plate 9). Unlike the other illuminati depicted in the crowded scene, these three Muslim leaders wear Oriental garb, in particular robes and turbans.

Before proceeding with a discussion of this pedagogical print's contents, a brief excursus into its particular depiction of Muhammad is in order. After all, the question remains to be posed: why did the French artist of this "Great Men" scene decide to depict the Prophet of Islam as a young gentleman standing upright and holding a standard? A preliminary answer can be offered here: by the middle of nineteenth century, the most likely pictorial resources for the French artist must have been illustrated travelogues, costume books, and even theatrical depictions. Although examples abound, perhaps the closest pictorial prototype of the Prophet in French prints is the depiction of an Ottoman Gentleman (*Agá*) smoking a long, thin pipe (Figure 2.4).[4] This illustration belongs to a series of twenty-eight prints made by the Italian artist Francis (Francesco) Smith, who accompanied British nobleman Frederick Calvert (d. 1771) to Istanbul in 1763–4.[5] These prints also served as illustrations in Calvert's travel account entitled *Eastern Costume*, published in 1768.

FIGURE 2.4 Agá *(Turkish Gentleman), in Frederick Calvert,* Eastern Costume, *Engraved from the Collection of Lord Baltimore, after designs by Francis Smith, (London: 1768). The Edwin Binney Third Collection of Orientalist Prints, Fine Arts Library, Harvard University, AKP287.235.*

Other eighteenth- and nineteenth-century French depictions of Ottoman rulers and individual types must have served as a visual reservoir for the artist's depiction of Muhammad in the "*Tableau des Principaux Grands Hommes.*" To give a second example, the similarities between an image of Sultan Sulayman II (r. 1687–91), made in 1825 to illustrate a French comedy entitled *Soliman II ou les trois Sultanes* that originally premiered in Paris in 1761 (Elmarsafy 2001), are quite striking (Figure 2.5). The Ottoman ruler, who was considered the ruling embodiment of Islam at the time, wears a similar *katibi* turban ornamented with a plumette, has a knife tucked into his waistband, and wears pointed shoes. In the French play's depiction, however, Sulayman II is shown with a well-trimmed mustachio, while the young Muhammad in the French "great men" print is shown forgoing facial hair.

In the pedagogical print (Plates 8–9), the artist has selected a standard decorated with a crescent finial and horse-hair ornament as an object-sign befitting the Prophet. Once again, a French pictorial source may have provided the impetus for the artist's decision to include a banner. One particular publication—i.e., Antoine Laurent Castellan's *Moeurs, usages, costumes des Othomans, et abrégé de leur histoire*, printed in 1812—may have served as a possible textual and visual resource. In his book on Ottoman customs, manners, and costumes, Castellant includes an entire chapter

FIGURE 2.5 *Depiction of Favart's comedy entitled* Soliman II ou les trois Sultanes, *illustration made by Sainfal, engraved by Mauduit, and published by Boulard, Paris, 1825. Bibliothèque nationale de France, Estampes et photographie, PET FOL-EF-266.*

dedicated to standards, banners, and flags, including those of the Janissary corps, pashas, and viziers. He notes that the "most noble" among them is the standard ornamented with a horse-tail (*though*), which is carried by the sultan (Castellan 1812: 237). Thereafter, he dedicates no fewer than four pages to a detailed description of the Prophet Muhammad's "noble standard" (*sandjac-chéryf*), the most important and respected of all banners in Muslim lands (Castellan 1812: 237–40). An illustration of such banners and standards appears in this chapter stressing both the *tugh* and *sancak* (Figure 2.6). As a result, within the mid-nineteenth-century French artistic imagination that this particular print captures, the Prophet Muhammad is

FIGURE 2.6 *Ottoman standards and banners, in Antoine Laurent Castellan,* Moeurs, usages, costumes des Othomans, et abrégé de leur histoire, *Paris: Nepveu, 1812, vol. 4, plate E, between pages 234 and 235. Edwin Binney Third Collection of Orientalist Prints, Special Collections, Fine Arts Library, Harvard University, AKP287.235.*

envisaged as a young Ottoman gentleman-sultan carrying the *tugh*-cum-*sancak*, a "most noble" object that elevates him to royal and prophetic rank.

Returning to the French print of the "Great Men," the concordance at the bottom of the image gives information about each of these great men, providing basic information about their birth and death dates, while also highlighting their most noteworthy accomplishments. The entry for "*Mahomet*" describes him as a "prophet and legislator of Muslims, and founder of the Arab empire" ("*Prophète et législateur des Musulmans, fondateur de l'Empire Arabe*"). It also notes that he is buried in a superb mosque in Medina and that he "wrote the Qur'an, the holy book of his followers" ("*Il écrivit le Koran, le livre saint de ses sectateurs*"). Both the image and the text in the French print of the "great men" of the world therefore eulogize the Prophet Muhammad in praiseworthy terms as a youthful and upright leader, lawgiver, empire builder, and "author" of one of the world's most influential holy books.

It is this highly acclaimed Muhammad depicted in post-revolutionary and Enlightenment-period French texts and images of the "great and illustrious men of the world," that somehow made its way to Iran, where artists and carpet designers adopted, altered, and expanded the print's figural representations and accompanying critical apparatus. Such Persian carpets were likely made at the behest of literate and powerful patrons, including members of the Qajar ruling family, provincial governors, and elite individuals who were elected to the newly established *majlis*, itself conceptualized in rhetorical strategies and visual products as a contemporary assembly of great men who achieved laudable deeds on behalf of Iranian citizens.[6] Via figural representation, photographic portraiture, and numerical concordance, these "great men" visuals attest to a Franco-Iranian encounter propelled to no small degree by revolutionary and constitutional fervor that intimately connected global movements during the nineteenth and twentieth centuries.

It is within this entangled political and cultural context that the image of a banner-wielding "Young Muhammad" migrated from France to Iran. In this regard, while 'Ali Khan Vali's note in his photographic album (Figure 2.2) insinuates that it was Nasir al-Din Shah who saw and recorded this alleged Byzantine icon during his trip to a museum in Europe, all evidence points to the "*Grands Hommes*" print of the mid-nineteenth century instead. Indeed, Nasir al-Din Shah photographed the French print while in Paris and brought a copy back to Iran, where today it remains pasted in one of his albums preserved in the Gulistan Palace (Khosronejad 2020). Once in Tehran, it is likely that the image was made accessible at the newly established Dar al-Funun—the modern Iranian equivalent of the *École des Beaux Art*—where it served as a catalyst for replicas in paintings, photographs, and carpets. This process of translating a European source in this elite school for modern sciences in Tehran should come as no surprise. After all, its curriculum included world history classes in which Persian translations of the lives of Alexander the Great, Peter the Great, Napoleon, and Columbus were all assigned (Ekhtiar 1994: 317–319). It is noteworthy that these world explorers and conquerors all figure in the "Great Men" carpets as well.

From France to Iran: Masonic pathways

By the 1800s, Nasir al-Din, Iranian diplomats, intellectuals, and students visited, studied, and lived for substantial periods of time in Paris. By then, within French literate milieus the Prophet Muhammad was conceptualized as an inspired uniter of peoples and founder of a world empire. No longer was he described as a trickster, heresiarch, false prophet, and impostor, as had been the case in European polemical writings from the twelfth to the eighteenth century (Tolan 2019; 2010). Instead, by the nineteenth and twentieth centuries Muhammad came to be admired as a "great man" worthy of admiration and accolades in his position as a religious reformer, statesman, lawgiver, and conqueror. As John Tolan has observed, these common tropes "allowed a relatively objective and irenic appreciation of the importance of the Prophet and of Islam on the stage of world history, avoiding the bitter religious polemics that had so often colored European discourse on Islam" (Tolan 2014: 269).

By the eighteenth century, French intellectuals started to include Muhammad in their works on the *grands hommes* of history (Bonnet 1998; Minois 2005). Such was the case for Claude Pastoret (d. 1840), who consecrated his 1787 study to Zoroaster, Confucius, and Muhammad. Later on, during the second half of the nineteenth century, French writers and educators continued the trend of describing the Prophet through a series of plaudits rather than repudiations. For example, the French writer and politician Alphonse de Lamartine (d. 1869) includes a lengthy discussion of Muhammad in *Les grands hommes de l'Orient* published in 1865. In his work, he rejects the notion of Muhammad's imposture, arguing instead for his unwavering conviction. He then concludes his discussion of the Prophet with the following enthusiastic words: "Philosopher, orator, apostle, lawgiver, warrior, conqueror of ideas, reviver of the human spirit, revealer of rational dogmas of a cult without images, founder of twenty world empires and one spiritual empire, that is Muhammad!" (de Lamartine 1865: 168). In de Lamartine's exposé, Muhammad again stands tall among the great men of the world as a highly gifted leader of peoples, places, and ideas.

Not confined to discussion in erudite spheres only, Muhammad also comprised the subject of learning in French elementary schools at this time. His life and deeds, along with the history of Islam, were taught in the *écoles* and *lycées,* in which a secular education was implemented by the late nineteenth century. To prepare and aid instructors in new teaching techniques, the French educational bureaucrat and Director of Primary Education, Ferdinand Buisson (d. 1932), pulled together with his colleagues the *Dictionnaire de la pédagogie* (1882).[7] Among the many entries can be found an article on "*Mahomet*" written by Maurice Wahl, who describes

Muhammad as a uniter of peoples with remarkable talent as a writer and orator who "spoke as much to the senses as to the spirit" ("*il parle autant aux sens qu'à l'esprit*"). In the entry's last paragraph, Wahl also notes that Muhammad established Islam, "under whose aegis states were organized and civilizations flourished." However, he goes on to lament that these states have remained stagnant since their heyday in the Middle Ages, and so Europe bears the responsibility to return the light that it inherited from Islam once upon a time (Wahl 1882). Thus, while certain French nineteenth-century discourses on Muhammad were on the whole quite favorable, the rhetoric on the stagnation of Muslim countries no doubt reinforced France's colonial projects and *mission civilatrice* in the Middle East.

The "Great Men" print reflects these contemporary historical and pedagogical discourses. However, it also diverges from them in two notable ways: first, in its emphasis on a large white temple as the convening ground of this brotherhood of great men and, second, in its visual coupling of Muhammad and 'Umar, the latter of whom played a significant role in French historical writing at this time. These two details strongly hint that this large-scale print was used in a Masonic lodge, perhaps the Sincère Amitié lodge in Paris that belonged to the Grand Orient de France league of Freemasons. Other Masonic visuals tend to follow a similar format, showing the great leaders—also known as Knights and Masters—of Freemasonry and affiliated Masonic organizations standing in a hierarchically stepped white structure meant to symbolize the Temple of Solomon, itself an architectural stand-in for a New Jerusalem that could be reached through progressive, enlightened, universal, and non-sectarian fraternalism (Beck 2000).

Besides sharing compositional characteristics with Masonic images, the "Great Men" print also includes a white structure reminiscent of the Temple of Solomon. Muhammad is shown therein with a crescent and scimitar, both of which are key Masonic symbols. Moreover, the inclusion of 'Umar points in the direction of Masonic texts, which laud the Muslim leader for having reconsecrated the Solomonic Temple in Jerusalem. This restorative act foreshadowed the efforts of the Knights Templar, through whom the Freemasons traced their mythical origins. Thus, the figural formula of Muhammad-cum-'Umar along with the glaring absence of Jesus Christ in the French print hail us to follow the next twist in this already complicated tale: namely, to trace the connections between French and Iranian Freemasons, because it appears most likely that the "Young Muhammad with Banner" image was imbricated in international Masonic channels.

Already since the early 1800s, Iranian diplomats, students, and intellectuals were initiated into Freemasonry during their stays in Paris. Upon their return to Iran, they carried with them French revolutionary and Masonic ideas, such that by 1858 the first Freemason lodge—known as *Faramushkhana*, or House of Oblivion—was established by Malkam Khan, who encountered Freemasonry during his diplomatic sojourn in Paris. As a leading faculty member at Dar al-Funun, he mobilized his colleagues and students to join his new secret organization, whose goals included implementing parliamentary reforms and spreading liberal ideas based on French models. In introducing the new republican notions of justice, equality, liberty, fraternity, and democracy, Malkam Khan went on the record as stating: "I knew that it was useless to attempt a remodeling of Persia in European forms, and I was determined to clothe my material reformation in a garb which my people would understand, the garb of religion" (Lambton 1987: 306; Algar 1970: 280).

While Malkam Khan's organization earned the suspicions of Nasir al-Din Shah, who banned the group in 1861, Freemasonry continued to spread its political ideas in Iran during the last few decades of the nineteenth century. Freemason groups and other secret societies (*anjumans*) encompassed an eclectic miscellany of ideologues. While most active in Tehran, secret societies also blossomed in Kirman after 1896 (Lambton 1987: 309). These Kirmani groups included not only *mullas* but also members of the carpet industry (Helfgott 1993: 422): the very same social and economic locus that gave birth to the "Great Men" carpets. Finally, by 1906 the first official Masonic lodge was founded in Tehran. Known as the "Reawakening of Iran" (*Bidari-yi Iran*), the lodge (*luzh*) boasted official affiliation with the Grand Orient of France.[8] By 1910, the Bidari Lodge included Qajar royalty and constitutionalists; as a consequence, it was a veritable "Who's Who of prominent constitutionalist figures, ideologically disparate, ranging from radical through moderate to conservative" (Bayat 2010), in which French revolutionary ideals were Persianized via Masonic channels.

Besides politicians, ministers, and princes, the Bidari Lodge also hosted famous writers and intellectuals, including the prolific lexicographer 'Ali Akbar Dihkhuda and the poet Adib al-Mamalik Farahani. In 1907, Adib al-Mamalik penned a poem on Freemasonry and the Bidari lodge. Comprised of 539 rhyming couplets, it is essentially a Masonic catechism, whose main goal consists in giving masonry a "Persian-Islamic framework of expression by incorporating Iranian and Islamic themes into its alleged proto-history" (Algar 1970: 288). In his poem, Adib al-Mamalik praises the inceptive fiat "*kun!*" (be), in which the *kaf* is equated to the set-square (*gunya*) and the *nun* to the compass (*pargar*), thus yielding the iconic double logo of Freemasonry (Adib al-Mamalik [1312] 1933: 575, verse 3). In addition, the poet informs us that the Prophet Muhammad inherited the Masonic light from Zoroaster, the father figure of Freemasonry, and that this light passed down to the twelve imams via the *ahl al-bayt* who are called the "people of the lodge" ("*ahl al-luzh*") instead. The trope of the *luzh*, or Masonic lodge, pervades his poem. To name just one other example, in praising Abraham as the founder of the Ka'ba, he refers to the holy site as the "Lodge of the Ancient House" ("*luzh-i bayt al-'atiq*"), thereby rhetorically couching the Ka'ba as the very first Masonic lodge in the world. He then continues to praise the return of the Masonic light from France to Iran thanks to the *luzh-i Bidari*, a center for fraternity and enlightenment at the very heart of Iran's constitutional movement.

These many Franco-Iranian historical, political, religious, cultural, and artistic conjunctions strongly suggest that a number (though not all) of the "Great Men" carpets belonged to Iranian revolutionary and/or Masonic milieus. Such items may have served as material mementos for the "big-shots" *(buzurgan)* who were initiated into Iranian secret organizations from the mid-nineteenth century until the first two decades of the twentieth century. They also could have been used as wall hangings in members' private homes and Masonic lodges such as the *luzh-i Bidari,* all of which could function as official or clandestine meeting places. While otherwise unknown and unstudied, depictions of Zoroaster, Muhammad, and 'Umar may have existed within Iranian Masonic lodges especially since a number of Masonic lodges in Europe and America depict similar subjects, albeit usually as frescoes (and not carpets) on walls (Cochrane 1934). In addition, that the formula "Muhammad-cum-'Umar" was retained—rather than replaced by the popular Qajar Shi'i duo of "Muhammad-cum-'Ali"—also intimates a non-Shi'i setting. Iranian Masonic milieus, populated by great men and potentially fitted with pictorial carpets, indeed can be understood as ecumenical yet clad in an "Islamic garb": in this instance, a "garb" personified by none other than the Prophet Muhammad.

A prophetic peg in the matrix of modernity

Structured as a forensic exercise, with no clear argument or hypothesis provided at its onset, this brief essay posed a basic question: why was Muhammad represented as a young man holding a banner in early twentieth-century Iranian visual culture? This deceivingly simple query took us on an expedition into the world of Iranian carpet-making, French print-making, Ottoman travelogues and costume books, the cult of the "great men" in post-Enlightenment France, Franco-Iranian Masonic relations, and secret groups laboring on behalf of the Constitutional Revolution in Iran. By following these disparate yet interconnected strands, the story of this particular prophetic image takes us on a winding trail, highlighting the many ways in which Muhammad could be conceived in different times and places.

Within progressive intellectual and political settings in early twentieth-century Iran—then known as *Iran-i Javan* or "Young Iran" (Vaziri 1991: 145)—the Prophet could be imagined and depicted as a youthful revolutionary founder of a new world order as well as a great lawgiver in a line of illustrious men who contributed to the progress of humanity across the globe. The Iranian urge to panegyrize and pantheonize the Prophet captures this highly dynamic moment in modern world history, in the process catalyzing a new heroic image that might be best called the "Masonic Muhammad."

This new image of a Masonic Muhammad emerged in France around *c.*1850, likely the result of a French artist creatively mining illustrated European travel accounts, costume books, and illustrated theater books.

This prophetic image then migrated east again, reaching Iran where it began to multiply in paintings, icons, and carpets during the early twentieth century. In the end, this "Young Muhammad" image, which traveled across media and within several circuits of exchange, proves not a foregone conclusion or the product of a modernity that can simply be called global, transnational, constellational, peripheral, alternative, or "liquid" in some fashion or another (Gaonkar 2001; Seggerman 2019; Bauman 2000). These images of Muhammad instead construct a larger modern matrix—a lifeworld in which people and objects operate through elaborate vectors of encounter and exchange.

CHAPTER THREE

Repetition and Relics: Tracing the Lives of Muhammad's Sandal

*Richard McGregor**

The thirteenth-century Damascene scholar Ibn 'Asakir, who made his living teaching hadith, recounts an episode related to him by the pious shaykh Abu Ja'far Ahmad ibn 'Abd al-Majid.[1] The shaykh spoke of the power of an image, more precisely, the power of an image created by tracing the form of the Prophet's sandal. 'Abd al-Majid's tracing was almost certainly made from another tracing rather than from a sandal relic. It may have looked much like the tracing in Figure 3.1.

> I made this copy for some of my students. One of them came to me, saying, "Yesterday I saw the wonderous blessings of this sandal!" I asked him what he had seen, and he replied, "My wife was suffering such pains that I thought she would die. I put (the copy of) the sandal on the spot that was hurting her, and said, 'O God, show me the blessings of the owner of this sandal.' and God cured her at once!"
>
> Ibn 'Asakir 2010: 59

The humble tracing of the Prophet's sandal was clearly a powerful relic in its own right. Ibn 'Asakir also quotes some of the poetic inspiration the tracing could elicit. The devotional tone is clear and intense: "O you who would gaze upon a tracing of the Prophet's sandal, / Wax not proud, but kiss its likeness. / Cleave to it! For as long as you do, / The footprint of the Prophet will revive and bless." (Ibn 'Asakir 2010: 62)

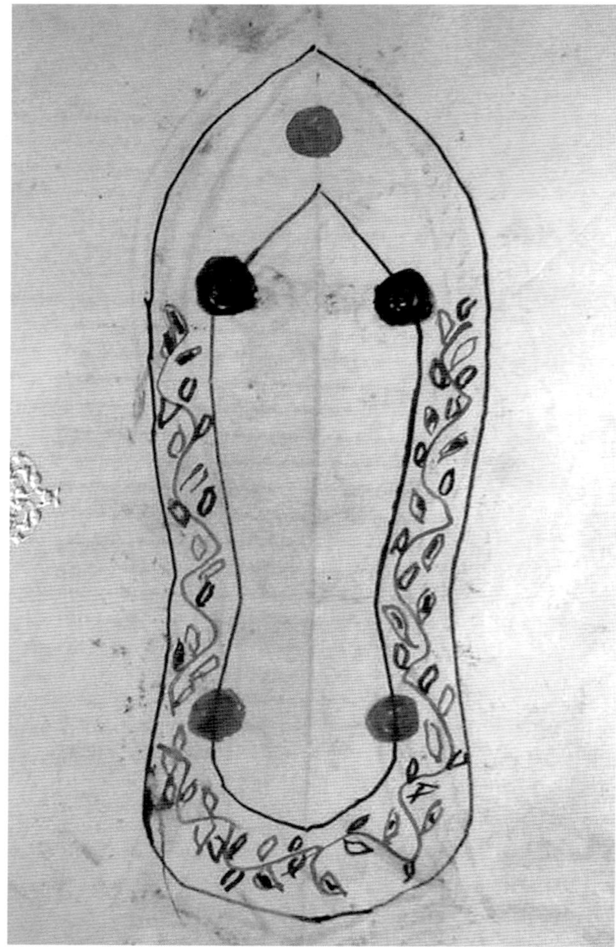

FIGURE 3.1 *Tracing of the Prophet's Sandal from al-Maqqari,* Fath al-Muta'al. *Al-Azhar University Library, manuscripts section (Al-Shawam,* raqam khass *5450).*

Ibn 'Asakir has put before us a narrative, a ritual practice, and an image—quite literally a copy of a copy—all of which may be approached from the perspective of studies in material religion. Healing practices, relics, and devotional ritual may have never been a primary concern for the discipline of Islamic studies, yet the recent turn to materiality in the humanities is opening many new avenues for research. As students of the Islamic tradition, though, we labor under a burden perhaps heavier than most. It is not an exaggeration to say that the dominant normative Islamic discourse from the early twentieth century onwards has pushed away the regional expressions of Islamic religiosity and pulled attention toward Islamic practice represented by modern Arabian reformers. As religionists we feel a certain obligation to represent the traditions we study in ways that are recognizable to so-called insider perspectives, but we have also been alerted to the methodological perils of taking one voice as representative of an entire religious tradition. Twenty-five years ago, Bruce Lincoln (1996: 26) called for the ideological critique of all sources, in order to not confuse a "dominant fraction" with the entire culture itself. The wider humanities were hard at work on this problem much earlier and would provide religious studies with some very effective tools in this endeavor. Feminist critique, and the recovery of marginalized voices through post-colonial studies, jump quickly to mind.

Another formative development was the linguistic turn in the humanities, which found one of its most powerful models in structuralism. Resistance to the mechanistic and determinative features of structuralism, however, gave rise to deconstructive critique, which in important ways has become an ally to the ideological critique advanced by Lincoln and others. One key element of ideological critique was the strategy of decentering, which sought to contextualize and even marginalize the most dominant voices. Normativity—the sense that a privileged narrative is an innocent and accurate mirror of the existing order—has become a hurdle that must be cleared before we can give voice to important marginalized agents. I believe this is where the turn to materiality comes in. Careful attention to the presence, demands, and perspectives, of objects can advance this decentering in surprising and productive ways (Ahmed 2008: 35). Jane Bennett puts this insight into ethical terms, when she claims that altering ourselves to the "vibrancy" of the material world around us serves to decenter our egocentric models. What she calls, "a bit of anthropomorphism" (2010: xiii-vi) will make conceptual space for the variegated web of bodies, ideas, environment, animals, and objects, which make up our worlds and cultures. In much the same spirit, Ian Hodder embraces new materialism for its promise to see the human-object interface from the perspective of things (Hodder 2012: 10, 13). Approaches to what he calls these "heterogeneous mixes" have been many, happily crossing disciplinary boundaries. Biology and feminist critique, physics and ethics, are just the tip of the iceberg (Wilson 2015; Ahmed 2008; Barad 2007).

It is with this sense of materiality that I turn to the topic of this essay. The current voices speaking for Islamic orthodoxy may thus be sidestepped for the moment, making room for the Islamic expressions that could be dismissed as "popular", outdated, or corrupt. More importantly, by putting emphasis on the object—in our case, copies of the sandal relic—we are forced to think about Islamic devotions in new ways. Instead of beginning with the privileged narratives of Islamic tenets, and forcing objects, images, and embodied practices into those frames, the current paper starts with the tracings of the sandal and builds out from there the many lines of meaning that present themselves. This decentering leaves the discursive space open and invites reconsideration of religious material culture. More specifically, the objects at hand for this study challenge us to account for their reproducibility. When considered historically, the practice of relic tracing does not sit easily in the existing conceptions of Islamic ritual and devotion. I will argue that the logic, experience, and "vitality" (recall Bennett's phrasing) of sandal tracing hinges on a deeper and more complex understanding of repetition. As we shall see, the historical record of this devotional practice resonates in irregular ways with Islamic understandings of repetition and with recent philosophical explorations of repetition.

The topic of relics in Islam is much wider and complex than most of us would imagine. Historians of Islam are no exception, but recent work has begun to fill out this picture (Wheeler 2006; Meri 2010; Gruber 2019; McGregor 2020). Some general framing, however, can be offered in brief. First, the wider Near Eastern context is relevant. The following passage from the Qur'an mirrors some of the ideas and objects circulating in that religious culture: "A sign (*aya*) of his kingship is that an Ark (*tabut*) will come to you in which are assurance (*sakina*) from your Lord, and the remnants (*baqiyya*) left by the families of Moses and Aaron, carried by angels." (2:248) From at least the first half of the eight century CE, exegetes identified these remnants as contact relics, with various lists being offered. Muqatil ibn Sulayman (d. 767) claimed these remnants included pieces of Moses' tablets, as well as his staff and turban, along with manna collected in a golden bowl. To this list al-Tabari (d. 923) added the staff of Aaron and the sandals of Moses. Qur'an commentators up into the medieval period, such as Ibn al-Jawzi (d. 1200), Fakhr al-Din al-Razi (d. 1210), and al-Baydawi (d. 1286), present variations on these lists.[2] In the late fifteenth century, the Egyptian exegete Jalal al-Din al-Suyuti also identified these remnants as relics, and added that the Ark contained images (*suwwar*) of the prophets, which had been sent down to Adam. Each prophet handed this collection down to his successor, until the Ark was lost to the Amalekites in battle.

The range of objects that can serve as relics is quite wide. Many personal objects can be enlisted, with the exegetes of Qur'an 2:248 enumerating several, that fall under the category of contact relics. These are objects that have acquired *baraka* or blessing because they have come into contact with a holy person. Bodily relics constitute another category, and include such things as fingernails, hair, and even heads. The imprints made by prophets and saints, usually into stone, are preserved and revered. Objects such as trees or stones that miraculously communicated have also been recognized and preserved. The commemorative marking of places from sacred history share some of the functions of portable relics (McGregor 2020: 122).

The category of contact relics is populated largely with clothing, and the sandals of Muhammad are well represented. The hadith and early histories of the Muslim community preserve a record of significant relic veneration. The hadith scholar al-Tirmidhi (d. 892), who compiled one of the six major Sunni collections of traditions of the Prophet, also composed *The Appearance of Muhammad* (*Al-Shama'il al-Muhammadiyya*), consisting largely of narrations from eyewitnesses of the details of the Prophet's appearance (Al Tirmidhi 1996). Between the ninth and twelfth centuries a number of such devotional works appeared (Al-Bayhaqi 1988; Ibn al-Jawzi 1976; Qadi 'Iyad 2006). The chapters of al-Tirmidhi's book deal with the personal manners of the Prophet (e.g. how he laughed, what he ate), his bodily proportions, and his personal items (e.g. his swords and clothing). In the tenth chapter, on the shoes of Muhammad, al-Tirmidhi presents eleven hadith reports describing the smooth leather of his sandals, and the two straps (or one only) fastening them to his foot.

With the modern emphasis on Muhammad as the desert prophet and iconoclast, it is not surprising that scholarship has made little of this devotional tradition, which relies on the objects, forms, and images associated with the holy figures of Islam. Part of any recovery of this tradition would include the medieval and early modern literature that propagated such devotion to holy objects (Gruber 2019: 253–369; Stetkevych 2010). One intriguing practice, which crossed the categories of object, image, and text, was that of tracing the Prophet's noble sandal (*al-na'l al-sharif*). In the historical record and the literary evidence we shall address below, there is a sense that such copying was a virtuous deed. To visit and venerate it did bring *baraka*, as with any other relic, but a unique aspect of the tracings is, of course, the reproduction of the relic.

Details have come down to us in the historical record attesting to relic veneration at the highest social and political levels. One intriguing account is from the early Abbasid period, and illustrates not only the popular interest in relics but also some of the political calculation that might come into play around their acquisition. At a public session held by the caliph al-Mahdi (d. 785), a man entered with a sandal wrapped in a handkerchief, and said, "Commander of the faithful, I present to you the sandal of the Messenger of God." Taking it, the caliph embraced it, kissed the sole and rubbed it against his eyes. He then ordered the man be paid 10,000 dirhams. After the man had left with the money, the caliph explained to his entourage that although he had his doubts about whether the Messenger had ever worn this sandal, since most people believed in it, it was best that he not reject it when presented to him publicly. In accepting this "gift" and tacitly acknowledging its authenticity, the caliph had bought the man's story to indulge the sensibilities of the commoners (Al-Safadi 1962–1981, 3: 302; Al-Baghdadi 1966, 5: 394).

The evidence for sandal and tracing relics in Syria comes later. In the mid-tenth century, the historian Ibn al-Faqih mentions a sandal at Abraham's mosque/tomb in Hebron. The earliest mention of the Prophet's sandal in Damascus goes back to the first half of the twelfth century (Ibn al-Faqih 1887: 101; Mouton 1993: 247), and the most prominent veneration of the Prophet's sandals and their public ritual copying seem to have taken place in the thirteenth-century. The Ayyubid ruler al-Malik al-Ashraf played an important role in the development of this practice. In 1228 he endowed a sandal to the college he had recently established under his name, the Dar al-Hadith al-Ashrafiyya (Ibn Kathir 1998, 17: 202, 232). Another madrasa in Damascus, the Damaghiyya, also apparently housed a sandal relic. Ashraf's relic enjoyed a high profile. A visitor to the Ashrafiyya in 1285 left a description of the sandal, housed in a niche, to the left of the mihrab, with Qur'ans stored in another niche on the right. A small door, gold in color, had been installed before the sandal's niche, which stood behind three silk drapes in green, red, and yellow. The sandal was housed in an ebony box with silver nails and a lock. Accounts of its ritual veneration tell us that crowds were allowed access to the relic only on Mondays and Thursdays, seeking to touch it and thereby acquire blessing (al Maqqari 2006: 279; Talmon-Heller 2007: 204; Meri 2001: 28–9; Humphreys 1977: 213). The sandal rested upon a stand, and its outline would be engraved upon an ebony tablet. The outline was perfumed, and the sweet smelling *baraka* would be transmitted to those who would kiss the outline. Ashraf seems to have promoted his relic actively, and on at least one occasion sent it to the home of an elderly devotee (Al-Yunini 1954–1961: 2:46). Devotion to the relic continued to the year of his death, when Ashraf is recorded in a public ritual of clasping the sandal to his breast and rubbing it against his eyes (Mouton 1993: 252).

Damascus would lose its sandal relics when the city was overrun by Tamerlane in 1401, but in the decades preceding, the sandal appeared in at least one important event. When the merchant elite and the religious class joined to publicly protest the local governor's excesses, the sandal was brought out of its niche in the Ashrafiyya college to join the procession. A mass of protestors gathered, led by the preacher of the Umayyad mosque. Along with them they took the flags of the mosque, a Qur'an allegedly in the hand of the caliph Uthman, and the sandal, as they marched to confront the governor. Their protest however, was not well received. The preacher was arrested and dragged to the governor's palace, while the sandal and the Qur'an were knocked to the ground. For the sultan Muhammad ibn Qalawun back in Cairo, the insult to the codex and the sandal was unforgiveable, and he had the governor publicly humiliated and thrown in jail (Al-Nabahani 2010, 3:215).

In its ritual function at the madrasa, the relic was doubtless enlisted in any number of personal petitions by anxious pilgrims. However, this location would not delimit the sandal's influence or presence. As we noted earlier, copies of some kind were being ritually made twice a week, and literary works like that of Ibn 'Asakir (d. *c.*1287), which we saw at the outset of this chapter, were also circulating the tracings. Significantly, these tracings were more than just copies, they were generally taken to be extensions of the relic. Traced and stylized representations were copied from each other, and handed down along with their chains of transmitters to guarantee authenticity. Plate 10 shows a sandal tracing from 1628. Ahmad ibn Muhammad al-Qadiri notes that he made his tracing according to one he found in the work of Ibn 'Asakir, *A Portion of a Tracing of the Prophet's Sandal (Juz' timthal na'l al-Nabi)*. At several points Ibn 'Asakir had discussed the provenance of the various tracings, including one that had come down from the early historian Ibn Fahd al-Makki, made from a sandal handed down by Talha ibn 'Abid Allah (d. 656) to the Prophet's wife 'A'isha and daughter Umm Kalthum (Ibn 'Asakir 2010: 53–4). Al-Maqqari extends this lineage of pious tracing to include al-Sakhawi (d. 1497) and al-Suyuti (d. 1505) in Egypt (Al-Maqqari 2006: 93).

Al-Qadiri mentions that more recently tracings have been displayed in Damascus, Alexandria, and Isfahan. On its efficacy as a relic, he notes the tracing is reputed to help with a wide range of concerns, from relieving any woman of the pains of child birth, to assuring victory in battle. Caravans are protected from attack, one's house is secured against theft, and safe travel by ship is assured. The owner of the relic will be rewarded with a successful pilgrimage to the Prophet's tomb in Medina, or at least a vision of him in a dream. This tracing (Plate 10) is clearly more than a simple outline. It includes two fine straps extending between the toes, and a band across the top of the foot at the ankle joint. The image is fairly ornate when compared with a tracing that appears in a later devotional work. Figure 3.2 is a nineteenth century tracing by 'Abd al-Qadir Habbal in his copy of Sulayman Jamal's (d. 1790) commentary on Muhammad al-Jazuli's (d. 1465) poem *The Signs of Blessing* (*Dala'il al-khayrat*), easily the most ubiquitous collection of devotional prayers in the Islamic world. The tracing is unadorned, without straps or holes, consisting simply of an orange outer line, with a black interior tracing.

An important work that disseminated the tracing throughout the Middle East and North Africa, was *The Divine Opening in Praise of the Sandals* (*Fath al-Muta'al fi madh al-ni'al*). The author was Ahmad ibn Muhmmad al-Maqqari (d. 1631), from Tlemcen, in present day Algeria. Al-Maqqari was from an established family of scholars, and had made his name as a historian. His description of Andalusia, entitled *The History of the Mohammedan Dynasties in Spain* (*Nafhu al-tib min ghusn al-andalus*), and his account of North African leading figures, *The Perfumed Myrtle Garden* (*Rawdat al-as al-'atira*), made him a valuable resource when he moved to Damascus and then Cairo. *The Divine Openings in Praise of the Sandals*, completed in 1624, presents scores of hadith relating to the Prophet's clothing, several historical episodes relating to the sandal in Islamic history, diverse poetry dedicated to the sandal and its tracings, and the various benefits and protections the tracings provide their owners.

Many manuscript copies have survived, and it seems all include a set of seven tracings. One early example was produced in 1657, copied by the hand of 'Abd al-Fattah al-Marhusi al-Azhari al-Ashmuni. Owned by Professor Muhammad bin Turki al-Turki, a current faculty member in the College of Education at King Sa'ud University, the text has been digitized and is available from the online depository alukah.net. An ownership stamp dating to 1762 indicates that the manuscript once belonged to a *waqf* endowed by Wali al-Din Efendi (Haci Veliyettin Efendi), the Ottoman Shaykh al-Islam from 1760 to 1761 and from 1768 to 1776. The first tracing

FIGURE 3.2 *Tracing of the Prophet's Sandal from al-Habbal's tracing in al-Jamal,* Al-Minah al-Ilahiyya bi-sharh Dala'il al-khayrat. *Ann Arbor, University of Michigan, Special Collections Library (Isl. Ms. 526).*

is fairly ornate, rendered in red, black, and gold, and framed with devotional statements of blessing for the Prophet. The second is rendered much the same, including two holes for the straps. Al-Maqqari supplies details handed down from various hadith authorities on the dimensions of the width of the heel, the middle section, and the overall length, which are variously presented in units of "hands" (*shibr*) and "fingers."

Al-Maqqari continues his presentation of the tracings, the second set of which he drew from the work of the thirteenth-century writer Sulayman ibn Salam al-Kila'i. Among the manuscripts I have consulted, the pagination and presentation of the tracings are not identical, meaning that it is not always clear to which of the tracings the author is referring. A tracing however from a seventeenth-century Berlin manuscript of the text does present some

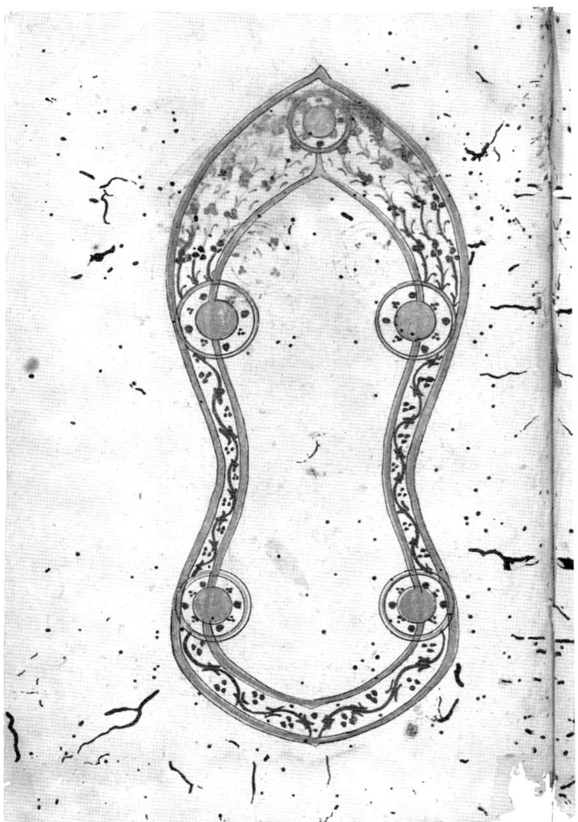

FIGURE 3.3 *Tracing of the Prophet's Sandal from al-Maqqarı,* Fath al-Muta'al. *Staatsbibliothek zu Berlin -Preußischer Kulturbesitz (Hs. Or. 10653).*

distinguishing features. Plate 11 is typical of all but one sandal – a double lined and embellished outline in red, black and gold color, showing only two holes for straps. Figure 3.3, the first tracing in the series, however, shows five strap holes, although the accompanying text does not explain why.

Another manuscript from the digital collection of Professor al-Turki—with similar *waqf* (endowment) stamps from the eighteenth century—presents one of the tracings with five strap holes, while the rest have two. These tracings are more ornamented than most of those appearing in later manuscripts. Gold, red, and blue paint are used, presenting not a double line outline, but rather a wide solid gold painted outline, decorated with flowers. A flowering plant in a small pot is present within each sandal outline, and flowering plants appear in the margins around the tracing. Thanks to the gold paint, the images are eye catching, but the execution is unrefined and amateurish. A copy made in 1690 by ʿAmir al-Ghamrawi, preserved digitally on al-mostafa.com, with a water mark "King Saud University 1959" along with illegible *waqf* stamps, presents the seven tracings in simple red ink, with little embellishment. The outlines are double lined, filled in with an undulating filler line. One tracing shows five strap holes, and all holes are filled in with very simple flower blossoms.

Three examples from the manuscript collection at al-Azhar university present the tracings in a range of styles. The undated manuscript 5883 was copied in a cramped but clear hand, and was designated as a *waqf* endowment to al-Azhar. The tracings are in red, green, orange, and black, but in execution they are quite rudimentary (Figure 3.4). Two strap holes on folio 30b seem to be flaming, but those on the facing page are simply colored blotches. Another set from the same manuscript (Figure 3.5) are messy and irregular. Eight strap holes are represented, although it is not clear whether the dots within the double outline should be read as holes.

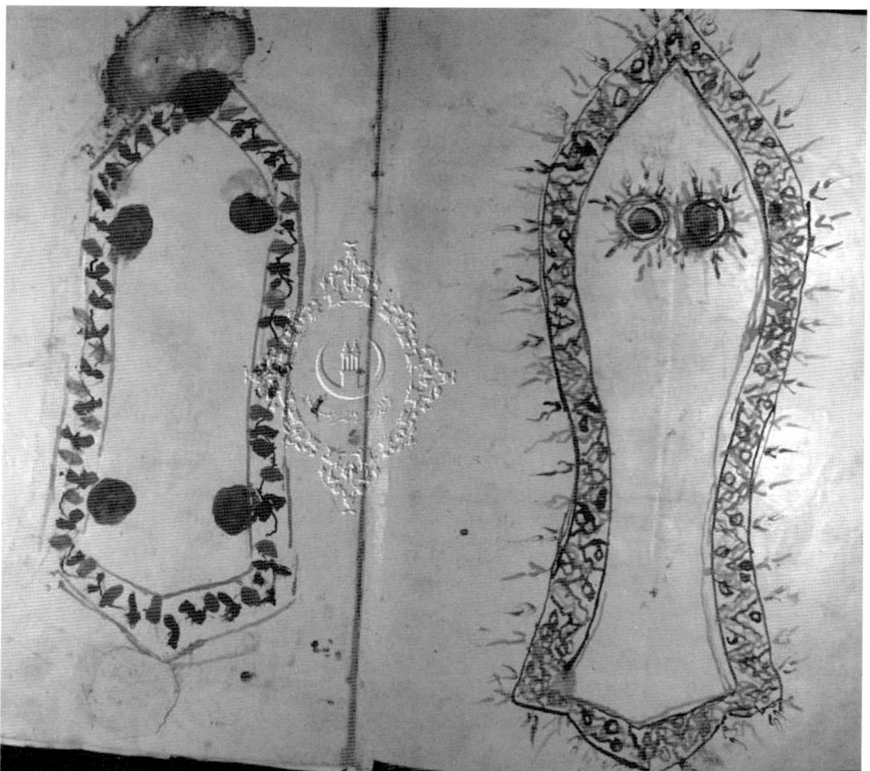

FIGURE 3.4 *Tracing of the Prophet's Sandal from al-Maqqari,* Fath al-Mutaʿal. *Al-Azhar University Library, manuscripts section (Al-Shawam,* raqam khass *5883).*

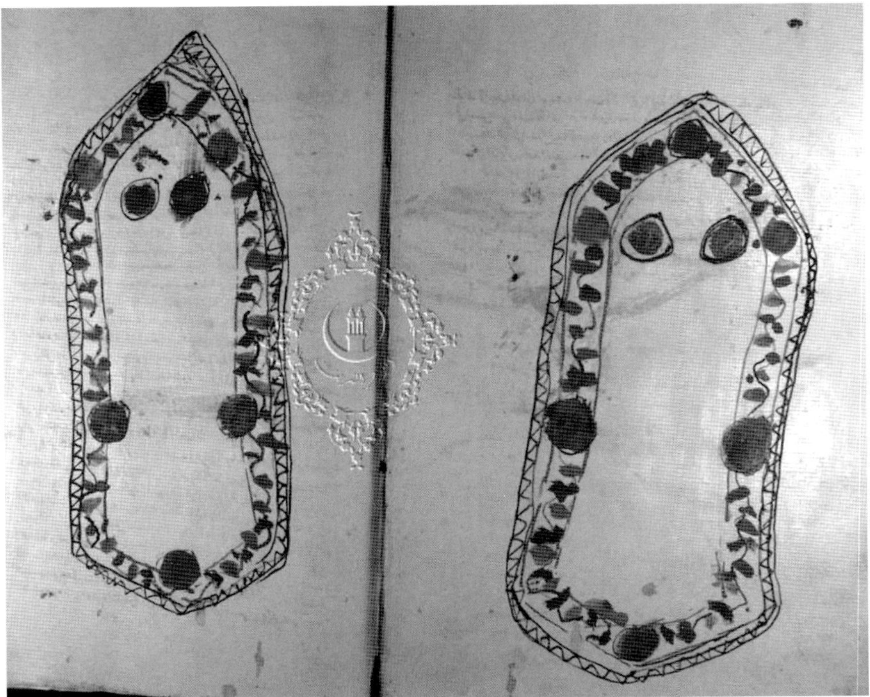

FIGURE 3.5 *Tracing of the Prophet's Sandal from al-Maqqari,* Fath al-Muta'al. *Al-Azhar University Library, manuscripts section (Al-Shawam,* raqam khass *5883).*

Manuscript 5450 is also undated and identified as a *waqf* to al-Azhar, but specifies that it should go to the benefit of the Syrian contingent (*riwaq*) of students. The tracings, all double lined outlines in black ink contrasted with orange, are rather simple and in places irregularly executed (Figure 3.6). The two-lined outline in black is repeated, with orange added for effect (Figure 3.7).

A third example from al-Azhar (MS 6299), this time dedicated to the Maghrebi *riwaq*, presents its tracings with attention to execution and design unseen in the others we have surveyed. The tracings are outlined by two gold bands, with the interstices filled by a finely rendered woven design in black and red (Plate 12). Dark green, orange, yellow, and red are used for the strap holes, which in one case number twelve, and start to look more like design ornaments rather than simply indicating structures for fastening a shoe. The tracing on folio 45b is more refined yet (Figure 3.8). The golden double outlines are decorated with a fine chain in black, and the woven designs are in black, red, and purple. What we have been calling strap holes now appear as celestial bodies, the middle unit in red, connected to three above and one below, all in gold color. The tracing in Plate 13 uses six

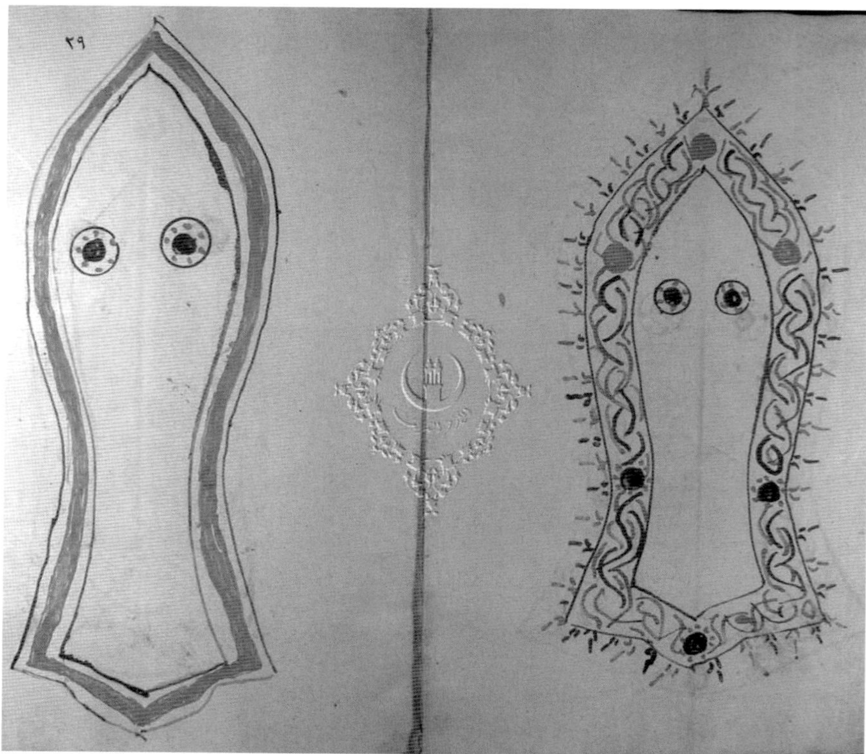

FIGURE 3.6 *Tracing of the Prophet's Sandal from al-Maqqari,* Fath al-Muta'al. *Al-Azhar University Library, manuscripts section (Al-Shawam,* raqam khass *5450).*

colors, and displays twenty strap holes. The interior is occupied again by five points, here connected further to each other, and through a red horizontal line across the middle, to the points on the outline band. Most remarkably, the outline is reproduced in a ghostly light brown, and inverted. It is essentially a tracing of the tracing. I would also argue that this an ingenious way for the image to represent its status as both an individual relic and part of the endless line of copies. As I will elaborate below, with this ghostly reversal of itself, the tracing image is engaging with the idea of repetition.

The tracing in Plate 13 alludes to repetition, a concept that has received significant attention in Islamic theology and philosophy. As early as the ninth century, Muslim theologians wrestled with the challenge to reconcile God's omnipotent will and humanity's agency over its own actions. In short, how could God be the only creator, while humans would in the afterlife be held accountable for their deeds? The simple answer that humans create their own deeds (thus explaining how they can be responsible for them) only opened up a greater set of problems, the first of which would be the apparent

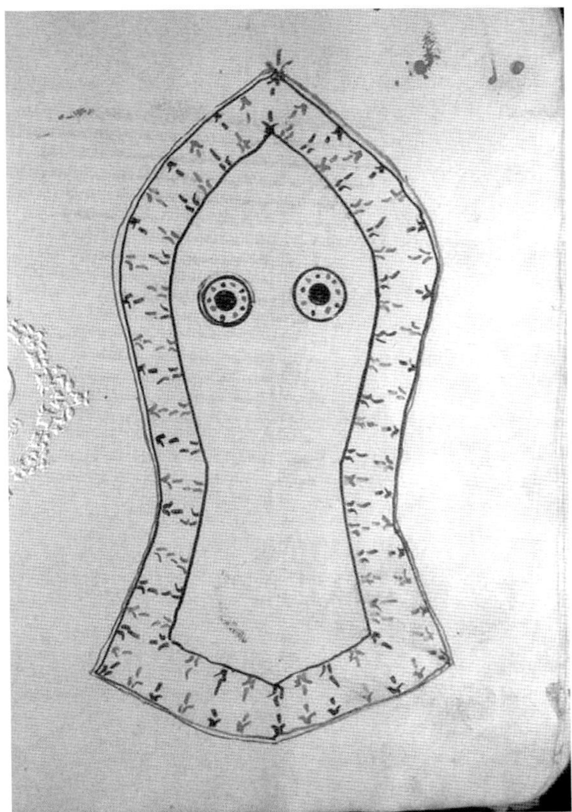

FIGURE 3.7 *Tracing of the Prophet's Sandal from al-Maqqari,* Fath al-Muta'al. *Al-Azhar University Library, manuscripts section (Al-Shawam,* raqam khass *5450).*

denial of God's omnipotence. Abu al-Hasan al-Ash'ari, the tenth-century founder of Ash'arism, took up the question, and he and his students developed a series of positions around *kasb*, or acquisition (Cahen and Gardet 2012). Generally, the position was that humans "acquire" their acts from God, rather than intending them and then creating and carrying them out. To make this understandable, al-Ash'ari had to reject the common experience we have of time as a linear continuity. In other words, one moment does not necessarily lead to the next; what seems like the flow of time to us is in reality a series of discrete moments that God just happens to create in an orderly sequence. Against our assumption that time, souls, or the universe, march along largely on their own momentum, the claim is that God recreates all from one moment to the next. In fact, one of the classic definitions of a miracle is *kharq al-'ada* or "disrupting the customary." A miracle is thus not a breaking of a natural law, but instead simply one moment being created after another in an unexpected way: at least unexpected to us. For the purposes of our discussion of repetition, the main point is that mainstream Sunni theology spilled much ink to unsettle the continuity we think we experience between one moment in a series from the next.

The Ash'arite theologians, however, were not the only ones trying to rethink the nature of repetition. The mystic Ibn 'Arabi (d. 1240) came to the question not to find the way out of a theological quandary, but in a more positive tone, seeking out the implications of an all-creating divinity. Reflecting on a passage from the Qur'an (55:29) "Each day He is upon some task" (*kull yawm huwa fi sha'n*), Ibn 'Arabi sees the need to reconsider our assumptions about repetition. In his reading, the Qur'an is saying that revelation is always new; and since existence is at heart the continuing process of revelation, everything in heaven or earth is new and never repeated. He is not using the same terms as al-Ash'ari, but his aim is similar. Continuity is impossible for creation, because it can never be its own creator; nothing can last for more than a moment before it needs to be created anew. The Creator has duration, while creation does not. Thus, Ibn 'Arabi says, "Know that nothing in creation repeats [*yatakarrara*]. Things are imagined to be identical with what resembles them and came before them. Yet in truth, they only resemble them and are not them. A copy [*mathal*] is not the thing itself" (Ibn 'Arabi 1854: 2:432). Elsewhere he adds, "No attribute or state endures for two moments, and no form appears twice" (Ibn 'Arabi 1854: 2:500).

These reflections from Ibn 'Arabi and al-Ash'ari should not be taken as explanations or even inspirations directly behind the practice of relic tracing. That would be an over-interpretation of the evidence. However, this conceptual work does show some of the range of thinking about how objects are related to each other, and to earlier or later instantiations of themselves. Some of this conceptual range has also been explored in modern philosophy, perhaps most importantly by Gilles Deleuze, who fully embraced the puzzle of repetition.

The idea of repetition is certainly a challenge. Al-Ash'ari and Ibn 'Arabi were trying to uphold the impossible but necessary position that things persist (e.g., I remain myself, for the duration of my life) and yet are grounded in specific and discrete moments (e.g., I am who I am at this moment, not the past or future me). It is this sense of objects in a series—be it temporal or spatial—being neither replaceable nor independent that Deleuze illustrates so well. One way he does this is by setting repetition into a structuralist model. Earlier in this chapter I noted the criticisms of structuralism, but here Deleuze is appropriating it to illustrate his point. Briefly, structuralism held that meaning is generated by the differences that stand between objects. (e.g., I am the father I am not because of my nature or fate, but because I have a child; and I am this father in particular because I am not any of the other parents in this neighborhood). Likewise, in linguistics, structuralism accounted for the meaning of words not because they have a necessary or indexical relation to their meaning, but because they stand apart and in relation to all other words in the language.

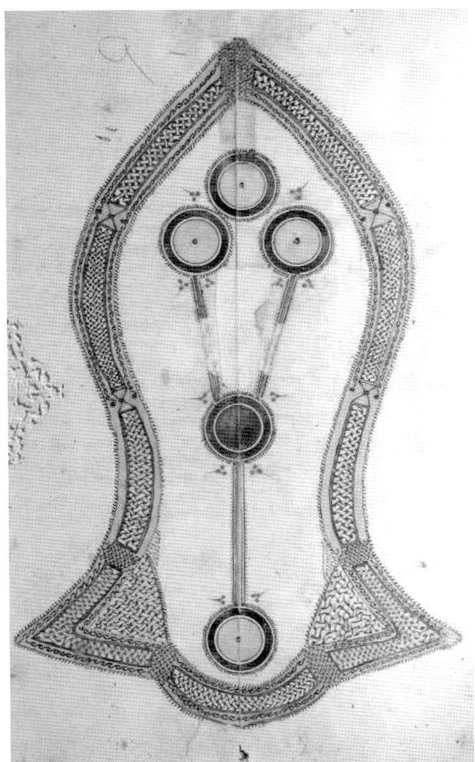

FIGURE 3.8 *Tracing of the Prophet's Sandal from al-Maqqarī,* Fath al-Muta'al. *Al-Azhar University Library, manuscripts section (Al-Maghariba,* raqam khass *6299).*

Here Deleuze, in considering repetition, notes a complex two-sidedness that emerges. To start with, he asserts that, "In every case repetition is difference without a concept." (Deleuze 1994: 23). Here he is pointing out that the difference at play within repetition (i.e. the relation between one moment or object and its processors and successors) is not actually discernable within the structure. That is, meaning or "concept" is not being generated in the simple procedure that say, "cat" has its concept thanks to its relationship to say, "bird" and "dog." The meaning at play in repetition is somehow generated by being at once all of the instances (in our case, all of the tracings), while also inhering in the concept itself. He builds out from his initial claim that, "In every case repetition is difference without a concept" by stipulating that, "in one case, the difference is . . . a difference between objects represented by the same concept. In the other case, the difference is internal to the Idea; it unfolds as pure movement, creative of a dynamic space and time which corresponds to the Idea" (ibid.: 23–4). So the "Idea" or the concept at play in our relic tracing(s) is both constituted by the standard structuralist notion of difference from its other, but difference is also a fundamental part of the concept itself. The former makes repetition discernable to a structuralist model, but the latter accounts for its unique status among phenomena, and captures, I claim, the open-endedness of our relic that is endlessly reproducible.

My reading of Deleuze on repetition may be an oversimplification, but in conversation with al-Ash'ari's emphasis on the discrete moments of existence, and Ibn 'Arabi's articulation of the newness of creation, I am trying to bring into focus the peculiar and complex phenomenon that tracing relics display. Such tracings then are not simply pious fictions, which make naïve claims to being accurate, or truer, representations of the Prophet's sandal. They are not metaphorical or indexical, making the lost beloved present. Deleuze here has helped us to see the concept of the tracing relic includes not only the endless instantiations, but that the meaning (the Idea) includes within it that unboundedness. The relic is by necessity unfinished and incomplete. Pulling back to consider this within the material culture of Islamic devotions, we can now draw a more fulsome picture, one that shows the objects and the pious bodies that interact with them in an embrace that eludes the static and the finite. To make a tracing is to fulfill and tend to the life of the relic, which from its side is forever leaning forward towards its next repetition. Through its ghostly self-tracing in Plate 13, the relic points directly to its other, which is itself the devotional act that is sandal tracing.

PART TWO

Identifying Objects

CHAPTER FOUR

"The Greatest and Only Flag Known:" The Lapel Pin in American Islam

Michael Muhammad Knight

The Supreme Wisdom Lessons, an initiatory text in the Nation of Islam tradition,[1] explains that because devils cannot be reformed, the Prophet Muhammad ordered Muslims to kill them: "Each Moslem is required to bring four devils, and by bringing and presenting four at one time his reward is a button to wear on the lapel of his coat, also a free transportation to the Holy City Mecca to see brother Mohammed" (*The Supreme Wisdom Lessons* n.d.: 10:14). Precise wordings of the text have varied. In 1932, one version reportedly commanded only that a "son of Islam" must gain "four victories" over devils to win an unspecified "reward" ("Raid Reveals Cult Practices" 1932: 3). According to a 1934 *Detroit Free Press* article, "Voodoo Catechism Says Heads of Four Devils Are Passport to Mecca," another variant read, "Each Moslem is required to kill four devils and by presenting the four heads he receives his reward of a button for his button-hole and transportation to Mecca to pass a visit with his brother Mohammed" (1934: 13). The *Lessons* became evidence in state prosecution of the Nation in 1934, when Sally Ali, a fifteen-year old student at the Nation's "University of Islam" testified in court that she had been taught that decapitating four devils would earn the free trip "and a button of some sort," possibly bearing the likeness of the movement's prophet and savior, Master Fard Muhammad (whom she apparently identified as "G.D. Farrand"). Ali also testified to Elijah Muhammad (who was cross-examining her as his own attorney) that "devils" meant "all wicked people," rather than a particular race ("Girl Recounts Lore of Islam" 1934: 1).

Sociologist Erdmanne Doane Benyon, who accessed the *Lessons* during his research of the community in the 1930s, remarks, "The entire teaching is symbolic and can be understood only by the initiates" (Benyon 1937–8: 901). Nation exegetes in the 1960s read the *Lessons* as a project of moral self-perfection (*Cooper v. Pate* 1964: 352, 390). Warith Deen Mohammed, who relied on his personal charismatic authority as Elijah Muhammad's son and supreme interpreter of the *Lessons*, to redirect the Nation towards what many would call "mainstream" or "orthodox" Islam, interpreted the devils as wicked states of mind (Muhammad 1975: 13). Louis Farrakhan has interpreted the devils in relation to the four beasts in Revelation, which he reads as oppressive nations (Muhammad 2018).

Nonetheless, accusations that Master Fard Muhammad promised a reward for murdering white people have persisted. This excerpt, referenced here as 10:14,[2] has become the most cited statement in the *Lessons* by outsiders seeking to implicate the tradition in anti-white violence. In 1963, the Louisiana legislature's Joint Committee on Un-American Activities subpoenaed materials from the Nation, quoting 10:14 as justification for its concern ("Activities of 'The Nation of Islam' or the Muslim cult of Islam, in Louisiana", 1964). In the 1970s, the "Zebra Murders," in which a small group of Black conspirators targeted white people for violence, killing fifteen and wounding eight, led to a new prominence for 10:14. *The New York Times* quoted 10:14 during its coverage of the Zebra Murders trial, reporting that prosecutors presented the excerpt from a conspirator's binder that he had used to indoctrinate the other killers ("'Zebra' Trial Ends its Ninth Month" 1975: 9). When a Five Percenter in the Virginia state prison system sued for the community's legal recognition as a religion, a change in status that would come with the right to possess the *Lessons*, the Virginia Department of Corrections cited 10:14 as proof that Five Percenters advocated violence against white people (*Coward v. Robinson* et al. 2017).[3] The idea that some might read 10:14 literally, has also appeared within the tradition as an urban legend, circulated in multiple versions, of a man who showed up at a Nation *masjid* in Newark, New Jersey (or the Nation's Salaam restaurant in Harlem, depending on the version) with a bag containing the heads of four white men, wanting his ticket to Mecca and lapel pin (Gardell 1996: 57; Magida 1997: 52; Noel 1989: 2). Though the Newark version ends with police arresting the man, there is no support for its historicity.

My interest in 10:14 lies not in the meaning of the four devils, but rather the significance of an ostensibly mundane reward for killing them: the lapel pin. How did the lapel pin become an artifact of American Islam? In lived practice, Nation of Islam members earn lapel pins bearing the Nation's flag, the National, for their memorization of the *Lessons*. The lapel pin in this context embodies both a personal belief and disciplined commitment. Participants in the Five Percenter tradition likewise earn their Universal Flag lapel pins for demonstrating mastery of the *Lessons*; to wear the lapel pin thus invites challenges to claims of authority and authenticity. As praxis rooted in the *Lessons*, the lapel pin speaks to the tradition's multiplicities and creative heterogeneities. As a performance of identity and visible marker of one's relationship to the truth, the lapel pin transforms and territorializes the body. Challenging academic master narratives that diminish the "Islamic" status of the Nation, Edward E. Curtis IV calls attention to the Nation's construction of ritual practices regarding the Black body, and includes in his analysis practices that might not be recognizable as "Islamic" for everyone, such as Nation members selling copies of *Muhammad Speaks* on street corners (Curtis 2002: 97–8). I extend Curtis's insight to the embodied practice of the lapel pin. The wearing of a lapel pin is not as instantly recognizable as an "Islamic" practice as the Nation's abstinence from eating pork, and is not directly traceable to a *sunna* of the Prophet or "classical" Islamic tradition but rather rooted in American Freemasonry, as we shall see; nonetheless, the lapel pin functions as an Islamic artifact. This discussion of the lapel pin contextualizes the artifact in Shahab Ahmed's treatment of the "Islamic" for its salience to the making of meaning in "terms of Islam" (Ahmed 2016: 71).

Prehistories

The Nation of Islam originated in 1930s Detroit, when Master Fard Muhammad embarked on his teaching mission, offering a materialist theology that denied the existence of an unseen "mystery god" and advocated a view of divinity rooted in the Black self. His teaching materials were eclectic, including Jehovah's Witnesses radio sermons, a collection of literature on Masonic symbolism, and an untranslated Arabic Qur'an, all of which required him to interpret for his followers (Benyon 1937–8: 900). While there remains uncertainty as to how much later Nation theology owed to Elijah Muhammad's elaborations rather than Fard Muhammad's teachings—it was after Fard Muhammad's disappearance in 1934, for example, that Elijah began asserting that Allah, still no invisible "mystery god" but a living man, was Fard himself—the mandate for killing four devils and earning a lapel pin as a reward dates to the Nation's formative period.

The lapel pin's meanings in Nation literature speak to the milieu in which Fard Muhammad began his mission. Well before the turn of the twentieth century, members of Masonic lodges, fraternal orders, and church groups had relied on lapel pins to mark affiliations and ranks on the body. Visiting the US in 1904, sociologist Max Weber observed the proliferation of lapel pins as markers of a successfully examined "moral worth" among the middle class. He would write,

> Many men among the American middle classes (always outside of the quite modern metropolitan areas and the immigration centers), were wearing a little badge (of varying color) in the buttonhole, which

> reminded one very closely of the rosette of the French Legion of Honor. When asked what it meant, people regularly mentioned an association with a sometimes adventurous and fantastic name.
>
> (Weber [1905] 2001: 132)

To Weber's eyes, the pins' primary function was to mark their wearers as having been endorsed by an institution that could vet their character: "the badge in the buttonhole meant, 'I am a gentleman patented after investigation and probation and guaranteed by my membership'" (ibid.: 133). This public expression of moral worth through membership also connected the pin's wearer to networks of fellow members—along with non-members who recognized the pin's claims—and possible social privileges that could come with affiliation, as promised in accounts of members finding job opportunities and friendship when strangers noticed their lapel pins (Beito 2000: 59–60). William D. Moore, however, argues that Weber misreads the lapel pin, placing "too great an emphasis upon the selection of initiates and inadequate stress upon the transformative effects of ritual. The lapel pin . . . was an external sign of an unseen transformation" (Moore 2006: 35–6). In the communities that I discuss here, the lapel pin carries a range of potential significations, signaling both exterior and interior meanings. The pin mediates relationships while also constructing and performing a particular vision of the inner self. These meanings are not mutually exclusive, or in tension, but authorize one another.

Discursive and aesthetic linkages between US Freemasonry and the African American Islamic renaissance of the early twentieth century have been well documented in academic literature. The Nation's lapel pin gives material expression to these connections, traceable to Black Shriner movements developing around the turn of the twentieth century. While white Shriners appropriated Arab and Islamic imagery as jest, Black Shriner groups from the 1890s onward treated Shriner claims of lineage from a Muslim East as a serious and legitimate connection to ancient Egypt and Islam. Contemporary to Noble Drew Ali's Moorish Science Temple of America (MSTA) in Chicago, Abdul Hamid in New York—claiming to speak as "head of all Masonic degrees in Mecca"—proclaimed that to become true Masons, Black Shriners must become Muslims and join the "Mecca-Medina Temple" in Arabia (Bowen 2011: 10).

For the potential of the lapel pin, fez, and other regalia to rewrite relations and map networks of power, white Shriners attempted to obstruct Black Shriners' access to these artifacts. In 1919, *The Chicago Defender* reported that a Black railway mail clerk in South Carolina was arrested for wearing a 32nd-degree Masonic ring and Shriner pin after a white Mason complained to police ("Arrest Man for Wearing Secret Order Regalia" 1919: 1). Two years later, the same paper wrote of a lawsuit filed in Arkansas by members of a white lodge, Al Amin Temple, Ancient Arabic Order of Nobles of the Mystic Shrine, against a Black lodge, the Mohamet Temple No.24, attempting to prohibit the Mohamet Temple members "from wearing Shrine pins and fezzes and from advertising and calling themselves Shriners" (Suit May Disband Souther Shriners 1921:1). Another suit, filed in Texas, saw a white order sue a Black order to prevent it from operating as a Shriner lodge and using Shriner regalia (Full Text 1929: 10).

The MSTA, popularly treated as a precursor to the Nation, performed a public embodiment of Islam through parades and sartorial scripts that were informed by Shriner imaginaries (Nance 2002: 643). Marcus Garvey's Universal Negro Improvement Association (UNIA), apparently viewed by Noble Drew Ali as the divinely arranged precursor to his own career, also echoed Masonic pageantry in its public presentations and Garvey's own regalia as the UNIA's "potentate." The UNIA's resonance with Masonic performative embodiment included members wearing lapel pins of the organization's red, black, and green pan-Africanist flag. UNIA lapel pins endowed their wearers with a mark of confirmed moral integrity and entered them into a network of social support. In her investigation of UNIA work in the rural south, Mary G. Rolinson provides an account of the UNIA's lapel pin saving one wearer from a vigilante mob, which decided upon observation of the pin that he could not have been the criminal that they sought (Rolinson 2007: 123).

Beyond Masonic and other fraternal orders, church groups, and Garvey's UNIA, the lapel pin's proliferation during the early decades of the twentieth century includes the Theosophical Society, which advertised pins bearing its symbol in affiliated periodicals (*The Messenger* 1919). The Nation's relationship to occult marketplaces of the early twentieth century and some of their prevailing themes—including the Theosophical metaphysics of race, theories of mystical magnetism and magnetic powers of thought, depictions of Moses as an occultist, and visions of Jesus as an esoteric master teaching "knowledge of self"—speaks to overlaps in lexicons between the Nation and Theosophy (Knight 2019: 183, 196).

In short, the Nation emerged from a setting in which lapel pins operated as embodiments of meanings for diverse groups: Masonic and fraternal orders, pan-Africanists, and Theosophists, not to mention "mainstream" church organizations. It is not my interest to single out one group as the source that "influenced" the Nation's lapel pin, but rather to set a stage for pins as preexisting items in the Nation's material vocabulary. The lapel pin was loaded with significations, making visible a secret of the wearer's interior condition as well as locating wearers within a network. Through the Black Shriners, these significations became meaningful to seekers of alternative Black worlds, enabling the pin's recoding as Islamic. The Black Shriners' lapel pin, linking to a genealogy within a timeless Black Islam—a connection that they would defend against white supremacy in court rooms—became an "Islamic" artifact in the definition laid out by Ahmed in *What is Islam?*: the lapel pin contributes to an individual's making meaning through Islam (Ahmed 2016: 450).

In Ahmed's terms, the lapel pin had become part of the Nation's Con-Text, "the full historical vocabulary of Islam at any given moment . . . a built environment of meaning" (ibid: 357). The "Con-Text" represents everything that the historical tradition offers for understanding the Text, including (but by no means limited to) classical commentaries and canonical literatures. Ahmed distinguishes between the Con-Text *in toto*—the totality of resources—and *in loco,* the accumulated tradition as accessible in a particular milieu. The Con-Text varies across historical settings, because not everything gets to be an ingredient in every locale; in some places, people read Attar, and in some places they don't. (ibid: 361) To ask "What is Islamic art?", for Ahmed, would really ask, "Of what consequence is Islam to the object?" (ibid: 409). The "historical vocabulary of Islam" in Detroit and Chicago included the lapel pins established in US Freemasonry, particularly Black Shriner groups. For the Nation, lapel pins inscribed visions of the self upon the body "in terms of Islam."

The Nation of Islam

"We come before you with the universe on our head or coat lapel," Elijah Muhammad declares in his *Theology of Time* lectures, "which means that we come to rule. That's what it means and nothing else" (Muhammad 2008: 26). Elijah Muhammad refers here to the National, the "holy flag of Islam," which Nation *masjids* displayed on chalkboards in opposition to the United States flag, between them the question, "Which one will survive the war of Armageddon?" The US flag signified "slavery, suffering, and death" and a fleeting empire, compared to the "greatest and only flag known," which represented a nation with "no birth record" (*The Supreme Wisdom Lessons*: 9:10). Elijah Muhammad disparaged those who wore patriotic or Christian lapel pins: "You put it [the cross] on your coat's lapel. You put it around your neck thinking that you're on the way to heaven, when you're on the way to hell. It makes sense for you to worship the Sun, Moon & Stars instead of the Stars & Stripes, because the Stars and Stripes is copied from the Sun, Moon and Star" (Muhammad 2008: 57). The National establishes the wearer as shareholder in an ontological Blackness reaching back "trillions of years" (*The Supreme Wisdom Lessons*: 10:40) (Figure 4.1).

If the lapel pin embodies variegated conceptions of Blackness and Islam, what would it mean, then, for a devil to wear it? In 9:14, the "degree" preceding the promise of a pin for killing four devils, the *Lessons* set conditions for white people to become counted as Muslims. Some white people have received privileged access to Islam and received tutelage from the Original Man. These exceptional devils become marked by their jewelry: after devoting "thirty-five or fifty years trying to learn and do like the original man," a devil can call himself a Moslem Son and thereby

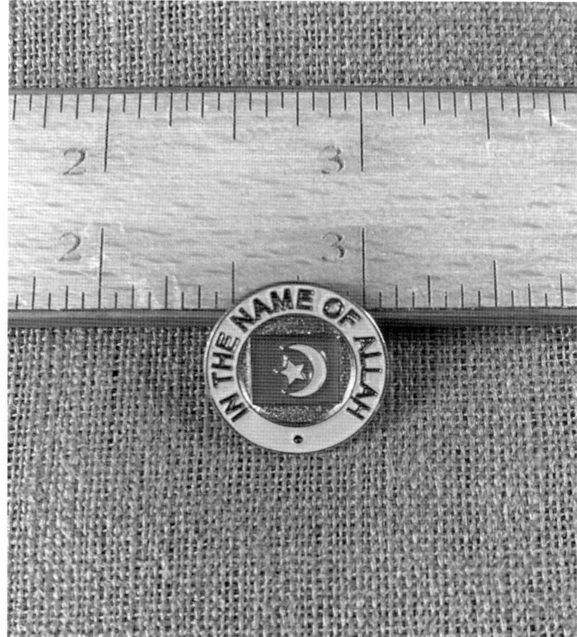

FIGURE 4.1 *Nation of Islam lapel pin. Collection of Michael Muhammad Knight (photo by Anna Bigelow).*

wear the flag of Islam—the "Sun, Moon and Star." However, the Moslem Son must "add a sword on the upper part" of the flag. As the *Lessons* explain:

> The sword is an emblem of Justice, and it was used by the original man in Mohammed's time. Thus, it was placed on the upper part of the flag so that the devils can always see it, so he will keep in mind, that any time that he reveals the secrets. We give him this chance so that he could clean himself up and come among us. His head would be taken off by the sword.
>
> The Supreme Wisdom Lessons: 9:14

Though the devils are not Muslims by nature, the flag marks them as having recognized the truth of Islam. These "Moslem Sons" who guarded their secret, in the Nation imaginary, were white Shriners. The Shriner emblem of a sword attached to the star and crescent reflected a mutual knowledge between Freemasons and Islam. In Elijah Muhammad's view, the bejeweled Shriner fez and lapel pin signified a public acknowledgment by white men (even if only as a subtle wink meant for those few who had already been initiated into understanding) of Black sovereignty over Islam:

> The high degree Mason takes our flag and puts it on their coat lapel and head, then walks out celebrating one day a year. Why doesn't he wear it every day? It doesn't belong to him. "So, Muhammad, when was the devil permitted to wear the flag on his head once a day?" He got permission when he began studying and trying to act on the principles for 35, 40 or 50 years.
>
> The Supreme Wisdom Lessons 2008: 58

The Five Percenters

In his collaboration with Ol' Dirty Bastard, "Cuttin' Headz," the RZA offers the verse, "Snatchin' devils by the hair, then cut his head off" (Ol'Dirty Bastard 1995). In the song, "I.S.L.A.M." from his *5% Album,* Lord Jamar proclaims, "To the four devils, yo I'm choppin' yo head" (Lord Jamar 2006). AZ, who appears in Nas's "Life's a Bitch" and recites, "We rolled beginners in the hood as Five Percenters," gives a spoken intro to Nas's "Affirmative Action" and declares, "Niggas don't understand the four devils: lust, envy, hate, jealousy" (Nas 1996). Like so many Five Percenter references in hip hop, the verses' full significance is lost to audiences that lack literacy in Nation tradition. Those who have studied the *Lessons*, however, recognize these lyrics as citations of 10:14. While departing from the Nation on numerous points (notably in Five Percenters' general denial of self-identification as Muslims[4]), Five Percenters preserve the Nation's investment in the *Lessons* and find meaning in 10:14 for their own praxis of the lapel pin.

The Five Percenter community, popularly known as the Nation of Gods and Earths (NGE), emerged in 1964 when Clarence 13X, a former member of the Nation's flagship Harlem mosque, Mosque No.7, during Malcolm X's tenure as its minister, renamed himself Allah and began teaching the *Lessons* to young men who had not registered as Muslims. Allah's followers became known as "Five Percenters" for their understanding of the *Lessons*, which refer to a "5 percent" who are "poor righteous teachers" and recognize the Black Man as God—in contrast to the 85 percent, "slaves to mental death and power" who believe in an unseen "mystery god" that the elite 10 percent weaponizes against them. While the Nation of Islam understood itself as constituting the enlightened "5 percent" mentioned in its own *Lessons*, Allah apparently perceived the Nation as containing its own 10 percent (Elijah Muhammad and his inner circle, getting rich from the Nation's labor) and 85 percent (the rank-and-file members selling *Muhammad Speaks* on the corner), both defined by their relationship to a "mystery god," the absent Fard Muhammad.

Allah concretized the border between his movement and the Nation. One elder recalls that when Five Percenters asked Allah about 10:14, reporting that a Nation minister had given the text a literal interpretation, Allah told them to no longer visit the mosque (Knight 2007: 61). His break from the

Nation would eventually produce a new flag and lapel pin. Early in the movement, Five Percenters appropriated the National as their emblem, wearing the star and crescent on a necklace, but Allah later adopted a new flag to supersede the National: the black and gold "Universal," which consisted of the number "7" projected upon a star and west-pointing (as in the National) crescent within an eight-pointed compass rose. Five Percenter tradition presents the flag as the design of Universal Shaamgaudd Allah, one of the "Medina First Born" (the original nine Five Percenters in Brooklyn). Universal Shaamgaudd Allah's design had reportedly amalgamated the National with the insignia of the Cross Park Chaplains, a Brooklyn gang to which several of the Medina First Born had relationships (ibid: 91).

The new flag marked the Five Percenters as a distinct tradition, not a "branch" or "offshoot" of the Nation, and designated an embodied territory via lapel pins. The first Universal Flag lapel pins materialized from Allah's work as a community liaison for City Hall. Ja'Mella God narrates that after receiving the design from Universal Shaamgaudd Allah, Allah handed it over to Mayor John Lindsay, whose people arranged for the lapel pins to be made by Eagle Regalia, which had produced pins and metalwork for the city, including, according to Five Percenter sources, New York Police Department badges. As a material artifact (at least for its earliest batches of pins), the Universal Flag finds an endorsement in its relationship to state power: "The United States government, the state government, and the city government had to authorize our flag," Ja'Mella God asserts. "That's why we qualify to be who we are" (Allahs' 2014: 332).

Barry Gottehrer, an official in the Lindsay administration who mediated the relationship between Lindsay and the Five Percenters, gives an account of the pin's origin in his memoir, *The Mayor's Man*. Gottehrer recalls Five Percenters asking him to get the Universal Flag made into lapel pins and encountering resistance at City Hall, which feared that an "official medallion" would empower the Five Percenters to start a new "recruitment drive" or "start a war." Gottehrer went ahead and had the pins made, without reportable incident (Gottehrer 2007: 102).

Five Percenter narratives describe Allah as requiring followers to write their adopted "righteous" names in a "Book of Life," which he would then get engraved onto the fronts of the pins. Whereas Nation pins featured the National with accompanying text, "In the Name of Allah," Five Percenter pins included the wearer's name as divine attribute: a god named Ja'Mella God would thus wear a pin reading, "In the Name of Ja'Mella God." The name, like the flag, signaled that the Five Percenters were not Muslims, as Allah had ordered followers to drop their "Muslim names" in favor of names drawn from Five Percenter culture. A Five Percenter who had adopted the name Bilal in 1964, for example, changed his name in 1967 to become Allah Born God (Knight 2007: 90).

Five Percenter tradition has seen longstanding debates concerning the meanings of the Universal Flag and the question of who could possess a lapel pin, and how exactly they earned the right to that access. While Muslims in the Nation earned the right to wear their National lapel pins through memorization of the *Lessons*, and Five Percenters maintained their vetting of students with the *Lessons*, Allah did not reserve his community's lapel pin only for those who had mastered the text. Allah Supreme God, a Five Percenter elder who joined the movement as a teenager in the 1960s, narrates that when he approached Allah for his pin, he still went by his "Muslim name," I-Jabar. Allah put a pin on I-Jabar's newborn niece Yakeema, told him, "that's hers," and said that I-Jabar would get his pin when he adopted a new name. I-Jabar dropped his Muslim name and became Allah Supreme God (ibid: 100).

Within Five Percenter sources, a tension persists between precedents of Allah giving the Universal Flag to non-Five Percenters or newborn babies and the tradition of Universal Flag lapel pins circulating in a regulated flow of teacher-student initiations. "Regulation" in this context remained decentralized, as there was no singular Five Percenter institution that could control the production and awarding of lapel pins. Shabu, a Brooklyn Five Percenter, remembers obtaining his pin from "half-original" (i.e., having one white parent) Monik, who would "come out to the park jams with some Universal Flags pinned inside of his coat with our names already on them, all we had to do is get 120 lessons in our heads" (ibid.: 146). The pin was earned with the student passing a test of his/her knowledge of the *Lessons*. Wearing the pin meant entry into a system of performance in which one embodied mastery over the *Lessons*, supported by a tree of teachers that traced back to the origins, and invited challengers. The teacher ("enlightener") who guided and tested the neophyte's memorization and qualified him/her for the pin, had presumably gone through the same process with his/her own teacher, and so on, embedding the wearer's knowledge within a genealogy, a Five Percenter version of the *silsila* or *ijaza*. Moreover, as the pin bears an engraving of the wearer's chosen name, the pin becomes a statement of the divine attributes its wearer claims. Five Percenter oral tradition abounds with stories of imposters finding their credentials questioned and ultimately losing their pins. Prince Allah Cuba, an author who became controversial in the 1990s for calling various Five Percenter "orthodoxies" into question, had allegedly first caused disruptions in the community in the late 1970s by selling Universal Flags from his Brooklyn store. Five Percenter sources claim that because Cuba was exploiting the tradition, a number of Five Percenters joined forces to destroy his shop (ibid: 147).

In *Knowledge of Self*, an anthology of Five Percenter essays, Victorious Honor Allah gives an account of the Universal Flag as a policed territory. During his first trip to the community's Harlem headquarters, the Allah School in Mecca, he purchased a headband bearing the Universal Flag; but when he later made a remark that exposed his lack of knowledge concerning the interpretation of the Universal, an elder god named Lord confiscated the headband, promising, "I'll give it back when you're ready." Victorious embarked on a study of exegetical material on the Universal. At the next community gathering, Lord saw him and asked, "You ready to build on the flag?" Victorious answered Lord's questions, including his "curveballs," and Lord returned the headband. "The system which so many had feared, rejected and misunderstood actually worked," Victorious writes. "It was fair. I didn't know the flag, so I shouldn't have worn it" (Allah 2009: 168–73). To wear the Universal Flag in any form did not serve merely to express support, but to make a claim of territory. This vision of the Universal caused some controversy in 2014, when Jay Z attracted broad media attention for publicly wearing the flag on a medallion. Though Jay Z's lyrics contain references to Five Percenter culture (in "Heaven," for example, he mentions the Five Percenter acronym for Allah, "Arm Leg Leg Arm Head"), he has not publicly claimed affiliation. Some Five Percenters charged that Jay Z's wearing of the Universal without knowing the *Lessons* amounted to disrespect (Autodidact 17, 2014).

Today, contests over the Universal Flag often take place in social media. In 2017, a Five Percenter woman sparked controversy when she posted a photo of her Universal Flag lapel pin. The pin conformed to normative community expectations with a significant exception: the pin read, "In the Name of Goddess," with "Goddess" appearing as her righteous name. The question of whether women could claim godhood reaches back to the original community, as Allah had reportedly termed one woman a goddess. While the dominant position claims divinity as a masculine privilege and regards women as Earths, Five Percenter women have asserted their rights to names such as Goddess, Al-Lat, and Al-Uzza, with or without preserving their identity as Earth (Knight 2007: 220–1). While that debate frequently elicits heated engagement in online Five Percenter forums, the roughly 800 posts responding to this image included commentary not only on the goddess question, but also the charge that theological offenses had been inscribed upon the Universal Flag. It appeared that for Five Percenters asking about the pin's origin and asserting that its maker should be "exiled," materially linking the goddess doctrine to the lapel pin was as offensive as the doctrine itself (Williams 2017).

As a rich interpretive tradition has developed around the Universal Flag, variations in the design can express a gendered theology. On the original Universal Flag, a sliver of the crescent moon could be seen behind the top of the "7". For some interpreters, this compromised the divine supremacy of the Black man (the "7") over the Black woman (the moon). A second design, in which the "7" completely covered the crescent's diameter, became popularly regarded as the "authentic" and "original" Universal Flag. Eagle Regalia, which still makes pins for Five Percenters, informed me that for some time, Five Percenters charged that the company had been printing the wrong design and insisted that the true flag was the "big 7" version. Eagle Regalia began producing the new "big 7" pins, but observed that in recent years, Five Percenters have come to prefer the "big moon" version as the original design (Author interview January 20, 2020).

In my own experience engaging the Five Percenters as an outside researcher, I encountered the Universal Flag as a marker of my status in relation to the territory. At community assemblies ("parliaments") that I attended in Harlem, vendors regularly sold items that included merchandise bearing the Universal Flag. Some vendors would sell me items bearing the Universal, no questions asked; this response became more common as I became more known in the community. Others would sell literature bearing the Universal, but not merchandise that I could wear on my body, so long as I had not mastered the *Lessons*. Still others would sell me the Universal on clothing or wearable accessories if I could demonstrate comprehension of the Universal's meanings, articulating the esoteric symbology that had developed around the Universal's details, such as its various angles and the meanings of its sun's eight points, the number "7", and the crescent and star. Vendors also vetted my knowledge by giving the price for an item in Supreme Mathematics. While it was theoretically possible for anyone to purchase merchandise bearing the Universal Flag, including plastic buttons, there were no enamel Universal Flag lapel pins for sale. Possession of the Universal in this iteration had to be earned. Less complicated was my purchase of pins bearing a drawing of Allah's face, captioned, "ALLAH," though vendors did occasionally quiz me to confirm that I had a basic grasp of the man and his name (Figure 4.2).

FIGURE 4.2 *Allah, the former Clarence 13X, lapel pin. Collection of Michael Muhammad Knight (photo by Anna Bigelow).*

Conclusions

The Supreme Wisdom Lessons, a foundational text for the Nation of Islam and Five Percenters, remains critically underexamined in the study of American Islam. Doubly neglected is the material practice, rooted in the *Lessons*, of embodying one's relationship to the tradition through the lapel pin. The pin emerges through a history of fraternal organizations, political movements, and church groups as a marker of initiation, social location, middle-class respectability, and internal transformation. In the Nation of Islam, the lapel pin of the National preserved these meanings and more, additionally recoded to signal membership in a nation understood to be "trillions" of years old. Five Percenters supplanted the National with their own flag, the Universal, but maintain the tradition of the lapel pin as an embodied performance of mastery over the *Lessons*. For the claims inscribed upon the body by the lapel pin, the practice requires the pin's wearer to remain rigorous in study of the *Lessons* and prepared to defend his/her right to wear it against challengers. The pin thus produces a materialization of ideas about authority, authenticity, and the policing of "orthodoxy" and its boundaries, inscribing these ideas on the wearer's body and thereby enforcing them in physical space.

CHAPTER FIVE

Tasbih in West African Islamic History: Spirituality, Aesthetic, Politics, and Identity

*Ousman Murzik Kobo**

Introduction

Beads have served multiple purposes in the material cultures and religious rituals of many societies since ancient times. Most religions of the world employ beads in their liturgies and to symbolize their unique spiritual and cultural identities (Henry and Marriott 2008; Dubin 2009). Molded from various materials—woods, stones, ceramic, glass, marbles, and even bones—beads, along with rare gems and other precious minerals, have also served as aesthetic items of wealth in many societies. Beads are therefore important in examining the spiritual and/or material culture of most societies, including African societies. For West Africa, the focus of this chapter, archeological evidence suggests that the use of beads as spiritual and cultural objects with profound aesthetic value has existed in the region for centuries. In many parts of premodern West Africa, beads served religious, political and cultural functions, demarcating social locations, political authority and religious functions within both centralized and decentralized societies.[1]

The expansion of Islam in the region starting from the ninth century CE initiated a gradual erosion of the traditional functions and symbolism of beads because Muslim scholars associated them with indigenous rituals, and therefore must not be conflated with Islam. Instead, Islam introduced its own strings of prayer beads (*misbah*) but known locally as *tasbih* or *tasbah*, which Muslims adopted to symbolize their conversion and belongingness to a new spiritual community. Today, *tasbih* is one of the most visible spiritual and material objects identified with West African Muslims, and perhaps Muslims throughout the world as evident in its vast market everywhere in the Muslim world, including Saudi Arabia, where the use of *tasbih* in prayers has been declared *bid'a* (reprehensible innovation), and discouraged. As demonstrated below, its resilience in the face of opposition from Salafi-inclined Muslims suggests that *tasbih* remains an important spiritual and material icon with deep history worthy of a careful academic analysis. In this essay I illustrate some of its various manifestations in West Africa's history. I begin with a brief description of the structure of *tasbih* and its usage in Islam generally. I also explain briefly some of the controversy surrounding its usage and why it has remained resilient. I then describe the Tijaniyya *tasbih* to provide a background to the narrative. Following this, I delve into some case studies to illustrate how a study of the different manifestations of *tasbih* helps to offer a nuanced narrative that highlights its multiple functions without overlooking its "affectiveness."

The general structure of *tasbih* includes the *imam* or head of the beads, a more elongated piece and shaped differently from the rest of the beads (Plate 14). This head-bead marks the beginning and end point of the recitation as the devotee counts the number of repetitive *dhikr* (phrases glorifying Allah). The string also includes the dividers or markers that group the beads into specific sets of numbers. The standard *tasbih* totals ninety-nine beads, representing the ninety-nine names of Allah (*Al Asma' al husna*), but grouped into three sets of thirty-three beads in each set. The name *tasbih* (also *tasbah* in West Africa[2]) is a verbal noun originating from the recommended basic *dhikr* recited after each of the five daily prayers in the following order: *subhana 'Llah* (glory be to Allah) thirty-three times; *Alhamduli'Llah* (All praise is due to Allah) thirty-three times; and *Allahu Akbar* (Allah is Great) thirty-three times (Al Tirmidhi, Book 48, Hadith 44).[3] Each of the three sets of thirty beads is separated by a marker (*alaama*) to reflect this commendable *dhikr*. There are also shorter *tasbih* with only thirty-three beads and these are sometimes divided into three sets of eleven beads. Other *tasbih*, mostly those identified with Sufis, contain one hundred beads because most of their *adhkaar* (sg. *dhikr*) are based on the multiple of one hundred. These are also divided into the standard three sets of thirty-three beads per set, with additional divisions depending on the *dhikr* formula of a specific *tariqa* or Sufi brotherhood.

Tasbih and its controversies

An analysis of the controversy surrounding *tasbih* in Islam is interesting but beyond the narrow scope of this chapter. It thus suffices to offer a basic outline that relates to the present topic: the relationship between *dhikr* and *tasbih*. *Dhikr* literary means remembrance. However, its diverse contextual appearances in the Qur'an (more than one hundred times) suggest a range of meanings, including glorifying or commemorating Allah through frequent utterances of His names and attributes, remembering and reflecting on His creations and bountiful mercy, and even offering admonition, as in Qur'an 87:9 and 10. The performance of *dhikr* by reading the Qur'an and or repeatedly uttering one or more of the ninety-nine names of Allah, is generally accepted by all Muslims regardless of doctrinal affiliation. However, the term has become associated with Sufism, Islam's mystical tradition, where chanting or uttering Allah's attributes remains the Sufis core voluntary spiritual activities, which they combine with the required supplications. Just as the word *dhikr* is generally associated with Sufis,[4] *tasbih*, whose diverse verbal meanings in the Qur'an, connotes glorification, is also associated with the Sufis. Indeed, *dhikr* constitutes the devotional pursuit of the Sufis' search for spiritual enlightenment and nearness to Allah, and *tasbih* is the instrument of their vocation.

The associational convergence of *tasbih*, *dhikr*, and Sufism, is evident in the ways many adherents of Salafiyya,[5] the doctrinal adversaries of Sufis, characteristically denounce Sufi *dhikr* and *tasbih* as innovations (*bid'a*) on the grounds that Prophet Muhammad neither used *tasbih* nor practiced Sufi mystical *dhikr* (plural: *adhkaar*). Consequently, Salafis in general tend to emphasize the recitation of the Qur'an and the standard *tasbih* (described above), while carefully downplaying the validity of elaborate *dhikr*. And in doing the standard *tasbih* after each of the daily prayers, they prefer to use the phalanges of the right fingers because Prophet Muhammad had recommended the use of the fingers, which will bear witness to the devotee's supplication in the hereafter.

However, recognizing that the Prophet neither fully rejected nor fully endorsed the use of *tasbih*, the Sufis insist on its assistive convenience in ensuring accuracy in *dhikr* involving large numbers. For them, the use of *tasbih* facilitates concentration on the phrases being recited without worrying about accuracy. From a Sufi mystical perspective, accuracy is important because each meditative utterance must conform to a specific mystical number constituting the phrase or attribute of Allah being recited. Everything in the universe, they argue, is based on mystical numeric values (what we may call algorithms in computer language today). Consequently, repeatedly uttering Allah's attributes up to precisely that mystical number, guarantees the acceptance of the devotee's spiritual or material intentions (*niyaat*). The resilience of *tasbih* in Muslim material culture, therefore, derives from its function as an assistive object, but not as an object of devotion, although, as explained, some attach spiritual and symbolic values to it beyond its material manifestation.[6]

Since references will be made throughout this essay to the Tijaniyya Sufi brotherhood[7] and its devotional litany, it is important to explain the

Tijaniyya *tasbih* in relation to its *dhikr*. The Tijaniyya requires its adherents to perform two major obligatory *dhikr* (called *wird*) each day. The first is the *laazim*, which involves repeating *istiqfaar* (beseeching Allah's forgiveness) one hundred times, reciting *salaatil faatih* (a specific Tijaniyya praise poem glorifying the Prophet), one hundred times, and *laa-illah-illa-lah* also one hundred times. The *laazim* is performed after the morning prayer (*fajr*) and repeated after the late afternoon prayer (*asr*). The second *wird dhikr*, called *waziifa*, is recommended to be performed in a group usually after the late evening prayer (*maghreb*) or after the morning prayer. In the *wazifa*, devotees recite *istiqfar* thirty times, *salaatil faatih* fifty times, *laa-illah-illa-lah* one hundred times, and *jawharatul Kamal* (the Pearl of Perfection) twelve or eleven times: the controversy surrounding the variation is a major subject of this essay. The Tijaniyya *tasbih*, therefore, has additional markers reflecting the divisions in this meditative formula and to ensure accuracy in the *dhikr*. The aid of *tasbih* is therefore important even for this relatively small number of repetitive recitations (other advanced *dhikr* involves thousands of repetitive phrases).

Another aspect of *tasbih* should be mentioned before we close this section. Although an important assistive object of *dhikr*, *tasbih* is not a sacred object and therefore is not required to conform to rules of ritual purity accorded to the Qur'an, for example. It is thus gender-neutral, allowing women to use it to perform *dhikr* even if they were in a state of ritual "impurity" due to postnatal condition or menstruation. It is also widely used for other mundane purposes such as decorating one's personal space. In West Africa, taxi drivers often hang *tasbih* on the inside mirrors of their vehicles for decoration or to express their doctrinal identity. Moreover, prior to the wide availability of calculators, Muslim moneychangers in West Africa used *tasbih* for calculations. *Tasbih* thus renders its service to both the mundane and spiritual needs of Muslims, further highlighting its importance in explaining Muslim material culture.

Tasbih has featured in the works of many Africanist historians and anthropologists that highlight its centrality in historical processes, colonial profiling of Muslims, doctrinal debates, religious affiliations, and identity formations (Harrison 1998; Diallo 1995; Hanretta 2009; Kobo 2012a and 2012b). However, no study has yet been conducted, as far as I know, that focuses specifically on *tasbih* to offer deeper historical insights. For example, as discussed below, the identification of specific *tasbih* with rebellion against French rule—that became central to French repressive policies toward a specific group of West African Muslims between the 1920s and the 1950s—has been analyzed by several scholars. Yet, none of these, including my own work, have looked closely at the core materiality of *tasbih* in these discourses. Perhaps most of these scholars assumed that *tasbih* is a static object without significant enough transformative structures and processes to offer an object-driven analysis. If the French had politicized the iconic symbolism of *tasbih* for their narrow political agenda, the narrative should be focused on the French and the Muslim leaders they repressed; framing the narrative around the materiality of *tasbih*, which was a mere symbol of that historical conflict, seemed unnecessary. Admittedly, this approach is ideologically and methodologically convenient because focusing on *tasbih* would distract from the larger questions of repression and victimization, which are the concerns of these scholars. However, a focus on *tasbih* to reveal its multiple manifestations in doctrinal debates and political conflicts, suggests that it transcends its material functions to also serve as a source for analyzing historical processes.

In his seminal work, Bernard Herman (Herman 2017) suggests two helpful methods for studying the materiality of objects and their relations to a specific culture: the object-centered and the object-driven approaches. An object-centered approach "seeks to represent the artifact in all of its materiality" such as its physical appearance, functions, and relationship to other objects within the specific culture (Herman 2017: 8). An object-driven approach, on the other hand, pays closer attention to ways by which the object provides clues to meanings and ideas within variable contexts (ibid.: 8). While the object-centered approach analyzes the object itself to provide meaning, the object-driven approach recognizes that objects embody questions that "offer unexpected avenues of inquiry and insight" (ibid.: 9).

In this paper I combine the two approaches proposed by Herman to offer deeper historical insights. Each of the two approaches offer a unique perspective to enhance our understanding of this resiliently controversial and conspicuous object in Muslims' spiritual and material cultures. For example, the object-centered approach allows us to pay attention to how the specific structure of a *tasbih* may suggest its liturgical functions within a Sufi group, as well as indicating doctrinal identity. Conversely, it may manifest itself as an aesthetic object adorned by Muslims for personal splendor free of doctrinal burdens. The object-driven approach, on the other hand, allows us to ask: what can *tasbihat* (sg. *tasbih*) teach us about cultural identity, social hierarchy, intellectual engagements, political conflicts, doctrinal contests, etc.? A *tasbih*, therefore, embodies multiple meanings that should be disaggregated to understand more fully some historical processes without overlooking its agency. Drawing on previously published and unpublished materials, and guided by the two approaches, this chapter illustrates that the *tasbih* is not a static object, and the history we construct around it is equally contextually variable and transformative.

Tasbih in religious reform and colonial discourse

The history of Shaykh Boubacar Sawadogo of Burkina Faso (Upper Volta during the colonial period and up to 1984) provides excellent examples of the ways by which *tasbih* offers a deeper understanding of some aspects of Muslims' spiritual, cultural, and political expressions. In the history summarized below, *tasbih* symbolized a group identity, commitment to peaceful proselytism and coexistence with members of all faiths, and a symbolic inspiration for self-restraint in the face of provocations from Muslim rivals, traditional rulers, and colonial authorities.

Boubacar Sawadogo (1883/4–1946)—Raguimia Sawadogo before his conversion to Islam—remains the most important Muslim reformer of Burkina Faso during the colonial period. According to oral sources, a Hausa merchant from what is today Nigeria secretly converted him to Islam when the merchant was lodging in Boubacar's family house (Kobo 2012b: 97–8). The young convert adopted the name, Boubacar (Abu Bakr, the name of the first Caliph of Islam after the Prophet Muhammad). During this period, the Mossi kingdom had resisted conversion to Islam for centuries despite their proximity to Islamized polities such as Mali and Songhay. Although the ruling elites allowed Muslim refugees from other societies to settle in their territories, they prohibited them from converting the indigenous people. In Boubacar's hometown, Namisguima, prior to colonial rule the penalty of conversion to Islam varied from death to banishment. Apprehensive of the risk to his life and that of his student, the Hausa merchant, known only as Abdul, advised his student to leave the territory to study Islam and to return to convert his people when the climate was conducive (Kobo 2012b: 98).

Boubacar left Upper Volta around 1900 to study in Mali and Fez (Morocco), after which he continued to Mecca on foot. The thousands of miles journey from West Africa to Mecca on foot lasted more than a year, requiring the pilgrims to settle briefly in some key towns to work and replenish their resources (van Duc 1995).[8] Boubacar settled briefly in Al-Fasher, the capital of the old kingdom of Darfur, now in Sudan, where he worked for renowned Tijaniyya Sheikh, Ahmad Salma (d. 1916).[9] According to the oral history, Boubacar refused to collect his salary at the end of his contract, requesting the Shaykh's *baraka* (mystical blessings) instead. Shaykh Salma accepted Boubacar's request and initiated him into the Tijaniyya tariqa at the rank of a *muqaddam* (deputy). Shaykh Salma offered his new student a *tasbih* with the following instructions recorded in Boubacar's hagiography:

> Go to your people and wage a *jihad*.
> But your *jihad* is a peaceful *jihad*.
> Call your people to true Islam with *la-ilah-illa-lah*
> They will respond in ways they never responded to any preacher before you.
> The *tasbih* is your weapon.
> Use it in all circumstances.
> Avoid aggression because aggressors are not among Allah's friends.
> To be among Allah's friends, you must avoid shedding the blood of fellow humans unjustly.

> Protect all of Allah's creations including plants and weaker animals.
> Restrain yourself against aggression and Allah will protect you against your enemies.[10]

According to colonial records, Boubacar returned to Upper Volta in 1920 (ANS 2G21, HV RPA 1921:8; ANS 2G30/10, HV, RPA, 1930: 53). He attempted to convert his relatives in Namisguima but encountered stiff resistance from the elders, who forced him to settle on a barren land in the outskirts of the town believed to be inhabited by dangerous jinns. However, their expectation that the jinns would destroy him was futile; the town he established, which he named Rahmatoulaye (Allah's benevolence), flourished and became arguably the birthplace of Islam among the Mossi, the largest ethnic group in the new colonial territory. He rapidly obtained converts from ex-slaves, members of marginalized ethnic groups, youths, as well as some of the existing scholars of foreign provenance (called Yarse) (Kouanda 1989), who agreed to renew their *shahadah* with him. Hanging their *tasbih* over the necks, chanting *laa-ilaa ha illa-lah* before the beginning of each of the daily *salaat*, and performing the group *wazifa* loudly, made their presence felt in neighboring communities. Even from the perspectives of the French, who had the tendency to dismiss Africans' practice of Islam as mediocre, Rahmatoulaye was a model Islamic community (ANS 2G36/18 RPA, Soudan, 1936: 85).

But the rapid growth of Boubacar's followers alarmed the French who had hoped the Mossi would continue to resist Islam in order to mitigate French fear of potential pan-Islamic rebellion in the region when the Muslim population grew. Boubacar seemed to heighten that fear as he gathered converts from across the region. However, since his teachings were not directed at the French, they continued their surveillance of his community, but otherwise left him to proselytize freely. The early 1920s was a transformative moment for Tijaniyya Francophone West Africa, suggested by its growing affinity with French colonial rule as well as tension among the leadership.

The Tijaniyya expanded into non-Arab West Africa through the aggressive proselytism and jihad of Shaykh Umar Tall (also Umar al-Futi (d. 1864). Umar Tall had embarked on a jihad to create a Tijaniyya state, imitating the Sokoto Caliphate founded by the Qadiriyya Shaykh Usman dan Fodio, in the area that is northern Nigeria today. His nascent empire began to disintegrate when the French colluded with his enemies in a siege that ended his life in 1864. Shaykh Umar's descendants and followers inherited his spiritual authority in most parts of West Africa, which by the turn of the century, they had transformed into a political authority under French tutelage. For decades after his demise, Umar Tall's legacy continued to shape the history and leadership structure of the Tijaniyya in West Africa, until the rise of Shaykh Hamallah.

Shaykh Hamallah had embraced the teachings of the Algerian shaykh, Sidi Muhammad Ibn Abdallah, known in West Africa as Shaykh al-Akhdar, who claimed to reform the Tijaniyya by requiring the recitation of the *jawharat al-kamal* (the Pearl of Perfection) eleven times during the *wazifah* instead of the widely accepted twelve times. The alteration of the recitation of the *jawharat* initiated what would become one of the most divisive and political episodes in the history of the Tijaniyya during the colonial period. Seemingly trivial, the dispute over the number of times the *jawhara* should be recited split the Tijanis into two major factions: the followers of Hamallah, called Hamawiyya, coined from the name Hamallah, the eleven-bead Tijanis; in contrast with the dominant and conservative Umarians, the twelve-bead Tijanis. Although French authorities in theory claimed to be neutral in religious and other local disputes that did not directly affect colonial rule, in practice they took the side of the Umarians in the dispute at Kaedi and declared the Hamawiyya fanatics (Hanretta 2009: 63). The number of beads in a *tasbih* reflected not only the dispute over the authenticity of an aspect of their liturgy as understood by most Tijanis, but also the descriptive names of competing factions within that dispute, and the association of that descriptive identity with fanaticism to justify French repression.

Boubacar visited Shaykh Hamallah (also Hamaullah) in the midst of this dispute to reinitiate into the Tijaniyya. It is unclear whether he was aware of the conflict prior to embarking on the journey. What the sources stress is that Shaykh Salma had predicted the rise of a young scholar from the Prophet's lineage and had advised Boubacar to reinitiate into the *tariqa* when that scholar emerged. Boubacar identified Hamallah as that predicted scholar. By the end of his visit, Boubacar had been appointed a *muqaddam* (deputy of the order), thus establishing him strategically in the hierarchy of a new "radical" movement led by Shaykh Hamallah. Boubacar thus became an important figure in the network of Hamawiyya scholars and reformers, contributing to its growth, benefitting from its ecumenical resources, and sharing with it the weight of French suspicion and ultimately repression. Nonetheless, the local French administration maintained a strategy of coexistence with him as long as he did not engage in anti-French activities. The 1930 Annual Political Report for example, summarizes the French perspective regarding his religious mission and contribution to the growth of the Hamawiyya. It noted:

> Sawadogo, an intelligent, ardent proselyte who hated Europeans passionately, had acquired a great deal of influence in the surrounding Mossi regions, up to Ouahigouya, as well as in the Fulbé districts of Todjiam, where his eloquent speech and energy attracted people who listened to him and believed him. The spread of eleven bead Tijaniyya in the region must always be attributed to his efforts . . . Whatever the reasons, out of the Muslim population of 109,000 in Ouahigouya, 67,000 were members of eleven bead Tijaniyya.
>
> ANS 2G30/10, RPA, 1930: 54

It is worth emphasizing that despite the widespread discourse of Hamawiyya threats to colonial order, the French did not summarily repress every Hamawiyya leader, preferring to deal with any threats based on specific local contingencies, as exemplified by the multiple exiling of Hamallah himself (Hanretta 2009). Boubacar, for example, continued to proselytize freely, and encouraged his followers to establish *zawiyas* (Sufi lodges) throughout the colony and neighboring Ghana and the Ivory Coast, where their eleven-bead *tasbih* distinguished them from other Muslims and reinforced their solidarity. However, the looming prospect of another world war in the 1930s heightened French apprehension of potential Muslim rebellion, leading to increasing surveillance of the Hamawiyya while pursuing diplomatic options. The weight of the diplomatic option was placed on none other than Seydou Nourou Tall, the grandson of Umar Tall, whom the French authorities in Dakar dispatched in 1933 to visit Hamawiyya leaders to convince them to reconcile with the Umarian branch and to support the French in case of another war in Europe.

Seydou Nourou Tall visited Rahmatoulaye in 1933 and advised Boubacar to abandon the Hamawiyya.[11] Boubacar Sawadogo agreed, or rather pretended to agree, and instructed his followers to add an extra bead to their *tasbih* to give the impression that they have abandoned the Hamawiyya (Plate 15). The French even noted Boubacar's cooperation in the annual report (ANS 2G42/3 RPA, Soudan, Province of Ouahigouya 1942: 52). However, the extra bead neither altered their *dhikr* nor diminished their loyalty to Shaykh Hamallah. Up to 1940 the administrative reports continued to emphasize Boubacar's peaceful sermons and confirmed his "conversion," which for the French, was testified by his rehabilitated *tasbih* (ANS 2G41/20, RPA 1941: 158). However, the rise of the Vichy regime in France in July 1940 changed the dynamics in West Africa, as local administrators intensified their surveillance of Hamawiyya leaders irrespective of their symbolic cooperation with the French. Thus, in 1941, all the Hamawiyya leaders were rounded up; Shaykh Hamallah was exiled to France, where he passed away in 1943, while the rest received various prison sentences, which they served outside their respective territories. Accused of deceiving French authorities in 1933 by pretending to abandon the Eleven Bead, Boubacar Sawadogo received a five-year sentence, which he served in labor camps in Mali from 1941 to 1946; he died shortly after his release.

While this history has been written using oral sources and colonial records, it seems that an object-driven approach helps to illuminate the centrality of Boubacar's *tasbih* in this conflict, highlighting not only its spiritual values, but also its symbolic representation in French discourse. In their attempt to profile Muslims based on the number of beads in their *tasbih*, the French transformed an object into an identity. But the *tasbih* had a deeper spiritual value to the followers of Boubacar Sawadogo. Shaykh Salma's instructions regarding the symbolic value of his *tasbih* became his community's mantra that guarded their religious behavior and practices, which included a deep commitment to the Shariah and self-restraint in the face of provocation. The community's hagiographical tradition was woven around the essence of the Tijaniyya *tasbih*, which every member of the community had to acquire as part of their spiritual identity.

Tasbih further symbolized not only the community's identity and loyalty to the Shaykh, but also a source of empowerment: the power of prayers which they believed shielded them from their enemies, and the power and security associated with belonging to a new and putatively powerful community of believers. For the youths, who constituted the majority of the new converts, a *tasbih* that had been blessed by the Shaykh embodied Allah's omnipotent presence that warded off the evils of the traditional deities they had fearlessly abandoned, and the mystical force that subdued the demons infesting Rahmatoulaye (Adam Zeigha, interview, May 3, 2002). The *tasbih* also epitomized their successful escape from the tyranny of gerontocratic rule of the elders and the traditional authorities.[12] Many elders I encountered in Rahmatoulaye insisted that their *tasbih* helped to temper their anger whenever they were provoked (Abdoul Salaam Ouedraogo, interview, May 2, 2002). Two veterans of the Second World War that I met in Ghana in 2005, credited their *tasbih*, which had been blessed by Boubacar before their departure, for surviving the war (Al Hadj Nouhou Zabre and Iddirisu Sawadogo, interview, August 23, 2005, Takoradi, Ghana). They noted rather posthumously, that while some "ignorant" soldiers carried talismans to protect them in battles but were gunned down by the enemy, they survived because of their *tasbih*, which had been blessed by Shaykh Boubacar. Moreover, contrary to the expectations of the elders of Namisguima that Boubacar would not survive the destructive powers of the jinns infesting the land that became Rahmatoulaye, his community survived and Rahmatoulaye is widely acknowledged as the birthplace of Islam and the Tijaniyya among the Mossi, Burkina Faso's largest ethnic group. The town is currently being considered for the status of World Heritage Site.

Tasbih and doctrinal contests

If the French politicized the external manifestation of *tasbih* by using the number of beads in a string of *tasbih* as evidence of acceptance or rejection of French rule, the advent of Wahhabi/Salafi reform declared the use of *tasbih*, *bid'a* and sought to banish it from their mosques. Identifying its use with members of the Tijaniyya, although non-Tijanis also used it for assistive purposes, *tasbih* became central to their polemics against the Tijaniyya. I cite two examples from Burkina Faso in the 1950s, to explain the centrality of *tasbih* in doctrinal polemics. It is generally noticeable in mosques in West Africa that, at the beginning of the congregational prayers, Muslims often place their *tasbih* in front of them, close to the spot where they would touch their foreheads during prostration. *Tasbih* is therefore among the materials, including the prayer mat, that devotees take to the *masjid*. It is thus possible to argue that *tasbih* represents ways of claiming one's space during *sujud* (prostration), a spot no-one is allowed to step or cross while the devotee is in the midst of *salaat*: a well-known hadith prohibits walking in front of the person standing in prayer. For West African Muslims, the *tasbih* conveniently served as the recommended barrier. By placing the *tasbih* in front of them they mark their space, thus making it permissible for someone to walk across in search for an empty spot.

However, despite recognizing the need for such a barrier in a crowded mosque, Salafi preachers forbade the use of *tasbih* precisely because of its connections with the Tijaniyya. In one masjid at Bobo-Dioulasso (Burkina Faso's second-largest city) in the early 1960s (the date is uncertain), the imam preached vehemently against the use of *tasbih* and encouraged his followers to fling them out of the mosque if someone were to place them in front of them as described above. This imam claimed that the use of *tasbih* was equivalent to idol worship (*shirk*), and his sermon initiated what one observer called the "fight over *tasbih*." Members of the community would routinely throw worshippers' *tasbih* out of the masjid by picking them up with their toes and tossing them to the next person in the direction of the exit door until it reached the person closest to the door, who would then fling it outside. In one instance, the individual whose *tasbih* was tossed out threw blows, inciting a brawl that resulted in the closure of the *masjid* for months (Kobo 2012b).

As argued elsewhere (Kobo 2015: 76) the late 1980s represented a moment of doctrinal reflection among Salafi scholars in Ghana and Burkina Faso, marked by a radical shift from provocative and divisive preaching styles pursued by earlier generations, to a non-confrontational approach that sought to promote doctrinal coexistence. In Ghana and Burkina Faso, for example, many younger graduates of Middle Eastern and Gulf universities preached against declaring other Muslims infidels because of their allegiance to the Tijaniyya. Coming from a new tradition even within Saudi Arabia that discouraged uncritical dismissal of fellow Muslims as infidels, the new Salafis considered the use of *tasbih* either detestable (but not a forbidden act) or even permissible based on good intention.

Tasbih in intra-doctrinal polemics

The debates by Salafi-inclined scholars in Ghana concerning *tasbih* reverberated among members of the Tijaniyya community as well, albeit in a distinct way, that is the Islamic rulings on men who wore *tasbih* on their necks. The debate began earlier in Nigeria, when in 2002 the notable Tijaniyya scholar Shaykh Tahir Usman Bauchi, discouraged his male followers from hanging their *tasbih* on their necks because it imitates women's adornment, which Islam discourages. In 2003, Shaykh Bauchi visited Ghana and repeated that pronouncement in support of the position of Ghana's National Chief Imam, and the de facto head of the Tijaniyya in Ghana, Shehu Usman Nuhu Sharubutu. This assertion offended the famous Azhari-trained scholar, Shaykh Abdullai Maikano (d. 2005), who was widely known to place his *tasbih* on his neck and wrap others on his wrist. Abdullai Maikano not only responded harshly, but also intensified his display of *tasbih* and instructed his students to wear theirs conspicuously because *tasbih* is the tool and symbol of the vocation of the Sufis, and the only object that distinguishes them from non-Sufis (Mallam Musah Abubakar, Interview, January 17, 2020, Accra, Ghana). His followers, particularly the youth, therefore adopted the wearing of *tasbih* as part of their Sufi identity and loyalty to their leader (Plate 18 and Figure 5.1).

FIGURE 5.1 *Praying with* tasbih. *Photo by author.*

The debate among Tijanis regarding the wearing of *tasbih* was not a particularly novel debate because it had been a common practice among Sufis at least since the medieval period. We recall Ibn Taymiyya's denunciation of the practice in Egypt and Syria on the grounds that it symbolized ostentatious display of piety. Many Tijanis in West Africa, including Shaykh Boubacar's followers, also wore their *tasbih* without incurring any opposition from fellow Tijjanis. Moreover, even in this specific example in Ghana, only the hardcore followers paid attention to this debate; most Tijanis continue to either wear their *tasbih* or place them in their pockets based on convenience. A deeper inquiry suggests that the debate was rooted in a simmering leadership contest between the two major Tijaniyya leaders (Dumbe 2013) and *tasbih* served as the object over which the contest became public, further suggesting how *tasbih* provides the lens for interrogating social, political, and intellectual dynamics.

Conclusion

This chapter has focused on selected episodes in the history of Islam in West Africa to accentuate the material agency of *tasbih* in historical processes. Although one of the most visible religious and cultural objects associated with Muslims, scholars of West Africa have not explored the stories hidden in the strings, shapes, number and colors of *tasbih* to offer deeper insights into those historical processes. Using a combination of object-centered and object-driven approaches proposed by Herman (2017), I illustrate how, in its function as a convenient instrument for conducting *dhikr*, *tasbih* reveals some processes and changes in Muslims' intellectual, political, and cultural history. For West African Muslims, the *tasbih* manifests itself simultaneously as a cultural icon, an instrument of religious practice, a marker of identity and doctrinal affiliation, an embodiment of passive resistance to colonial rule, and an aesthetic object for adornment and decoration. The various cultural, doctrinal, and political interpretations derived from the number of beads in a string of *tasbih* in the historical episodes analyzed here, further suggests that it is not a static but an active transformative object in those historical processes, and thus a source for historical inquiry.

As illustrated, during colonial rule the French in West Africa added *tasbih* to the profile of Muslims to identify potential "troublemakers," and in doing so, transformed an innocuous spiritual object into an identity marker that helped them, often wrongly, to distinguish between loyalists and potential adversaries. For French colonial administrators, Tijanis whose *tasbih* had twelve beads in the final division represented colonial loyalists, while the Hamawis, whose *tasbih* had eleven beads in the final division, were declared adversaries of French rule, despite the overwhelming evidence in French records and in oral testimonies that the Hamawis had no political intentions vis-à-vis the French. I demonstrated with the brief history of Shaykh Boubacar of Burkina Faso, that *tasbih* also embodied Boubacar's commitment to peaceful proselytism. His appointment to the position of *muqaddam*, and the symbolic *tasbih* offered to him during his first initiation into the Tijaniyya, demanded his solemn commitment to the *tariqa* and its peaceful disposition.[13] Yet, it seemed more convenient for the French in West Africa to create an identifiable Muslim enemy and to associate that enemy with a visual marker: the *tasbih*.

On their part, the Hamawis inverted *tasbih* to evade French harassment and repression. As illustrated, Shaykh Boubacar instructed his followers to change the symbolic representation of their *tasbih* by adding an extra bead to it to deceive the French into believing that they had abandoned the Hamawiyya. In this context, *tasbih* became the object for constructing and deconstructing identities. First, they changed the structure of their *tasbih* from the twelve beads in the final marker to the eleven-beads to reflect their allegiance to Shaykh Hamallah, and then reverted to the twelve-bead to avoid colonial repression. Here, the object-driven approach allows us to assess the competing strategies between the French and Muslim groups seeking to confuse French surveillance while retaining their ritual practices.

The case of Salafi/Wahhabi preachers who forbade the use of *tasbih* in their mosques, also mirrors French profiling of Muslims based on *tasbih*, although for different purposes. *Tasbih* also emerged as an object of internal doctrinal debates among members of the Tijaniyya in Ghana over the permissibility of wearing *tasbih* over one's neck. As noted, this internal debate revealed simmering leadership contests between the two most prominent Tijani leaders in Ghana, as each leader subscribed to the opposing position. Here too, *tasbih* became the object of doctrinal contestation, further indicating its myriad, albeit conflicting, positions within Islam.

While the *tasbih* functions as an assistive object for counting *dhikr*, the examples in this essay clearly suggest that it transcends this parochial function. Using a combination of object-centered and object-driven approaches, this chapter highlights not only the objective materiality of *tasbih*, but also its multiple manifestations that provide clues for deeper historical inquiries. In the cases examined here, the structure of *tasbih* suggest its liturgical function while allowing historians to further interrogate social relations and hierarchies, political conflicts, intellectual debates, doctrinal contests, and competition for the authoritative voice. Similarly, a debate over its display on the devotee's body provides some hints to further interrogate the roots of that debate. A study of *tasbih* therefore contributes enormously to our understanding of Muslim material culture.

CHAPTER SIX

Caps, Heads, and Hearts

*Scott Kugle**

Introduction

The matter of this essay is a hat. Wearing a cap is ubiquitous for Muslim males and passes unnoticed, while veils on Muslim women attract inordinate attention. Recent scholarship on Islamic dress discusses "fashion" exclusively through women's clothing (Tarlo and Moors 2013). Yet its connecting aesthetics and ethics serves as a useful theoretical reminder for this essay about men's caps (Tarlo 2010; Lewis 2015).[1] It discusses caps in general and traces a single distinctive cap: the one that I wear as a legacy from my Sufi teacher in India, a cap of simple design but complex symbolism.

The tall, peaked, yellow Chishti cap is very distinctive and gives us insight into both Sufism and hats in general. This archival exploration of the Chishti cap, its material design and its symbolic meaning, will try to get inside the heads that wear them. I was initiated into the Chishti Order and this cap was placed on my head by my own Sufi teacher, in a ritual that goes back many centuries. If Chishti lore is to be believed, the ritual goes back to the Prophet himself, who was crowned with a cap of light by the angel Gabriel during his heavenly ascension. That is heavy symbolism for a light piece of cloth. It feels strange to turn an analytic gaze upon my own hat, but the invitation to contribute to this book on material Islam made me think about what objects represent Islam in my own imagination. I only had to look at my own head to find the answer (Plate 17).

What's in a hat

Clothing matters. Clothing is also matter: supple matter, concrete but not rigid. It lies somewhere between animate matter (body) and inanimate matter (object). It moves but not of its own volition. It is designed to clothe, to be a fabric that simultaneously conceals the body and reveals it. It moves with the body, giving the body identity and expression, even as it removes the biological body (or important parts of it) from sight. Clothing is to the body what a mask is to the face: it both disguises it and makes it more expressive than it otherwise would be. Clothing is an integral part of self-enhancement. Jane Schneider observes that two aspects of cloth and clothing—their spirituality and their aesthetic characteristics—are crucial to self-enhancement.

> Self-enhancement loosely refers to energizing the self and close others, perhaps organized in small groups, through life-affirming practices and rituals. Examples involving cloth and clothes include transforming the body and its surroundings in ways considered aesthetically or sexually attractive; dressing well to accrue prestige, the respect of others, a sense of worthiness or empowerment; generously distributing textiles to consolidate friendships and followings; and signaling through clothes an identification with particular values or constituencies.
>
> Schneider 2006: 203

This article focuses on a cap that performs several of these functions at once.

Hats are clothing but are distinct from other types of clothing, just like the head is part of the body but distinct from the rest of the body. The cap deserves our phenomenological attention, for it crowns the head at the very top of the body and frames the face, the expressive focal point for bodily sensation and recognition. Hats are the focus for intense symbolism because they adorn the head: they emphasize it and express its wearer's power. Officials often wear hats, especially those who wield authority and exercise violence. Royalty relies on hats to display their wealth and might. Sufis wear hats and cloaks to display their embrace of poverty. The poet Hafiz (d. 1389 in Shiraz, Iran) illustrates this in the *ghazal* (the mystical-erotic genre of lyric poetry), which he sent to the ruler who invited him to India.[2]

> Getting a world of joy is not worth even a moment of pain
> Sell my Sufi cloak for a bottle of wine?—that's a net gain
>
> A sultan's crown is radiant but constant fear of death lurks in it
> A much-coveted headdress, for sure—but will the head remain?
>
> Browne 2000: 285

The Sufi cap is made of cloth rather than the metal of a soldier's helmet or the jewels of a ruler's crown. Traditionally, Sufi caps and cloaks were made of woolen cloth (hence the name Sufi, from *ṣūf* or wool). In India, wool is a luxury rather than a symbol of ascetic poverty, so most Sufis wear cotton. Fabric itself is a metaphor for the body. Cloth that moves is an allusion to life itself. One particularly eloquent Sufi, Maulana Rumi (d. 1273 in Konya, Turkey) illustrated with a cloth flag embroidered with a lion how the material body is animated by the immaterial spirit.

> We are just like lions that men paint on their flag
> Who only charge when wind should make it sag:
> Our charge is visible, while wind is not
> May that which is invisible be sought!
> This wind, our very being, blows from You
> You brought to life our whole existence too.
>
> Rumi 2004: 40, Couplets 606–9

Rumi specifies that the human body is like the lion-emblazoned flag: it flaps in the breeze making the lion appear to run, leap and attack just like our body moves by our thoughts. It could be a gentle easterly wind that causes kind and compassionate actions, or it could be a severe westerly wind that causes harsh and discordant actions. The harsh westerly wind is like thoughts that are driven by the ego (*nafsani*), while spiritual forces (*ruhani*) are like those impelled by the gentle easterly wind.

> The banner's lion's playful movements show
> The ways in which the winds behind it blow
> If those winds moving it weren't really there
> How could drawn lions leap up in the air?
> The body's like the lion on the banner:
> Thought moves it at each moment in some manner
>
> Rumi 2017: 182, Couplets 3052–5

Explaining the body-spirit interface through wind-rippled fabric, Rumi exhorts us to be lions like the one that appears to leap on the flag, meaning bold people who identify with the spirit that blows through them and thus transcend their physical form. Sufism is a system of initiation and training to effect this transformation. It was first taught by ʿAli ibn Abi Talib, who was known as the Victorious Lion of God (*asad allah al-ghalib*). He was the closest follower of the Prophet who was taught meditation (*dhikr*), contemplation (*muraqaba*), and wisdom (*maʿrifa*), and in turn taught his followers; they form a *silsila* or 'chain' of initiating teachers that form Sufi Orders.

Bestowing inner wisdom was symbolized by gifting a cloak (*khirqa*) and peaked cap (*kulah*). Masters of the Chishti Order gave initiation and successorship by clothing their disciples, as recorded in *Siyar al-Awliya*.[3] It explains the origins of the cloak by recounting a teaching of Nizam al-Din Awliya (d. 1325 in Delhi), the fourth master in the South Asian lineage.

> God granted the Prophet, upon him and his family be peace, a cloak on the night of his ascension. This is called "the Cloak of Poverty" (*khirqa-yi*

> *faqr*). Each of his companions requested that he give it to them because he said, "The Lord has granted me this cloak and told me to give it to one of my companions." The Prophet said to Abu Bakr, "If I grant this cloak to you, what will you do?" Abu Bakr replied, "I will practice sincerity, worship and liberality." Then the Prophet said to Umar, "If I grant this cloak to you, what will you do?" Umar replied, "I will enforce justice." Then the Prophet said to Uthman, "If I grant this cloak to you, what will you do?" Uthman replied, "I will behave equitably and practice generosity." The Prophet turned to ʿAli and said, "If I grant this cloak to you, what will you do?" ʿAli replied, "I will veil myself from the sight of others and cover over the faults of God's servants." So, the Prophet granted the cloak to ʿAli, may God ennoble his presence, stating, "God ordered me to grant the cloak to one who answers in this way".
>
> Amir Khurd 1884: 341–2

The cloak indicates heavenly return through utter poverty. The Prophet said, "Everyone is cloaked by something and my cloak is poverty and struggle, so those who love the impoverished are close to me in love and those who despise the impoverished are far from me in hate" (ibid.: 546). The Sufi cloak is an otherworldly mirror-image to the royal robes that kings gift to their clients to cement this-worldly political solidarity (Gordon 2003). Just as the cloak covers the body, the cap covers the head; both symbolize poverty. Nizam al-Din Awliya taught that, "All sin is in one storehouse and the key to its door is love for this world. All worship is in one storehouse and the key to its door is love of poverty" (Amir Khurd 1884: 544). The cap worn by Chishtis is distinctive in style: it is a peaked cap called a *kulah*.

Nizam al-Din Awliya culminated the initial cycle of Chishti masters in India who lived in five generations (from 1200-1350) and taught by stories, poem, and ritual music. The next cycle of Chishtis, including Zia Nakhshabi (d. 1350 in Badaun), wrote in prose. Nakhshabi explains how the cap worn by Chishtis is distinctive in style; it is a peaked cap called a or *turki topi*, and it fuses elements of a raised crown with elements of renunciant humility (Rizvi 1978: 131).

> Poverty's caretaker pronounces that those caps donned by the dervishes can be divided into two types: flattened or raised. Flattened caps (*latiba*) are those that adhere directly to the scalp like a skullcap. Raised caps (*nashira*) are those that stand up off the scalp with a little loftiness. He who is crowned with the compliment of "If not for you I would not have created the heavens," namely the Prophet Muhammad, used to wear a flattened cap rather than a raised cap. The Turks from Central Asia used to wear a different style of cap called a *turki topi* or four-cornered peaked cap. Its name has an alternate derivation—not from *turk* but from *tark* (not from an inhabitant of Turkistan but rather from an act of renunciation). This cap symbolized renouncing the world which is the

> essence of all worship.[4] The Turks say that wearing this cap [with four corners] symbolizes [four principles]: never ask for anything from anyone, never store anything with himself, so that none ever ask anything from him, and never should he waste a moment of time.
>
> Nakhshabi n.d.: 149; Urdu translation n.d.: 195

Nakhshabi's prose explanation is actually poetic. He makes a play on the word essence (*ra's* in Arabic). It means head, and also essence and value. The cap is the essence and the value of the head that wears it. The cap stands for the wearer in a relation of synecdoche. The part stands for the whole. A piece of clothing represents the persona of one who wears it. The cap symbolizes the mind-set of the person's head who bears it (Plate 18).

Crowns, turbans or four-cornered caps

I was stimulated to think more deeply about the cap by Shahzad Bashir's essay "The World as a Hat" (Bashir 2014: 343-65).[5] I was moved by his attention to how headgear stands in for the body and expands its expressive possibilities. Some hats, like crowns, symbolize possession of the world. Others represent the mythological crown symbolizing world transcendence. In Sufi retellings of the *mi'raj* (the Prophet Muhammad's ascension to God), he wears a crown of light. When the Prophet first touched the mystical steed Buraq who bore him on this journey, it spooked and shook its mane in agitation, having never before encountered a human body. The angel Gabriel calmed Buraq so that the Prophet could mount, saying, "This is Muhammad son of 'Abd Allah, beloved of the Lord of the worlds, master of all of creation, and possessor of intercession, crowned by the crown of noble favor" (Colby 2008: 198). This narrative is a favorite for pictorial representation; in one illustrated manuscript, Muhammad is called "the possessor of Kawsar [the fount of eternal life], the staff and the crown" (Gruber 2010: 81). In Chishti gatherings, a prayer for blessings on the Prophet is recited, called *Durud-e Taj* or "Benediction of the Crown"; its first lines praise the Prophet as "Master of radiant crown, heavenly ascent, lightening steed and victory banner, who repels disasters, afflictions, scarcity, illness and suffering of every manner" (Kugle, forthcoming).

Despite his crown of light in spiritual realms, the Prophet Muhammad never wore a crown in this world. Hadith relate that he wore a turban or *'imama*: he said, "The turban is the crown of the Arabs" and enjoined Muslims to wear turbans to differentiate themselves from others (Patel 2018b). When he exhorted his followers to follow his cousin and son-in-law 'Ali at a well called Ghadir Khumm, the Prophet tied a turban around his head as a mark of distinction; the Prophet's praise of 'Ali at this event became the foundational hymn in Qawwali music as performed among Chishtis Sufis. Underneath the turban, it was common to wear a *qalansuwa* (cap worn under the turban, probably from Aramaic with similar words derived from it in Greek, Hebrew and Arabic). This cap, common to many communities in the region, was likely what the Prophet was thinking of when he asked Muslims to differentiate themselves from others (Patel 2018a).

The urge to differentiate did not always prevail. The Arabic word for cap is *taqiya*, derived from the Persian word *taq* meaning dome or arch. It describes the domed shape of the hat that is raised slightly off the head, symbolizing connection to the celestial world. The Hebrew term *kippah* for a skullcap preserves some of the same meaning, likening the cap to an architectural dome (similar to *qubba* in Arabic). We find vernacular terms for this model of cap: *topi* (in Urdu, Hindi and Bengali) and *kufi* (in Swahili), both of which have come into popular usage in North America. The cap is ubiquitous, spurred in part by legal rulings that the Prophet prayed with his head covered so that wearing a cap for worship is *mustahabb* (favored though not required). In South Asia where the Hanafi school of Sunni law is strong, the cap is required and one might be "coercively capped" by elders at a mosque, madrasa, or Sufi shrine. Caps woven from palm leaves are stacked at the door for occasional communal use. Recently, biodegradable palm leaf caps are replaced by neon green plastic caps imported from China emblazoned with the Saudi flag.

Because wearing caps is common for Muslim males, they become a malleable medium to advertise identity and difference. Chishti Sufis revere ʿAli as their charismatic leader and fountainhead of saintdom. The cap and cloak that Chishtis give as a sign of initiation are understood to be continuations of those the Prophet gave to ʿAli. Yet Chishti practice evolved in ways that differentiate it from other Sufi orders. The Chishti cap is a *kulah*, a distinctive style of cap that is peaked, which was a sign of power in Turkic communities who ruled India. It is usually yellow, a sign of joy at the onset of spring when the mustard flowers bloom during *Basant*, an Indian festival associated with love and beauty that was celebrated by Nizam al-Din Awliya and his follower, Amir Khusro, who composed songs alluding to the celebration. It is said that Nizam al-Din Awliya wore his *kulah* tilted awry in a jaunty style, and Amir Khusro wrote songs about that, too!

Beauty and love in the cap awry

The Chishti cap is a peaked *kulah* built of four gores (*tark*). This contrasts with the Turkic *kulah* of Anatolia which evolved into a conical shape with no gores or pleated angles (Geczy 2019: 37). A Persian ghazal alludes to this cap—which is simultaneously a symbol of renunciation and of fascinating beauty—that is sung in Qawwali and attributed to the Chishti master, Qutb al-Din Bakhtiyar Kaki.

Each one who finds a way to sip the wine of love for you
Wears on his head, like the prince of poverty, a cap askew

No one set upon this earth can find lasting security, yet
One who has a friend like you finds aid and help anew

He is ruler of the world who sits begging at your door
A fortunate beggar is he who attends on a king like you

Why should the sins of Qutb al-Din, done or left undone,
Cause him sorrow when his God is as merciful as you?

Faruqi 1972: 88

The four-cornered peaked cap represents the worldly renunciation of its wearer. It rises from the head in a gesture of high aspiration; its four corners represent the four-fold renunciation of never asking, never storing, never being admired, and never being distracted. Some modern Chishti teachers explain this as *chahar-tark* or four aspects of renunciation: renouncing ambition for this world, renouncing hope for the next world, renouncing expectation of reward, and renouncing the act of renunciation.[6]

Symbolism is stitched into its material construction with a subtle linguistic pun. *Tark* in Persian means "gore" or pleated fold (what we call a "dart" in English tailoring), which creates an angle or corner in a fabric construction. Yet *tark* in Arabic means renunciation, a "leaving aside" of worldly ambition or selfish concern. *Tarki Topi* means a hat with pleated angles while it also means a hat worn for world renunciation! In India, the word *tark* is sometimes pronounced as "turk," so the hat with pleated angles becomes the "hat of a Turk." This alludes to the Turkic origins of the peaked cap, for in Persianate culture that developed among the powerful Turkic Sultans in India, Iran and Central Asia, the peaked cap became a symbol of ruling authority (Flood 2009: 92). As this culture took root and developed spiritual and literary currents, the cap fused images of power with those of beauty. In this environment, the most handsome man was imagined as a young Turk, fierce and loyal. The Sufi paragon of love mysticism, Ruzbihan Baqli (d. 1209 in Shiraz) saw God as a Turkic youth who wore his cap awry (Ritter 2003: 462).[7] Two elements have changed in Ruzbihan's visionary encounter: the ethnicity of the beauty and the style of the cap. From an Arab ideal of beauty, he marked the radical shift in culture which had taken place after the Abbasid era, and now the Turk stood for ideal beauty. Yet the cap itself is a heavy symbol, one already loaded with ascetic and mystical meaning, regardless of which ethnic beauty wears it. As a crown, the cap symbolizes world domination. But if made of wool, felt, or other common cloth, it symbolized world renunciation. In Sufi thought, of course, the two are intimately connected: one who renounces desire for worldly goods is given authority over the world and all that is in it (Lawrence 1992: 95–96).[8]

When the cap is worn awry, it is inflected. The symbol of renunciation becomes a sign of beauty and devotion (Ahmed 2016: 200-210). The one who renounces the world and its conventions becomes a radiant beauty that attracts the world's attention. Sufis echo this imagery when they grant caps as signs of world-renunciation and initiation. Islamic tradition preserves a saying attributed to the Prophet Muhammad, in which he declares, "I saw my Lord in the shape of a beautiful young man with his cap awry" (De Sondy 2014: 165). Some specify that this beautiful young man was the image of Dihya al-Kalbi, reputed to be the most handsome youth among the Arab tribes of the Prophet's community. Many interpreters explain that this vision occurred during the *miʿraj* when the Prophet faced the divine throne in God's presence; some circulate a hadith that the Prophet said, "Looking upon the Kaʿba is worship, looking at one's parents is worship, looking at greenery is worship, and looking at a beautiful face is worship" (Ritter: 473). The cap awry is a material object full of symbolic value that covers the head and frames the face. The cap awry, though a material object, is often transposed into immaterial forms in word or song, conjuring its meaning even if the object is not physically present. The crooked cap is woven into the fabric of discourse, which is indeed more pliable and durable than the fabric of clothing.

When singing poems by Amir Khusro and other South Asian Sufis, Qawwals often introduce the main lyrics with a couplet or quatrain from other poets. In particular, Amir Khusro's poems are often paired with couplets by Saʿdi, the Persian poet from Shiraz who preceded him. Amir Khusro was inspired by Saʿdi and inflected the Iranian's romantic style in a more Sufi mystical direction; there are traditions which state how Nizam al-Din Awliya urged Amir Khusro to adopt Saʿdi's sweet and romantic style with a mystical twist (Sharma 2006: 21). Amir Khusro's friend, Amir Hasan, was often called "the Saʿdi of India" to seal the importance of Saʿdi as the inspiration for the love mysticism of Chishti Sufi poetry (ibid: 50). Saʿdi highlights the religion of love, which is the wider complex of associations to which the crooked cap belongs. The religion of love is associated with a string of images, of which the face of the beloved plays a prime role. The face of the beloved is compared to pages of the Qurʾan. Turning to face the beloved is compared to orienting oneself to the Kaʿba in Mecca. Submitting to love, no matter how it might outrage the narrowly pious, is equivalent to sincere worship.

The crooked cap frames the beloved's face and accentuates the beloved's curling locks. It serves as a signpost and a marker for love, just as the Kaʿba serves as an orientation point for those who pray. Indeed, we find that the ghazal poetry of Saʿdi includes references to the crooked cap, as it sings of "a tyrannical lord, a cap-tilted beauty, a seeker of brawls," as in the following poem by Saʿdi.[9]

A strolling cypress stole my heart in a garden of temptation
Gold of hip, silver of breast, waist like a hair in expansion

A tyrannical lord, a cap-tilted beauty, a seeker of brawls
Sugarcane in appetite, arrow in stature, bow in compression

With his ringlet then his cheek then his ruby lip, Saʿdi is reduced
To a sigh and tear descending, then dust and smoke in ascension

Saʿdi (1955: 1113)

Similarly, another ghazal by Saʿdi praises the beloved as the "moon at full wearing a cocky cap." Poems such as this serve as the direct predecessor for the Indian poets Amir Khusro and Amir Hasan.[10]

See how gracefully along the path that cypress does prance
See how doe-like is his eye if he graces you with a glance

Do you see a cypress lean with belt tightening the mean
Or is it the moon at full wearing a cocky cap perchance?

Once more I rouse myself to say, "To recover from lost love
The only way, oh Saʿdi, is with another love to take a chance"

Saʿdi 1955: 724

The image of the crooked cap was taken from Saʿdi's romantic poetry and forged into a symbol for Sufi poetry. The cap becomes a tangible and concrete symbol for the more abstract idea of the *qibla*, the direction to which one turns for prayer and devotion, which is usually marked with an arched recess in the wall of a mosque, called the *mihrab* (Figure 6.1).

Sufi imagery of the *qibla* is much older than Saʿdi's romantic orientation to the beautiful man with the rakish cap. The very earliest Sufis, to shift mystical discourse from asceticism to love, as in Rabiʿa of Basra, used this image (Lings 2003: 3). When Sufi orders were being organized around a master with disciples, the *qibla*, or direction of devotion, becomes embodied in the Sufi master, and the master's body—as the locus of beauty and power—becomes concretized in the symbol of the cap (Lawrence 1992: 82-3). The cap takes its form from the body of the Sufi master, from his most essential and top-most part: his head. Yet it can be removed and gifted, making it a flexible and malleable substance full of symbolic potential. Amir Khusro and Amir Hasan used the romantic image of the cap on a beautiful beloved in a spiritual valence, creating a poetic parallax in which romantic excitement and spiritual agitation were incited by one single image. From its origins in the prose of Ruzbihan Baqli and the poetry of Saʿdi, the image of the crooked cap (*kaj kulah*) persisted in Persian poetry in South Asia and it is perpetuated later in Urdu poetry, which adapted Persian models. The crooked cap image persisted in Sufi poetry, right up to

FIGURE 6.1 *The author's Sufi teacher, Pir Rasheed Kaleemi, wears a white four-cornered* kulah *while praying over the tomb of Amir Hasan Sijzi in Khuldabad, Maharashtra, in 2008 (photo by author).*

the advent of the modern period. Bahadur Shah Zafar, the last Mughal emperor who wrote at the end of an era, still used the image of the crooked cap in poems that are found in Qawwali songbooks today (Faruqi n.d.: 225).[11] The toppled emperor, who was more importantly a poet and Chishti Sufi, takes us into the colonial era with his reign: from 1837 to 1857 (Plate 21).

Modern mentalities

Modernity was ushered into the Islamic world through colonial catastrophe. Crowns fell to conquest. Some heads—like those of Bahadur Shah Zafar's male relatives—rolled on the ground. Other heads remained on their necks but had to adjust their minds to new circumstances: changing minds meant changing hats. In the early twentieth century, India witnessed "cap wars," as Hindus and Muslims experimented with how to be nationalist and anti-colonial, while reforming religion to suit political purposes (Pernau 2010: 249-67). The Gandhi-cap made of homespun cotton, *khadi*, became increasingly identified as "Hindu," while Muslim participants in the anti-colonial struggle increasingly adopted the fez, identified with Turkey and Islamic modernism (Tarlo 1996: 100-2). After the Ottoman defeat in World War One, the secularist Ataturk banned the fez in Turkey even as it became popular internationally as a symbol of Islamic solidarity and nostalgia (See Plate 3). As the Nation of Islam emerged in the USA, its leader often wore a fez (see Wheeler and Knight in this volume).

In Turkic regions, wearing a cap was a defining feature of Islamic identity. Uzbeks continue to wear a four-cornered cap similar in design to Chishti hats, while in Turkic areas controlled by China, Uyghurs are being identified as Muslims if they wear caps, often leading to their oppression (Kaltman 2007: 11, 43). For Muslims in North American and Europe, wearing Islamically-marked clothing can be a way to confront the double-standards of Western secularism (see Margariti, in this volume, for a deeper discussion of the "Islamic versus Islamicate" debate). That is, what Christians do and wear is "normal" and passes as secular, while what other religious communities do and wear is distinctive and "religious," a marker of difference and fanaticism and the inability to be assimilated (Kolig 2012: 185-226).

The present is a rather bewildering moment of diversification. When I last visited Sufi dargahs in India, during the *'urs* of Amir Khusro at the Dargah of Nizam al-Din Awliya in 2018, a wide variety of male head coverings were to be seen. While most men covered their heads, it is evident that this is no longer standard behavior: the non-covered are mostly men who are incidental visitors, those simply accompanying their female family members, those who are young, or tourists. The Khadims, hereditary custodians of the Dargah, are also not uniform. Most of them wear a simple white cotton *topi*, cylindrical in shape, that denotes urban middle-class respectability. Only during ceremonies do elder Khadims wear the high Chishti *kulah* (sometimes wrapped with a turban cloth of yellow or brown) as they lead the ceremony, offer prayers, or head the Qawwali sessions (Figure 6.2).[12]

Many of the men who visit the shrine simply tie a handkerchief around their heads, to cover the forehead as a mark of humility. Younger men wear American baseball caps, with the visor turned to the back to allow for prostration. Others purchase gaudy versions of the *kulah* that are on sale at shops all around the dargah, usually made of green, yellow, or orange velvet; these bright peaked caps—sometimes featuring sequins marking out the shape of the dome at Mu'in al-Din Chishti's shrine at Ajmer, or the numbers 786, representing the phrase "Bismillah al-Rahman al-Rahim"—are trophies to be shown off back home (Plate 20).

One can often see men carrying baskets of flowers, to offer at the tomb, on their heads as if the offerings were a kind of cap. It is as if the blossoms absorb the prayer, petitions, thoughts and concerns of the ones who bear them. They become consecrated offerings more valuable than one's own head, to be scattered over the tomb as one pronounces blessings on the Prophet, his family and his followers (Plate 21).

FIGURE 6.2 *Man in meditation while listening to Qawwali songs at the Dargah of Nizam al-Din Awliya in Delhi, wearing a conical* kulah *(photo by Adeel Amjad Ghaznavi).*

FIGURE 6.3 *A boy prays over the cloth-covered tomb of Pir Rasheed Kaleemi (died 2013) in Hyderabad, with a baseball hat turned backwards so that he can prostrate toward the tomb (photo by Mohammed Mubeen).*

Conclusion

Some coverings reveal what they cover, expressing what is covered by the qualities of the covering: its contours, colors, composition, texture, design, and inscription. This essay has explored one kind of covering—the Sufi cap—as an expressive material. Like the poetry that memorializes the awry cap, this covering "rhymes" with many layers of covering and alludes to them; these layers include the natural environment, built structures, psychic ideas, and sartorial material. The canopy of the sky covers the earth, and between them we humans move; indeed *adami* ("human being" in Arabic, Persian, and Urdu) is derived from "the surface of the earth" that receives moisture from the sky, indicating the muddy clay from which our bodies were formed (Kugle 2007: 29-33). Some humans move into and through shrine buildings, whose domes spread over the saints' graves that they cover; indeed, kings bowed their crown-wearing heads to saintly tombs and expended enormous wealth to build architectural approximations of the heavens over the blessed earth of their graves. As ordinary humans move through such shrines, they cover their heads to express humility and reverence. If they hold allegiance to a Sufi order, their head covering may take on a distinct shape; in this case, the covering expresses the ideas and teachings—the psychic structure or "mentality"—of the person whose cranium is covered (Figure 6.3).

Such a Sufi cap does not merely display its wearer's allegiance to others. It also reminds its wearer—by the very pressure of its matter against his forehead—of the ideals of the order to which he took vows. These ideals are easily neglected because they urge one to forget oneself; the process of being reminded, whether by one's clothing or other skillful means, is the essence of *dhikr*, remembering God and thus being reminded of the nothingness of one's own mind. Purifying one's heart of the pollution of the egoistic mind is grueling and difficult; progress along its path is marked by backsliding as much as progress, and without love there is little hope for success, for only passionate love can push us toward effacement. For this reason, the Chishtis celebrate the cap that is awry, raised like a dome, peaked like a goal, cornered like a system, but tilted to show deference to beauty and love within the material constraints of this embodied world.

PART THREE

Objects in Practice

CHAPTER SEVEN

What Comes to Light When a Lamp is Lit in Bektashi Tradition

*Mark Soileau**

The dervish strikes a match and touching it to the tip of the wick of a candle held upright in a small brass holder utters the words:

> Lamp of the lords, lord of the lords, lover of the lords
> Quintessence of existence, intercessor of the day of reckoning
> Knower of the secret and the hidden
> To the truth of the light of Muhammed–Ali, a loud salutation![1]

And all present respond in unison with the salutation formula—*Allahümme salli 'ala seyyidina Muhammad ve 'ala al-i Muhammed* ("O God, bless our lord Muhammad and the People of Muhammad")—as the now burning candle sheds its light before them. Such is the scene when in a Bektashi setting a candle is lit or, in Bektashi parlance, a lamp is awakened (Figure 7.1).

That a simple everyday material object like a candle can in its utilization generate this much cultural elaboration is testament to the ingenuity of religious traditions to embellish things and what is done with them—when in the appropriate context and among the proper people—and to associate them with significances beyond their bare utility. But the depth of this particular elaboration might also depend upon the profundity and unique expressiveness intrinsic to the thing in question: a burning candle. In the terminology specific to Turkish Bektashi discourse, a candle is not referred to by the usual Turkish word for candle (*mum*) but rather by the Persian-derived word *çerağ*, which carries the broader meaning of lamp. The category of lamp, which would also include an oil lamp, could then be defined as a small-scale implement for maintaining a controlled flame for the purpose of

FIGURE 7.1 *Taht-ı Muhammed, Hacıbektaş, Turkey (photo by author).*

giving off light. A basic lamp consists of fuel (solid in the case of a candle, liquid in the case of an oil lamp), a vessel or holder for the fuel, and a wick. The wick is actually what gives integrity to the lamp, maintaining the fire and limiting it to a single thin flame. The flame is the visible manifestation of a process of combustion, as it draws the fuel upward through capillary action and consumes it, burning and giving off light in the process. The flame is fire, so it gives off heat—which can be felt—but the lamp's primary purpose is rather to give off light, enough light to see in a space that would otherwise be dark.

Lamplight has two properties of note: it is itself visible, and it allows other things to be visible through it, things that would otherwise lie in the dark. Being both luminous and illuminating, light is thus the quintessential sign of presence, as opposed to absence, since as it shines forth its own presence it allows other things to be seen as there, and not remain hidden; and thus it is also a sign of perception, of knowledge, and of awareness. This is why light is a common discursive metaphor in many religious and especially mystical traditions, signifying the presence of the divine or the knowledge that humans can have of it (Kapstein 2004). But the metaphoric power of light can also be put into play via its actual manifestation in a material lamp, in which case the presence becomes, in a more material sense, real.

A presence, in a material sense, is something that is available to the senses, in the here and now, so that it can be seen, heard, felt or otherwise perceived and experienced; a present thing thus requires a perceiving subject, to which it is present in relation. Things that are present in a religious setting are often, though, associated with other things that are absent, like a god, saint, narrative, truth, value, or other bond. These may be absent because they are dead or otherwise immaterial, but here the concept of absence implies that, while not sensorily present, they are intended or desired to be present, or are thought to be ultimately present but somehow hidden from view, lying latent in the dark. When the materially present things are, in religious practice, engaged, and their associated absent things are summoned through the form of this engagement, the intended absences are made present through them, brought into the perceivable here and now, before a perceiving audience or cast of participants who have come prepared with the expectations for them. We can refer to this process as presentation, or, more simply, making present. It has been described in similar ways by several scholars of religion and in particular ritual (Morgan 2010; Orsi 2005; Meyer 2012).

Often what is made present through things in religious practice is an otherwise absent sacred person: a god or saint or spirit or ancestor, such as with the *praesentia* of saint cults that Peter Brown (Brown 1981) describes, the presence of God in the African church studied by Matthew Engelke (Engelke 2007), or the Imams and the Ahl-e Bait that Karen Ruffle (Ruffle 2017) finds made present among Shi‘is in India. In many cases, especially when what is absent is a person, the material object presenting it bears a pictorial resemblance to it, as in an image—such as the icons of the Virgin Mary that Robert Orsi (Orsi 2005) analyzes—or else has been in physical contact with the person, as with relics (Korom 2012; Ruffle 2017). But things like a candle with a flame, with no obvious association with a particular person, have less exclusive referentiality, and thus allow for the presentation of a more complex web of absences and, in the case of a lamp, of presence itself.

Lamps are used in many different religious traditions for a variety of purposes, with myriad meanings and forms of presentation. What exactly any burning lamp makes present is influenced greatly by what people, especially the tradition's specialists with authority, have said it makes present, or symbolizes, or means. Other relevant absent things can be found in the lore of the tradition: those elements that homologize in some way with the lamp. Others still can be discerned by observing the lamp in its context: the ordered time and space in which it is employed. A key aspect of its spatial context is its emplacement; the lamp is not only placed in the space, but at the same time in an arrangement that comprises other objects, so it has spatial and contextual relationships to them. And within this configuration people too have places, have positional relationships with the things arranged, and assume bodily attitudes vis-à-vis the lamp. When the time for action comes, the lamp can be lit, held, offered, bowed down to, or put out, and the manner in which these actions take place can help illuminate what is thereby being presented. Often accompanying ritual action is ritual speech, and the words spoken are perhaps most effective in drawing out the significances of things and actions, recalling explicitly or metaphorically the absences through verbal cues. Besides the words themselves, the genre of speech—invocation, supplication, prayer, praise, scriptural passage, narrative—and the language, style, tone, and register can all serve to negotiate the interaction among things, people, actions, and ideas, and to make present what is absent (Keane 2008). Speech does this in part through triggering and guiding emotions in the audience, and these emotions, along with sensory perceptions—especially visual and aural—and proprioception constitute the medium through which the absent becomes present to subjects.

By following such a course of inquiry, we can discern the sorts of things the lamp makes present when it is set alight in a Bektashi context. The lamp is ultimately a simple everyday object: a candle in a holder. But when it is employed within the context of the Bektashi tradition, at a specific time and in a specific setting, it takes on and gives off a particular array of meanings and references. The material lamp is present, and its activation makes other things present, just as its light can be seen and can make other things seen. What becomes present when it burns is what is absent before it is lit.

The lamp and its absences in Bektashi tradition

Due to the practicality of the lamp as a source of light, and the fact that Sufi gatherings tended to take place indoors at night, it would seem likely that from the first Bektashi ritual meetings or their precursors, the lamp—whether an oil lamp or a candle—was already there. But as the lamp continued to serve its practical purpose, developments in the configuration of its emplacement and the ordering of its practical application, such as the words spoken when it is employed, came to reflect key elements that the shapers of the tradition felt deserved engagement; the lamp and its use thus became ritualized. With its formative development occurring in Turkish-speaking Anatolia between the thirteenth and sixteenth centuries, the Bektashi order brought together various streams that congealed into a unique system that drew heavily from Islamic lore while often diverging from mainstream Islamic practice. The resulting cosmology, mythology, and expressive idiom share much with those of related traditions emerging in the same cultural milieu, such as that of the Alevis. The Bektashi order would go on to spread throughout western Anatolia and the Balkans, especially among Albanians. Many of the key elements and themes of the system that developed can be drawn out through reference to the light of a lamp, and these therefore constitute some of the absences which the lamp makes present when it is ritually lit.

Bektashism takes as its ultimate scriptural reference the Qur'an, and one verse that has particularly captured the Bektashi imagination, as it has that of all Sufis, is the one known as the Light Verse, which goes:

> God is the light of the heavens and the earth, the likeness of his light a lamp in a niche, the lamp in a glass, the glass as if a glittering star, lit from a blessed tree, an olive not of east nor west, its oil would glow though fire not touch it. Light upon light. God guides to his light whom he wills. And God strikes similes for humankind. And God is knower of every thing.
>
> 24:35

This finely woven verbal representation of God's light draws a vivid picture of an oil lamp shining through a glass within a niche. As the description moves inward from the enclosing niche to the glass to the lamp to the fuel and its source, the descriptive style moves upward from the concrete and real to the sublime and ethereal. Its verbal imagery thus unites the world of the materially present with the world which was to us absent, which seems to follow the theme the verse begins with, that God is the light of both realms: the heavens and the earth. The verse also highlights the fact that the lamp image is here being used as a metaphor for the otherwise ineffable divine light, beginning and ending with the idea of likeness or simile (*mathal*). Perhaps this interplay between the real and the metaphorical is what is alluded to by the elusive phrase 'light upon light' (*nurun 'ala nur*): the absent over the present. The Arabic word used in this verse for light—*nur*—has come to be used in Turkish religious and mystical discourse to refer to the light emanating from the divine source, and operates at a higher register than the everyday word for light, *ışık*. Turkish Sufi terminology also utilizes the Arabic phrase *nurun 'ala nur* to refer to the extraordinary light as described in this verse.

Another Qur'anic reference to a lamp occurs in the Ahzab surah 33:45-6, as God is listing the roles he has sent the Prophet Muhammad to fulfill: following those of witness and bringer of good tidings and warner and inviter to God, is that of "a luminous lamp" (*sirajan muniran*). Here it is the Prophet who is being likened to a lamp, and given that the other roles listed each have him as mediator in some way between God and humankind, the light this lamp gives off would presumably be that of God; though this is not explicitly stated, the word for luminous, or giving off light—*munir*—derives from the same root as *nur*. The divine light now being associated with the Prophet as its bearer, and thus linked to revelation, comes to be known in Sufi cosmology as the Light of Muhammad (*nur-ı Muhammed*). The word used in this verse for lamp is *siraj*, unlike that in the Light Verse, which was *misbah*. *Siraj* derives from the Persian word for lamp, *chiragh*, probably via the Aramaic-Syriac *shraga* (Jeffery 2007: 166-7). In Turkish *chiragh* takes the form *çerağ*, though the Qur'anic phrase *sirajan muniran* is often used in Turkish religious and mystical discourse.

The Islam that developed in the Bektashi tradition is a specifically Shi'i-inflected one, emphasizing the figures of Ali (cousin and son-in-law of Muhammad), his wife and Muhammad's daughter Fatima, and their sons Hasan and Husayn, who constitute the Ehl-i Beyt ("people of the house"), along with the Twelve Imams: the lineage of leaders beginning with Ali. Besides the ubiquitous use of the number twelve as an organizing principle, a key outcome of these emphases is the elevation of Ali to a cosmological position alongside the Prophet, so that the two complementary realities are often combined into a single joint mystical figure: Muhammed–Ali. We thus see the Light of Muhammed continue, but it is often linked with that of Ali, being referred to as *nur-ı Muhammed–Ali*; we see this phrase appear for instance in ritual formulae. The nature of this cosmological complementarity is complex, but it is often likened to that of the sun and the moon. Muhammed is here the sun, shining forth from the source, which illuminates the otherwise dark and hidden moon, likened to Ali as reflecting the more esoteric, mystical aspect of the truth, allowing it too to shine forth and also be seen. Drawing this dynamic into a more comprehensive cosmogony, we see the process also often include God—either as Allah or as *Hakk*, the True or Real—so that we hear of Hakk–Muhammed–Ali; thus the other ubiquitous numerical organizing principle of three. This might then account for a cryptic line in a poem by the sixteenth-century Bektashi poet Kul Himmet: "Three lamps burn in a glass / Lions hidden in the oak / In the seven climes, the four corners / I've seen my elder Ali." In an apparent allusion to the Qur'anic image, the lamp now becomes three, but still contained within a single glass.

Besides the Shi'i elements, the Bektashi tradition shares many inclinations with other Sufi traditions. One is reflection on the dichotomy between the concepts of *zahir* and *batın*. *Zahir* carries the meanings of manifest, appearing, visible, and outer, while *batın* is the hidden, the secret, the inner. In Sufi discourse, these terms are employed, for example, when contrasting exoteric (*zahir*) and esoteric (*batın*) interpretations of the Qur'an, narratives, practices, or truths. Sufis thus often seek to uncover the deeper *batın* truths hidden below the *zahir* surface. The binary can also be applied to the light of a lamp, so that while the *zahir* comes to light and shines forth, the *batın* is hidden and dark; this would correspond to the sun–moon dynamic, with Muhammed as the *zahir* sun and Ali the *batın* moon. Related to the *batın* is the *sırr*: the secret or mystery. This the Sufi hopes to have revealed, but then should keep concealed.

In addition to the Islamic, Shi'itic and Sufic elements it has incorporated, Bektashi tradition has features informed by the closer cultural milieu in which it formed, especially in terms of its mythology. The mythic movement that marks its genesis is the migration of its thirteenth-century founder Haji Bektash Veli from the mythical homeland of Khorasan in Central Asia to the land where his tradition was to take hold: Anatolia, then known as Rum. This movement, as recounted in the hagiography of Haji Bektash, the *Vilayet-name*, is portrayed as being a mission given by the great master Ahmed Yesevi. Haji Bektash is chosen among the other deputies (*halife*) after he performs a miracle, and his selection is then marked also in miraculous fashion by six items coming to him of their own accord: the headgear comes to his head, the cloak to his back, the prayer rug comes beneath him, the banner is planted before him, the tablecloth is spread out before him, and the lamp (*çerağ*) becomes illuminated (*ruşen*) and comes before him (*Velâyatnâme* 2007: 157-65). Each of these items, whether vestment or implement, is a sign of the authority of a Sufi master, and just as the tablecloth (*sofra*) symbolizes his capacity to share spiritual nourishment, the luminous lamp expresses his ability to enlighten. The *çerağ* as sign of the authority and power to enlighten disciples appears again in the episode in which Haji Bektash arrives in Rum and finds that the saints already there, the *Rum Erenleri*, are jealous of his powers and challenge him; so he blows and all of their lamps are extinguished, until they come and submit to him (ibid.: 174-85). Then, at the end of the hagiography, we learn that Haji Bektash in his 36-year career in Rum, having shown miraculous signs both *zahir* and *batın*, has "awakened 36,000 lamps, and installed 36,000 *halife*s," employing once again the lamp as a sign of the spiritual authority of a master and his power to enlighten disciples. One of the five *halifes* mentioned by name is Pir-Ab Sultan, who had served Haji Bektash in the capacity of *çerağcı*, lamp-tender (ibid.: 554-8, 609).

The best-known of the teachings attributed to Haji Bektash is a set of concepts known as the Four Doors (*Dört Kapı*): *şeri'at*, *tarikat*, *ma'rifet*, and *hakikat*.[2] These Arabic terms can be understood and used in many different senses, but based on their literal meanings and the ways they have been employed in Bektashi discourse, they can be seen as a series of levels of understanding and the means to achieve them, progressing respectively from the outward law to the inward rites to direct knowledge to the experience of reality itself. These concepts and their progression from *zahir* to *batın* have been explicated by Bektashi masters through many different metaphors (Birge 1937: 102). One is the analogy told to me by Nevruz Baba of Istanbul, in terms of the *çerağ* in its candle form: the wax candle in its materiality is *şeri'at* (Arabic *shari'a*, law or way), the wick within it is *tarikat* (the path, here the Sufi path), its "awakening" or burning is *ma'rifet* (knowledge or gnosis), and its melting is *hakikat* (truth or reality). Besides being the frequent subject of Bektashi discourse, the theme of the Four Doors and their progression plays out in Bektashi ritual as well, and has led to yet another numerical organizing principle.

A final element of Bektashi cosmology that is relevant here is the ubiquitous but multivalent concept of the *erenler*. Literally meaning "those who attain," this term is used in reference to various figures or groups of figures, such as the *gaib erenler*, those unnamed "absent" saints who exist in the world, but are hidden, unseen. It is also used in the form of *aynü'l-cem erenleri* to refer collectively to those individuals present in the *aynü'l-cem* ritual: that in which lamps are lit. And its usage for living, present people is seen in the fact that Bektashis address each other as *erenler*, and address the *baba* (master) as *babaerenler*. So, the *erenler* can be beings both present and absent.

A few notes can here be made about the actual forms the lamps take as objects, and some particularities in their usage. *Çerağs* are today almost always in the form of wax candles held in holders, usually of brass or a type of onyx that is known as Hacıbektaş stone because it is worked in the town named after Haji Bektash. It is likely that before the proliferation of wax candles, oil lamps were used; Ibn Battuta, while visiting a hospice of the Akhi brotherhood in Antalya in the fourteenth century, describes a kind of lamp on a stand made of brass that burned melted grease,[3] and given that the Akhis were an institutional precursor of the Bektashis, this form of *çerağ* may have passed into Bektashi practice and been the type mentioned in the hagiography of Haji Bektash. Ibn Battuta also records the title of the person charged with tending the lamps as *jaraji*, which approximates to the Turkish *çerağcı*. There are reports of lamps burning olive oil being used in Bektashi rituals in the early twentieth century (Atalay 1921: 10), probably in the case of the three-wick lamp, and there are in fact a few examples of these in the Hacıbektaş museum, having a figure of the twelve-seamed Bektashi headgear at the cap. The three-wick lamp is today almost always in the form of a three-branch candelabrum, and wax candles are now ubiquitous for all forms of the *çerağ*. One Bektashi village in Denizli province has recently begun using electric light bulbs for their twelve-*çerağ* configuration, and the late Bektashi leader Bedri Noyan Dedebaba (d. 1997), very much the modernist, had promoted this innovation (Noyan 2010: 64). Other Bektashis, though, have insisted on the importance of maintaining the match-lit, flame-burning, slowly melting candles.

When lamps are talked about among Bektashis, a special set of terms and expressions are employed. For the lamp itself, as has been mentioned, the word *çerağ* is used, rather than the usual Turkish word for candle (*mum*) or oil lamp (*kandil*), marking the candle used in a Bektashi ritual context as distinct from ordinary candles. In ritual formulae, *çerağ* is often qualified with the Persian adjective *ruşen* (bright, lit, luminous) and placed in the proper Persian grammatical construction, rendering *çerağ-ı ruşen*. This would appear to be a direct translation into Persian of the Qur'anic "luminous lamp"—*sirajan muniran* (33:46)—and the same Persian phrase is in fact used among Central Asian Ismailis, and also in the context of a lamp-lighting ritual (Khan 2013; Saidula 2015). Its ritual use among otherwise Turkish-speaking Bektashis raises the image of the light-giving lamp to a higher register and toward its associated absences. When it need be understood more explicitly it can be expressed closer to everyday Turkish, as in a line from a poem by Turgut Koca Baba (d. 1997): *Nur-ı Muhammed haktır / Nur saçan bir çeraktır* ("The Light of Muhammed is real / It's a light-shedding lamp").[4]

The terminology used for *çerağ* practices is likewise taken seriously by Bektashis. The lighting of the lamp is referred to not with the usual Turkish word for this act—*yakmak*—but rather with *uyandırmak* or *uyarmak*, meaning to awaken, emphasizing the homology between the burning of the flame and the spiritual awareness which is sought. Likewise, when a lamp is put out it is not "extinguished" (*söndürmek*), with the finality that implies, but rather it is "put to rest" (*dinlendirmek*) or "concealed" (*sırretmek*), with the implication that it can again be awakened or revealed. The use of these terms suggests that the lamp is understood as something that can come and go, be manifest or hidden, present or absent. When a lamp is indeed "concealed," the flame is decidedly not blown out with the breath, but rather pressed out between the thumb and forefinger, or else waved out with the hand. After all, the Qur'an (61:15) declares: "They want to extinguish the light of God with their mouths, but God will perfect his light, although the disbelievers dislike it." This is reflected in a poem by the sixteenth-century Bektashi poet Pir Sultan Abdal: "The lamp won't go out by the denier blowing / When it catches, it burns, the kindling of love."[5]

The lamp-lighting rite

In order to see how these lamp associations and other themes that lie dormant in Bektashi tradition come to the fore, we can turn to the ritual use of the material lamp. *Çerağs* are utilized ritually in many circumstances, and in fact a candle can be lit any time a Bektashi master (*mürşid* or *baba*) meets with disciples. Such meetings will often involve a shared meal, and a candle will certainly grace the table.[6] And initiated members may light candles on their own for spiritual practice purposes or out of personal motives, doing so while reciting the standard *çerağ* formula. But it is during the *aynü'l-cem* that the most elaborately ritualized use of *çerağs* occurs, and consequently that the process of presentation is best illustrated. This ritual series is performed by Bektashi communities with some periodicity, such as once a month among more active groups, in conjunction with calendrical events, and on special occasions, as in initiations.

The *aynü'l-cem* (or *ayn-ı cem* or *ayin-i cem*) ritual takes place in a specially designed space called the *meydan*, a rectangular room arranged so that seating is along the four walls with participants facing inward. Traditionally seating was on the floor or on cushions on the floor, but today chairs or benches are often found along the walls. Still today participants' seating places are marked with a sheepskin (*post*), the *post* of the *mürşid* being in the corner opposite the door. Many of the *post*s in specific spots are associated with past saints of the order, like Haji Bektash, Abdal Musa, and Seyyid Ali Sultan, so that when these are occupied or referenced in the ritual, the saints too are made present.

Besides the *post*s, the layout of the *meydan* prominently features candles placed in particular locations and in specific configurations. Hanging next to the door is a glass lantern housing a single candle, known as the Khorasan *çerağ*, after the Central Asian mythical homeland of Bektashi Sufism. This is the only *çerağ* already burning before the lighting rite begins, and so it serves as the source of flame. It is also the only *çerağ* enclosed in glass, so it most directly recalls the lamp from the Light Verse. Across the room, to the *mürşid*'s left, is a wooden structure consisting of three steps and called the *taht* ("throne") of Muhammed, and on it are arranged twelve candles, recalling the Twelve Shi'i Imams (Figure 7.2). Amidst the twelve candles is the candelabrum of three branches—the number a reference to the triad of Hakk–Muhammed–Ali—called *kanun-ı evliya*, "the Law of the Saints." Often placed on one of the steps between candles is a copy of the Qur'an, open to the Light Verse. At the base of the *taht* stands a single candle called the *baba sancağı* ("the banner of the baba"), and on the sides of the *taht* are four more candles, the number evoking the Four Doors of Bektashi understanding. To the right of the *mürşid* is a structure resembling a fireplace (formerly an actual fireplace) called *küre*, on the mantel of which are a pair of candles, associated with Hasan and Husayn, along with other implements that are used in the ritual, such as the rose water dispenser (*gülabdan*) and incense holder (*buhurdan*).

It is in this setting that the *aynü'l-cem* takes place, and among the several parts that the ritual consists of is that in which all these candles are lighted: *Çerağ Uyandırma Erkânı*, the Rite of Awakening the Lamps. It is in the performance of this highly ritualized sequence that the latent lamp associations are activated along with the material lamps, and what is absent is made present. Along with the action of lighting the candles—performed by the dervish charged with this office, the *çerağcı*—the presentation is given precision with the ritual verbal pronouncements made by the *mürşid* (called *gülbank*) and those by the *çerağcı* dervish (called *terceman*, literally "interpreter"). Some of these formulae or portions of them are given in the description below,[7] but it should be noted that all *terceman*s are introduced with the invocation *Bismi Şah Allah Allah* (the Bektashi and Alevi version of the Islamic *bismillah* invocation), and they are followed by the call to praise: "On the beauty of Muhammed, the perfection of Imam

FIGURE 7.2 *Taht-ı Muhammed, Manisa, Turkey (photo by author).*

Hasan, Imam Husayn / To the truth of the light of Muhammed–Ali – a loud salutation." And to this all present respond with the Islamic salutation to the prophet: *Allahümme salli ʿala seyyidina Muhammad ve ʿala al-i Muhammed.* Besides answering the *gülbanks* and *tercemans* with their own set of formulaic responses, non-officiating participants also watch and listen to the sequence and at some points ritually prostrate themselves. So the ritual is the performance of the interaction among people, things, actions, and words within a particular spatio-temporal arrangement, and there presentation takes place.

When the *aynü'l-cem* is to begin, it is the *mürşid* who first enters, alone, and he lights the Khorasan *çerağ* in the lantern near the door. As he does so, he recites the formula:

> The lamp of the light of Muhammed–Ali is what is pre-eternal
> Unceasing at the stage of "God is the light of the heavens"
> In the *aynü'l-cem* is seen the mighty hand of Hakk
> The rule of the rite, Lord Haji Bektash-i Veli
> Attaining to the secret of "But for you" the lights of manifestations shining

He thereby links the light of the lamp just lit to that of Muhammed–Ali, and to the Qur'anic reference to God as the light of the other realm. With only the Khorasan *çerağ* burning, the participants then enter through the door one by one, and walk with measured steps to bow and make prostration to the *mürşid*, to certain *post*s, to the *çerağ* configurations, and to their own *post*s as they take their seats.

Once all have entered the *meydan* who are to enter and the door is closed, the *mürşid* calls for the dervish charged with lamp-lighting duties—the *çerağcı*—to rise. The *çerağcı* approaches the *mürşid* in the appropriate manner and from him takes the thin, holderless and unlit candle called *delil* ("guide") that he will use in lighting the *çerağ*s. He takes the *delil* to the already burning candle near the door, the Khorasan *çerağ*, and touches the *delil*'s wick to its flame, so that he takes a *zerre* ("particle") of it, and the *delil* too now burns. In accompaniment of this action, he recites the *terceman*: "From the lamp of the light of Muhammed–Ali is born the sun and the moon / Let this poor one take a particle – by your leave, Allah *eyvallah*."

Having thus taken flame from the source to the *delil* and verbally identified its light as that of Muhammed–Ali, which cosmologically gives rise to the shining sun and the reflecting moon, the *çerağcı* next moves to a *post* in the center of the *meydan* called *dar* ("gallows") and there recites in Arabic the Qur'anic verses 36:45-7, including the reference to the Prophet being sent as a luminous lamp: *sirajan muniran*. He now progresses towards the main *çerağ* configuration on the three-step *taht*, pausing at certain of his own steps on the way to recite *terceman*s, such as the one beginning: "Your face is the candle of the success of guidance / Your face is a sign from the image of Hakk . . ." and at one step calling out: "Lovers, loyal ones, burning ones, woken ones – to their rose-faces, love!" Reaching the *taht*, the *çerağcı* first lights the single candle at its base with a *terceman*, and then the three candles of the *kanun-ı evliya* while reciting a *terceman* that begins with the phrase *çerağ-ı ruşen*: "Luminous lamp, pride of the dervishes, manifestation of faith / Opener of the meydan, law of the saints, moment of glory / Power of the Abdals, Pir Balım Sultan."

He then begins to light each of the twelve candles arranged on the three steps of the *taht*, repeating as he does so the basic *çerağ terceman*:

> Lamp of the lords, lord of the lords, lover of the lords
> Quintessence of existence, intercessor of the day of reckoning
> Knower of the secret and the hidden
> To the truth of the light of Muhammed–Ali, a loud salutation!

He then moves to the fireplace (*küre*) and lights the two candles on its mantel. Once all of the *çerağs* have been awakened, a series of ritual formulae are spoken that consummates the lighting rite and further expounds on the significance of the lamp. The *çerağcı* recites a *terceman* beginning: "For the lamps have become luminous on the Law of the Saints / Become proof to the poor ones, and a sign of the guide . . ."

The *mürşid* then recites the Qur'an's Light Verse in Arabic: "Allah is the light of the heavens and the earth, the likeness of his light a lamp in a niche. . . ." This is followed by a *terceman* from the *çerağcı* which begins "For we have awakened the lamp of pride for the love of God." This is a poetic *terceman* that continues this pattern in successive lines, "for the love of": Muhammed, Ali, Khadija, Fatima, Hasan, Husayn, the Twelve Imams, the Fourteen Pure Innocents, and Haji Bektash, before ending "Until resurrection may it burn, be lit for the love of the lovers."

As the lighting rite comes to its end, the purpose of the *delil* has been served, so its flame is "put to rest" or "concealed"—snuffed out between the fingers of the *çerağcı* and not by blowing—and as the *çerağcı* performs this act he recites: "*Batın iken çerağ-ı Şah-ı Velayet / Zahir oldu şems-i nur-ı Muhammed*" (While hidden the lamp of the King of Sainthood / Became splendent the sun of the light of Muhammed). This is spoken as the *delil* is concealed, so it in fact marks the moment when the material light goes from *zahir* to *batın*, but the verbal movement seems to be at the same time from *batın* to *zahir*, as if in the other realm the dormant lamp of Ali (the King of Sainthood) is filled with the shining light of Muhammed.

The *delil*, no longer alight, is handed carefully back to the *mürşid*, and the *çerağcı*, before taking his post, recites his final *terceman*: "*Zahir-batın, hazır-gaib aynü'l-cem erenlerinin gül cemallerine aşk!*" (Manifest–hidden, present–absent – to the rose-faces of the *erenler* of the *aynü'l-cem*, love!) With the lamps thus awakened, the rest of the *aynü'l-cem* can now take place.

Illuminations

At one level, the use of candles in this ceremony is addressing the basic need for a lighted environment so that participants can see each other and what is happening, and not sit in the dark—necessary for any indoor gathering of people—and for this purpose the material lamp is fully functional. But the tradition has built upon this material presence and organized its employment to reflect its mythology and cosmology, and those values and truths it has deemed worthy of engaging. It has arranged the candles in configurations of one, two, three, four, and twelve: numerical sets that homologize with groupings of mythic figures and espoused principles. It has elaborated the simple task of lighting all of these candles by slowing down the process and making each step deliberate and full of attentive weight, and by accompanying each act with verbal markings of the mythical, mystical, scriptural, and instructional relevance they bear for the tradition, so that the objects thereby become material manifestations of these relevances, presenting what is absent when activated. A lamp lit outside of this arrangement, or without the proper people, actions, words, or intentions would not illuminate the same things.

The intended world that has developed in Bektashi tradition is made up of a set of mythic figures, narratives, images, values, and truths—lodged in place through repeated association—that are absent until activated through discourse and practice. The specific absences that become present in the lamp-lighting rite include God, the unity of Muhammed–Ali, the Twelve Imams, Haji Bektash and other named saints, and the elusory *Gaib Erenler* ("hidden saints"). Besides these figures, the lamp also presents right guidance, whether coming from God, Muhammed as the Luminous Lamp, the past masters of the way, or from the *mürşid* physically present in the ritual. In this regard, the ritual taking of the flame from the source of the Khorasan lamp and spreading its light throughout the room arranged in a specific configuration replicates the narrative of Haji Bektash coming from the mystical homeland to spread his guidance—also marked in the narrative with a *çerağ*—in the present homeland. The diffusion of the flame in this setting in this way brings the absences of the intended world to the ritual world in the here and now, disseminating the guiding light to participants present. All of this occurs through the performance of the ritual in the space by the people with the things and with the words.

The particularity of an actual lamp is that it gives off light, so what its use in Bektashi ritual most obviously makes manifest is the idea of divine light, that which the Qur'anic passage had expressed with a similetic image of a lamp, but now is presented through a material lamp seen giving off real light as it is lit and the Qur'anic passage is heard read out, activating the association. The Bektashi ritual, in enacting this practice while repeating these words, continues to use the Light Verse as a vehicle for understanding the absent light, but by grounding the image in a material, sensible lamp and the physical act of lighting, it makes the light present in a deeper dimension: one that can be seen with the eye. The lamp that the Light Verse shows to the mind's eye as shining out of its niche, is here and now shedding actually visible light spreading throughout the *meydan* room. As a realization of the intended light, it can be physically seen, and in fact experienced in a more encompassing sense because participants are there in the midst of the light and see each other in it. With its unique combination of materiality and light in the process of happening and being consumed, the actually burning lamp perhaps presents presence itself. And if the subjects involved in these presentations—the ritual participants—are in fact attentive to all of this going on, the lamp can be said to make present their awareness.

Throughout these processes appear pairs of opposite ideas—material and ethereal, present and absent, manifest and hidden, real and metaphorical, the heavens and the earth, light and dark—and their subtle interplay. Their oppositions are then resolved through various forms of a discursive shift to a higher register, as with the invocation of concepts like God, as having dominion over the heavens and the earth, or love, which brings together two into one, or by their combination through imagery in simile or metaphor. And here we see all of these come together through the performance of traditional practice involving real things, a point which is highlighted by the formula with which the lamp-lighting rite ends: "Manifest–hidden, present–absent – to the rose-faces of the *erenler* of the *aynü'l-cem*, love!"

Here, as what is hidden is made manifest and what is absent becomes present, the absent (*gaib*) *erenler* now take the form of the present (*hazır*) *erenler* of the *aynü'l-cem* ritual, having been united through a process that brings space, things, people, actions, words, ideas, feelings, and the past together in the here and now: a process likened to love.

CHAPTER EIGHT

The Agency of the Material *Taviz* (Amulet) in a South Indian Healing Room

Joyce Burkhalter Flueckiger

The first time I entered Amma's healing room in 1989, in the South Indian city of Hyderabad, not knowing who or what was under the Islamic green flags that had called me there,[1] Amma was sitting at a low wooden desk, surrounded by a group of about ten Muslim and Hindu women. I was alerted to Amma's professional status first by the number of women waiting to see her, and then by the stacks of slips of paper on the desk in front of her, held down by chipped, glass paperweights (Plate 22). After she had welcomed me and called for tea, she introduced herself as someone who "did *ilaj*" (healing, treatment) for patients; later she identified as a *piranima* (wife of a *pir*, a Sufi teacher/master). She specified that her treatments were based on the Qur'an and were effective for illnesses caused by negative spiritual forces.[2]

It took me many months, upon return, of long-term research to learn the basic contours of Amma's diagnostic system. The slips of paper that are given as prescriptions are called *taviz* (amulets), upon which are written numbers for particular verses of the Qur'an, names of Allah, and/or the names of Allah's *maukil* (Arabic *mu'akkal*; Urdu pronunciation *maukil*), or deputies (including the four archangels and powerful *jinn*). Under each paperweight is a different kind of *taviz*, each prescribed for a different problem or for use at a different time of day in conjunction with others.

Amulets are material objects worn on the human body for purposes of healing or protection; they are often procured from powerful religious persons or at powerful sites of worship. In the case of their use in Islamic traditions, amulets are most often a materialization of the Qur'an that transmits Qur'anic *baraka* (spiritual power or blessing) (O'Connor 2001). In her healing rhetoric, Amma extends the word *taviz* to include both written amulets worn on the body and other forms of protective or healing writing, such as slips of paper that are hidden under a rock or piece of furniture, hung from a doorway, or smashed with a shoe. Amma's written prescriptions also extend beyond what she calls *taviz*, but these share with *taviz* the agency of the material written word. She writes on paper that may be burned over coals and the smoke inhaled by the patient; she writes on saucers or paper that is washed over with water that is then ingested, and she writes on green gourds and flat breads.

Amulets are common throughout South Asia, and, significantly as material objects rather than verbal rhetoric, they quite easily cross religious traditions. For example, to deflect the evil eye, many babies of all religious identities commonly wear a small metal canister that holds herbs or a written mantra or *taviz*, attached to a black string tied around their necks or waists (Figure 8.1). Amma's patients include Hindus, Christians, and Muslims, suggesting that, from an indigenous perspective, the amulets she prescribes and writes have their own agency that does not depend on knowledge or acceptance of the specific belief system of the persons wearing them.

The legitimacy of using amulets has been debated in Muslim circles since the time of the Prophet himself, beginning with debate about the legitimacy of pre-Islamic practices of *sihr* (magic, sorcery) (O'Connor 2001: 164-6)

FIGURE 8.1 Taviz *canisters (photo by author).*

and continuing through to contemporary internet, on-line Muslim discussion groups.[3] The primary issue of debate centers on the danger of *shirk*: associating anyone or anything with God and, by extension, attributing to another person or material object a quality or agency that is attributable only to God. Amma's frequent assertion that all of her practices are based on the Qur'an would be one defense against the claim that she may be committing *shirk* in her healing practices. I also frequently heard non-theological critiques against healing practices like Amma's that asserted they were "backwards," "superstitious," or "not scientific." Criticism does not, however, preclude a critic's participation in healing practices like Amma's or *dargah* (shrine) visitation. Visiting a famous Hyderabadi *dargah* one Thursday night, I met one of these critics, who had earlier chastized me for conducting research on a healing practice that was "only superstition." He was embarrassed to see me, but explained that his daughter-in-law was having trouble conceiving a child, that the family had run out of other healing options, and that they were coming to the saint here who had a reputation for answering entreaties for health and fertility.

This essay analyzes the agency of the material *taviz*. While from the perspective of Amma's patients, the *taviz* are the primary agents of healing as, quite literally, the word of God, analytically the work of *taviz* depends on the "distributive agency" (Bennett 2010: 9)[4] between the *taviz*, Allah and his deputies, the healer, and even the patient (whose compliance in following prescriptions is crucial). The primary data of this essay is drawn from long-term fieldwork in Hyderabad, conducted first with the female healer whom I call Amma and now, after her death and the death of her son (who also wrote *taviz*), with her grandson Akber, who has inherited her charisma and healing position.[5] I use the present tense in describing Amma's practices that are ongoing in the healing room in which her grandson and daughter-in-law now sit.

The use of writing—in both diagnosis and prescriptions—was striking to me as an ethnographer who had, prior to meeting Amma, observed traditional Hindu healers who rely on possession by a deity to diagnose a patient's problem and to identify appropriate ritual prescriptions. I learned that while writing is characteristic of many Islamic healing traditions, not all Muslim religious healers employ the written word.[6] I met several Muslim healers who relied solely on blowing prayers (*dua*) on patients; another healer interpreted the patterns of dried lemons for the diagnosis of patients' illnesses. Still another female healer diagnosed patients' problems through dreams, and she prescribed patients to sleep at a *dargah* (where she lived with her husband as caretakers of the shrine) for a certain number of nights. When Amma heard of my visits to these healers, she chastized me for giving them any consideration at all. She would often make a comment like, "But what do they *give* [materially]? Nothing!" She implied that they were not worth my time since they did not write or give anything material, such as her *taviz*.

Amma is distinguished, in part, from other female professional and lay Muslim healers I met in Hyderabad in three ways: she meets non-family members and non-Muslim men and women; she charges fees for her services; and her diagnoses and prescriptions are based primarily on writing. Amma is the only female healer I have met who incorporates writing into her practice, and this practice associates her with Muslim male healers. Amma's husband, Abba, although a *pir* (ritual specialist and religious teacher), was not literate in the Arabic/Urdu script,[7] and so he gave his permission for her to meet the public in a religious healing practice that depends on writing and is traditionally male. Theirs was a symbiotic relationship—Amma often emphasized that she could only practice with Abba's permission, and most of his disciples came to him through Amma's healing practice.

Physicality of the written word in a healing repertoire

Before we shift to writing in Amma's healing practice, it is important to note that in Islamic traditions, the liturgical oral recitation of the Qur'an *(tajvid)* and names of God (*zikr*) may also be considered to be effective in protection and healing (O'Connor 2001: 170, 172); and Amma and Abba and their disciples participated in these oral practices. For example, to purify and protect the site of Abba's monthly *sama* (ritual performance of *qavvali*), a group of female disciples participates in the ritual of *dastarkhwan*. During this ritual, the women recite the *kalima* (creed of faith) over and over, with each repetition counted by placing a smooth, dark brown seed[8] in a pile in front of individual reciters gathered around a *dastarkhwan* (lit., cloth spread out, over which blessings are recited).[9] Both laywomen and Amma also orally recite Qur'anic verses and blow their now-sacralized breath over a person for healing or a blessing. Amma also recites Qur'anic verses and blows prayers into bottled water that patients take home to ingest themselves or give to family members (Urdu: *dua phunkna*; Arabic: *nushra*).

Several years after I had first started working with Amma, she gave me two white-metal amulet canisters for my children. While I had often answered questions about whether Amma uses herbs in her prescriptions in the negative, when my daughter popped off the end of the amulet to see what was inside, out spilled dried leaf pieces. Upon returning to Amma's healing room the next year, I asked her about this; she explained that she had started to use herbal prescriptions (*jari-buti*) as a supplement to the written word (Flueckiger 2006: 101). She reminded me, "You always have to keep learning." But several years later, the *jari-buti* treatments disappeared from her healing repertoire, and her grandson has not continued with *jari-buti*. Amma's primary and consistent diagnoses and prescriptions are based on the written word.

Geert Mommersteeg distinguishes written prescriptions of Qur'anic verses from their oral recitation for the former's capability to be physically manipulated in different ways and in different patterns: "When written, words of a single formula can be separated and then distributed according to various geometric designs" (Mommersteeg 1990: 66). Many of the *taviz* Amma writes do just this; they separate and codify in numerical form Qur'anic verses and names of Allah that are then distributed on a piece of paper (or on saucers, gourds, or flat breads) in particular designs that break up their semantic whole.[10] *Taviz* are not meant to be read for their semantic value; individual letters, numbers, and words are spatially manipulated across the page so that they cannot, in fact, be read semantically from right to left (for example, see Figure 8.5).

Further, each form of amulet is folded in a unique way and is physically employed so that reading it would be difficult: they are worn on the body, or burned, buried, or hung in the wind. *Taviz* worn on the body are folded into a tiny square that is wrapped in plastic with a black cotton thread; these are tied to a woman's wedding necklace or a child's or man's neck or waist (Plate 23). Amma sometimes surmised some patients may be "too modern" to wear *taviz* on their body and told them they could carry the plastic-wrapped *taviz* in their pocket (for men) or purse (for women). When they get home, many patients sew the plastic-wrapped *taviz* in protective cotton cloth (Figure 8.2). The patient never sees what is written on the *taviz* after Amma has folded it, nor do they pay attention to what she is writing as she is doing so. The spatialization of writing on the *taviz* and the fact that they are enclosed in protective plastic are clues pointing towards the agency of the material *taviz* itself—the material word of God—rather than the semantic meaning of what is written on it. A caveat is warranted here: I am not a textual scholar of Islam and I do not read Arabic. Had I known Arabic, my focus would most likely have been on the semantic value of elements of the *taviz* and their textual sources, which of course would have its own value, but I may have missed the performativity of the material *taviz*, the focus of this essay.

In the context of talking about *taviz* written with pen on paper, Abba once explained the unique force of writing:

> Allah gave power to the pen and paper. To the pen. He gave strength to the pen. And the paper. *Taqat*—power. He didn't give power to the tongue. If someone gets angry, what happens? You take him and report him to the police . . . Then they look at the petition. They don't listen to the word of the tongue, only the written word. The judge can send you to the gallows. And if he wants, he can bring you down from there with the stroke of a pen . . . it's all in the pen, in the pen and paper. Only these two things.
>
> Flueckiger 2006: 66

FIGURE 8.2 *Child's* taviz *wrapped in cotton cloth, 2018 (photo by author).*

On another occasion Abba elaborated further on the power of the written word: "It's like if I write a letter to you and tell you to come; it's urgent—a telegram. You can't refuse . . . And on [your] name, like if we know the name of your mother. Reading that and reading your name, we make an attack."

Amma explained, "We call the *maukil* and they do the work. We write their names [on the *taviz*] and they do the work." Certain *maukil* are known to be particularly powerful for certain kinds of problems; for example, Abdul Jinn does the work of healing relationships, and Badru *maukil* calls runaway or missing persons back home. However, Amma frequently reminded me, ultimately the *maukil* are doing the work of Allah; it is his power that effects the healing. Amma's daughter-in-law (who now sits at the healing table with her son) emphasized many years later, perhaps fearful of being accused of *shirk* and wanting me to fully understand: "It's all Allah's *shifa* (healing); the paper (*khagaz*; i.e., the *taviz*) [only] brings him close." From this perspective, the paper *taviz* is like a prayer (*dua*, calling out to God, through his *maukil*.

I became interested in the agency of the material *taviz*—how did it work? —when I noticed that none of the Muslim and Hindu patients who came to Amma's healing room asked about or read what was written on the *taviz* that Amma customized for them. They seem to accept the agency of the *taviz* without consideration of the semantic value of what is written on them or *how* their materiality is effective. When I recently pointed this out to Amma's grandson Akber, he explained: "To write is *our* [healers'] work, to put in knowledge is *our* work," and then he proceeded to distinguish several different kinds of *taviz*, saying after each name, "this is *our* work." He explained, "Just like patients who go to doctors don't know what is in their medicines, our patients, too, don't know what is in their medicines. This is *our* work." Patients do not have to understand how *taviz* work (or even agree with an implicit theology behind them); they only have to follow instructions about what to do with them. Whereas the healer must learn and understand the entire system of diagnosis and prescription.

The written word through healers' perspectives

Diagnosis

While not all Amma's prescriptions incorporate the written word, her diagnostic methodology for adult patients always begins with writing, using a system called *abjad ka phal kholna* (lit., the opening of the mystery of numbers). (For children, she often makes a diagnosis simply by looking at their eyes and tapping their stomachs). Her desk is cluttered with pieces of scratch paper upon which she has written letters, numbers, and mathematical calculations (Figure 8.3). She begins by asking the patient's name and their mother's name and writing down each name in the Urdu/Arabic (what she called "Arabi") script.[11] By tradition, each Arabic letter has a numerical value, which Amma adds together for each name before adding the values of the two names together with the value of the lunar day of the year. Then Amma divides the total sum by three or four (reflecting, Amma explained, the three levels of the universe or, variously, the four directions or the four elements that make up a human: earth, air, water, and fire) until the quotient is a single digit number (zero through four). Amma explained, "If you don't get it one way [dividing by four], then you get it this way [dividing by three]."

If the final quotient is zero, the diagnosis is that the patient is not experiencing illness due to spiritual forces. This is not to deny the existence

FIGURE 8.3 *Lateefa writing* falita *and sheet of* abjad ka phal *calculations, 2018 (photo by author).*

of a problem, but only that it has been caused by a solely physical rather than spiritual cause (these biologically caused illnesses include four that Amma enumerated as those over which her healing practices had no effect: cancer, typhoid, heart disease, and polio). Patients are often dissatisfied with a diagnosis calculation of zero (no spiritual cause) and Amma usually gives them a protective amulet to wear on their body, at the same time often referring them to specific allopathic doctors or clinics by name.[12] However, a quotient of one, two, or three means that the illness has been caused by different kinds of evil eye or, more generally, a negative force cast by a human or nonhuman (jinn, ghost, or devil, etc.), cast purposefully or unknowingly. Each kind of evil eye requires a different prescription/*taviz* or set of *taviz*—that is, it is rare for a patient to walk away with only one kind of *taviz*.

Less we conclude that the diagnostic system is just mechanical addition and division, Amma asserted, "Anyone can *read* [*parhna*; also implying, can write], even a parrot. It's understanding [that's difficult]." That is, Amma suggests that anyone who is literate in the Arabic script and knows the basic system of *abjad ka phal* can write names and add up and divide the mathematical values of their letters; this person may come up with a quotient but would not know how to interpret it. She explained that spiritual training—by sitting *chilla* (forty days of meditation and fasting) and reciting the Qur'an every night—gives nuances to the seemingly mechanical prescriptions of *abjad*. This spiritual wisdom is needed to decipher the "weight" of the evil eye, to know its source, and to know, then, what kind of *taviz* or other treatment to prescribe. These are the skills of a professional healer.

Taviz can work, according to Amma, at the hands of non-professionals who have not sat *chilla*; but these *taviz* are not as powerful as those of professionals. Amma periodically gave me stacks of *taviz* to bring back with me to the US, telling me that I could use them for my children or close family members if they are sick. When I said that I did not know how to write their names in Urdu, Amma reassured me that the effect of the *taviz* would be the same whether I wrote names in Urdu or English. However, it became clear that while this level of healing may be effective for everyday illness, it would not be so for "heavy" illnesses; for these, Arabic writing of the name would be needed. On another occasion when I explained to Amma that many English names could be written in a variety of ways, or Urdu names written in English could be spelled differently, she told me that English and its various spellings would work if I had the right intention (*niyya*). Here, she implied that the person writing the *taviz* (her intention) is as important as the writing itself;[13] again, the intention or belief of the patient is not implicated in successful healing.

Prescriptions

Four stacks of *taviz* are laid out across the desk behind which Amma or her daughter-in-law, son, or grandson sit (Figure 8.4); other *taviz* less frequently used are stored in plastic bags on a shelf behind Amma's desk or in one of its drawers. Amma's daughter-in-law, Lateefa, showed me a notebook to which she regularly refers, in which Amma's son Shaykh Khalid had written pages and pages filled with specialized *taviz* designs that, if needed, she copies. One *taviz* in the stacks on the table is given to almost all patients to wear on their body or otherwise keep close to them, no matter their individual problem. These are protective as well as healing. Then there are two kinds of *falita*, always given in pairs, to be burned as oil wicks every morning and evening over the period of a week depending on the diagnosis—either in coconut or sesame oil, the specific kinds of oil having different effects. Amma writes the patient's name on the front side of the pre-printed *falita*. On the backside, she writes a word or words that reference the healing that is desired, often naming the person who is causing the problem, such as an abusive husband or quarrelsome neighbor. That is, every falita is personalized. *Falita* are prescribed to effect change in another person; for a change in the patient themselves, a slip of paper called *dhuan* (lit., smoke) is placed in burning coals and the patient inhales the resulting powerful smoke.

FIGURE 8.4 *Akber and Lateefa at healing table, 2007 (photo by author).*

Amma instructs patients to recite an oral incantation, of sorts, as the *falita* burns: "may so-and-so's mouth be shut," or whatever end the patient desires—an oral version of what has been written on the *falita*'s back side. These statements are performatives that (help to) effect the healing, similar to Amma's performatives that end every patient interaction: "You *will* get pregnant"; "Your husband *will* stop arguing with you", etc.

Other *taviz* involve the writing of magical squares (called *naqsha Qur'an*, lit., diagrammatic Qur'an) or the outline of a fish (Figure 8.5) that is dissected by lines, the intersections of which are filled with numbers representing verses of the Qur'an and/or the names of God and/or his angels (O'Connor 2001: 169). For missing children or animals, a *hava taviz* (lit., breeze *taviz*) should hang unfolded from the doorway of the patient's home, to flutter in the wind; the written words will be carried to and cause the missing child to return. For childhood fevers, a small paper *taviz* is written with the child's name on it, which should be folded up in a tiny square and smashed three times with a sandal, thus destroying the fever.

Amma writes not only on paper, but also on flat breads (*chapati*) to be fed to a dog as treatment for an errant husband: the husband will be faithful to his wife in the same way that a dog will be faithful to whoever feeds it. For failure-to-thrive babies, she writes on a long green gourd, wraps it in white

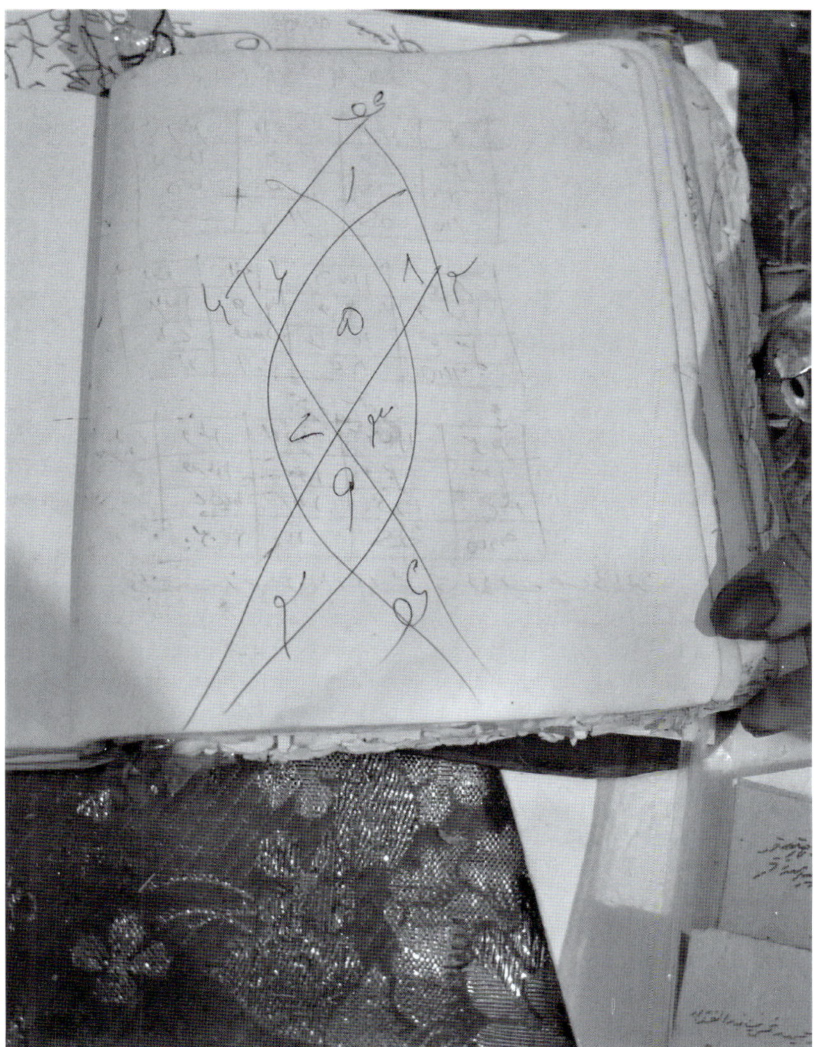

FIGURE 8.5 *Fish shaped* taviz *(photo by author).*

cotton cloth, sprinkles it with oil-based perfume, and gives it to the patient to lay next to her baby for forty days; the strength of the gourd and the powerful words written on it transfer to the child. Amma writes on lemons that are buried with other ritual ingredients in the corners of the rooms of a house for which she performs house exorcism (*bandish*, lit., binding the house). She also writes on saucers into which the patient is instructed to pour water, which dissolves the written words that the patient now drinks.

On several occasions, I asked Amma to explain to me what she wrote on *taviz*. I wanted to learn what particular numbers stood for beyond the generic answer of "verses of the Qur'an" and "names of God." (I had been told from one of Amma's disciples that most commonly used verses were the last two chapters of the Qur'an.) She replied with a sigh, "These are heavy [*bhari*] matters, Jo-ice. One day I'll teach you." That day never came. The next generations—Amma's son, daughter-in-law, and grandson—have been reluctant to talk about the specifics of the written *taviz*; they may have assumed that I had already learned these basics from Amma.

Technologies of the written word

When I first met Amma in 1989, she was writing all *taviz* by hand, with the aid of carbon paper that permitted her to make six copies at a time. Over the years, the technology of production of the most commonly prescribed *taviz* changed from handwriting to photocopying to printing. The handwritten and photocopied *taviz* were black and white; the printed ones range in color from white, bright pink, to green (whatever color is cheapest at the print shop, Amma's son told me). When I wondered aloud if the handwritten *taviz* may be more effective than printed ones, Amma's son thought the technology of writing did not make a difference. However, it is significant that Amma and her son, and now her grandson and daughter-in-law, always hand write the patient's name and/or the name of the person who may be implicated in the illness on each *taviz*. Of course, for *taviz* of erasure, Amma handwrites with delible ink that washes off into water.

Not all healers would agree with Amma's son that the materiality of the writing is not significant. In 2018 I met a male Muslim healer in Chhattisgarh (central India) who wrote all of his *taviz* with saffron ink (saffron threads soaked in oil), resulting in a pale golden, scented ink. This healer explained that were he to use regular ink, he would not be able to guarantee its purity; he said nothing about the purity of the paper on which his *taviz* are written.

Written taviz *from the patients' perspectives*

Most Muslim and Hindu patients are not literate in the Arabic script in which Amma writes; nor would they necessarily be able to read her handwriting if they were. Amma often declares that her healing is based on the Qur'an, characterizing it as a "Book of Service" (*khidmatwali kitab*), so we can assume patients know the words are powerful in the Islamic tradition. However, many patients told me that they came to Amma not because of her skills of writing, but because of her reputation for success; most importantly, they said, they were drawn to her for her reputation of unusual love and patience. Amma understood this when she observed that her son was like an express train who "quickly-quickly" (*phat-a-phat*) asks the name of the patient and their mother, makes the diagnostic calculations, and prescribes *taviz*; whereas Amma said she is like a passenger train, asking her patients how they are, taking time to listen to their stories, reassuring them: "They come crying and they go away laughing."

Patients' primary concerns are that their troubles will be identified and that they will be relieved of their suffering. The only attention patients seem to give the material *taviz* is to the instructions about how to use them, instructions that may be confusing to first-time patients. Their confusion was often a moment of humor in the healing room: "No, no," one patient told another; "didn't you just hear what Amma said?!" and then proceeded to explain the difference between the *falita* to be burned in the morning and those to be burned in the evening, distinguished by the way they are folded. When a patient periodically comes back with a complaint about the prescriptions not working, Amma repeats her ritual instructions and asks if the patient had followed these carefully; usually the patients' answers indicate they had made one mistake or another in the implementation of her prescriptions.

While patients do not talk about Amma's writing, performatively the highly technical, differentiating diagnostic and prescriptive systems that Amma uses—including the sheer array of all the pieces of paper and writing—identify her professional status and help to create her spiritual and healing authority. *Abjad ka phal* only produces four diagnoses, and yet Amma distinguishes many more diagnoses within each category. It is like many patients giving an allopathic medical practitioner more authority if they use an MRI or X-ray rather than a simple physical exam, or giving them more authority if they prescribe specialized medications rather than simply an aspirin for every kind of problem. Each patient walks away with a little plastic bag filled with different kinds of folded paper *taviz* and specific instructions about when and how to use them differently.

The written word as the word of God

The words of the Qur'an are believed by Muslims to have been orally transmitted by the angel Gabriel to the Prophet Muhammad as the word of God, written in Arabic, which was pre-existent to the revelation as a "preserved tablet" (Qur'an 85:21). When Amma narrated the creation of Adam and Hava, she described the moment Adam first opened his eyes after his creation and saw the *kalima* (creed of faith) written across the sky—in Arabic; this would be a moment *prior* to the revelation of the Qur'an to the Prophet. Ibn Ishaq, first biographer of the Prophet (704-61 CE) narrates the revelation of the Qur'an to the Prophet as written words that are materially pressed into the body of the Prophet:

> While I was asleep (Gabriel) came to me with a (coverlet of brocade) upon which was some writing. He said, "Read! [Recite!]" I said, "What

> shall I read?" He squeezed me so tightly that I thought it was death, then he released me and said, "Read!" I said, "What shall I read?" He squeezed me again until I thought I would die, then he let me go and said, "Read!" I said, "What shall I read? He squeezed me a third time until I thought I would die and said "Read!" I said, "What then shall I read?" I said this only to save myself from him, in case he would do the same thing to me again.
>
> cited in Mattson 2008: 18

If the written Arabic words on Islamic amulets are considered to be, quite literally and physically, the word of God, then issues of purity/pollution could (and according to some, should) come into play. The Qur'an as a physical book (*mushaf*) should be treated carefully to preserve its purity: it should never be put on the floor, and anyone touching it should be in a state of ritual purity; when a copy needs to be disposed of, it should be buried or burned (Mattson 2008: 153-6). If *taviz* are the materialization of sacred words of the Qur'an, then the question arises: how should they be treated with regard to purity-pollution practices? Can they be worn by menstruating women, for example? In the case of erasure, do the fluid words risk pollution as they pass through the (presumably polluted interior of) the human body?[14]

While these are interesting theoretical questions, the only visible or audible hint of them being relevant in Amma's healing room were instructions about the correct practice of disposing of old or damaged *taviz* and the prohibition of menstruating women entering the healing room (although they could lean their upper torsos through the doorway to talk with Amma). When this became an issue for me one day in the healing room, Amma explained that it was alright if I entered the healing room and sat at her desk when I was menstruating; the real prohibition, she explained, was against touching the *taviz*, which she could not guarantee if menstruating women entered the room. It was unclear if *taviz* worn by menstruating women should, then, be removed from around their necks for the duration of their menstruation; perhaps the plastic tightly wrapped around them protected against such pollution. There were surely unstated assumptions about the care of *taviz* on the human body beyond this that I did not hear or think to ask about. As for ultimate disposal of a *taviz* that falls or is taken off a human body, Amma's son explained that it loses its power at this point and is no longer sacred. Nevertheless, as material on which Qur'an is written, he said that it should be buried or disposed of in a body of water to preclude its misuse or it being the recipient of the evil eye.

Conclusion

In conclusion, we return to the question of agency in Amma's healing room: how is healing effected, through whom or what? Amma would surely answer that the primary agent is Allah himself and that the material *taviz* she dispenses are his words—the Qur'an materialized. At the risk of committing *shirk*, Allah as primary agent must be the answer for Muslims. When Amma writes their names on *taviz, maukil* are compelled to come close and follow the orders of the writing, although they work at the bidding of Allah. And so *taviz* and *maukil* are both sub-agents in effective healing, who work in the service of Allah.

However, it becomes clear in Amma's own narratives of healing and in the testimonies of her patients, that—at least performatively, if not theologically—a key agent in the healing process is the healer herself. As Amma said, even a parrot can do the necessary calculations of diagnosis. It is because of her spiritual training and practices that the *taviz* Amma writes are more effective than those that can be purchased in bazaars surrounding *dargahs*. Amma's professional status and authority as a healer who treats "heavy" illnesses, and who can differentiate the weight of the illness and refine her prescriptions accordingly, is performatively created and reinforced by the stacks of different kinds of *taviz* sitting on her desk, sheets of paper filled with mathematical calculations, and the small plastic bags filled with their unique sets of prescriptions that patients carry home.

However, as she is writing and folding *taviz*, Amma also does something else—she patiently listens to the stories of suffering her patients bring to her and assures them that healing will be effected. Her diagnosis of evil eye takes away, on one level, agency or fault from the patient, even as that same patient has exerted agency though the choice of coming to Amma's healing room. From both Muslim and Hindu patients' perspectives, Amma is the primary agent of healing; or at least her reputation for love, patience, and success are the stated reasons they come to that particular healing room for treatment. However, while patients do not read or ask Amma about the semantic content of the *taviz* she writes, they they do want/need the materiality of the *taviz*; the more slips of paper patients walk away with, the more satisfied they seem to be. Both for Amma and her patients, the material *taviz* is a necessary but not sufficient component of successful healing in a continuum of distributed agency.

CHAPTER NINE

The Life of a Tablet

Aomar Boum

Last summer, Nouria Riyadi, an acclaimed specialist of Islamic calligraphy (*al-khat al-islami*), organized an exhibition of Moroccan calligraphic styles of writing on Qur'anic tablets at Abdellah Guennoun Cultural Building in Casablanca. In association with a group of female students from 'Ubayy Ibn Ka'b Quranic School in the neighborhood of Ain Chock, Riyadi and her novice female collaborators showcased their skills of Islamic calligraphic styles on a series of wooden Qur'anic tablets (*alwah*, singular *luha* or *lawh*) in July 2019 (Plate 24). The event lasted for days attracting a large number of visitors including religious scholars and imams who celebrated and applauded the initiative (Les Site Infos 2019). This is not the only unusual context where Qur'anic tablets feature as objects of celebration and appreciation of Moroccan religious and cultural heritage. In markets and bazars throughout many traditional Islamic cities such as Marrakesh and Fez, shopkeepers display new and sometimes old samples of wooden tablets featuring handwritten Arabic calligraphy and Islamic geometric designs. In the age of globalization and a worldwide tourism industry the Islamic wooden tablet has gained new meanings and functions as a material object sold and exhibited outside traditional Islamic contexts of learning.

Yet, despite these new meanings and social manifestations, wooden tablets remain today an integral part of Islamic learning in Qur'anic schools and madrasas throughout North and West Africa (Brigaglia 2017). In southeastern Morocco, where I conducted the larger part of my ethnographic research (Boum 2008, 2013), families place decorated tablets used by their children in Qur'anic schools on shelves or hang them on walls in living rooms as a token of family pride in their educational achievement. In this ethnographic account of Islamic education in southeastern Morocco, I adopt the concept of *isnad* (chain of transmission of hadith) to trace the narrative of a Qur'anic memorizer through different generations of ordinary transmitters. In this transmission network I rely largely on the oral accounts I collected from different oral and written sources between 2004 and 2010, especially based on interviews with Ziri, my primary informant.

In this chapter, I trace the social transformation of Bakki, a former slave in the village M'Ghimima, southern Morocco, just a few miles from Tissint (Bellakhdar et al. 1992), through the different stages of his initiation to official Islamic learning. During the fifteenth century, religious brotherhoods had expanded their networks in southern Morocco calling for jihad against the Spanish and Portuguese colonial interests in the coastal cities. In Imi n'Tatelt, Sidi Mhammd U Ya'qub established one of the first *zawiya*s (Sufi centers) on the south slopes of the eastern Anti-Atlas among the Sektana tribe (Berque 1982; Boum and Park 2016: 497; Naji 2011; Lévi-Provençal 1922). By the sixteenth century his students built and expanded a large network of satellite *zawiya*s. At M'Ghimima, Sidi Mbarak ben Abdellah, one of the disciples of Sidi Mhammd U Ya'qub, quickly established himself as a religious figure in the Anti-Atlas in M'Ghimima. His spiritual influence grew and so did the numbers of his followers in the region of Sous and the Sahara. For years, Berber and Arab tribes fought over grazing lands and water; throughout the south Sidi Mbarak ben Abdellah became known for his mystical powers and peacemaking between fighting tribes. After his death a generation of descendants maintained the economic and religious prestige of the *zawiya* throughout the south.

As I transmit the story of Bakki using his preserved Qur'anic tablet as the story thread, I am conscious of the reliability of the transmitters. However, I also acknowledge that in the traditional historical account of North and West Africa, marginal voices require attention. In the words of Eric Wolf, I make sure that "the people who claim history as their own and the people to whom history has been denied emerge as participants" (Wolf 1982: 23). The story is not only about the tablet as an object that indexes different phases of Islamic learning, it is also a moment to rethink how we study Islamic communities and societies by shifting our focus from the mainstream structure of power and ideology to marginal groups and objects. I stress here that the story is told mostly based on a third person account. In this chronicle, I describe the corporal and sensory dimensions of stages and practices of Qur'anic memorization and Islamic learning as hypothetically experienced by Bakki. I use the tablet as a historical source that allows us to put voices of a marginal group—slave and *Haratine*—back in the larger and mainstream narratives of southeastern Morocco.

The tablet as historical document

In 2010, during an interview with Ziri (a Berber name meaning moonlight), a local farmer from the Anti-Atlas, about Islamic knowledge and scholarship, I was informed of cases of descendants of slaves who excelled in Qur'anic memorization. I paid little attention to this ethnographic story largely because

I thought that Ziri was just trying to respond to the widely circulated social and conventional stereotypes that black people are by nature not capable of learning the sacred text like local individuals who claim descent from the Prophet, also known as *shurfa*. Ziri was among a generation of blacks known as *Haratine* who launched a public campaign against negative stereotypes about families of sub-Saharan descent. The *Haratine*, a black ethnic group indigenous to southeastern Moroccan oases, have generally been regarded as an inferior social stratum in comparison to the light-skinned *Shurfa*, who claim descent from the Prophet Mohammed, and through this claim had special status within the community (Ennaji 1998; Becker 2002; Ilahiane 2004; Boum 2013; El Hamel 2002, 2013; Aouad 1973). Over many weeks I succeeded in building a social rapport and bond with Ziri. He trusted me and believed that I could help him write about his community. He also thought that it is important that we record the history of the region, including what he dubbed as its "shameful" past of slavery (Figure 9.1).

Usually I accompanied Ziri during his daily tours to check if his small field needed to be watered. We spent our time chatting about the social and political memory of his village. One day, thinking that I would walk with him to his field of maize, Ziri led me into a dark room in his humble adobe house and opened a chamber inside a mud-brick wall. He set aside a group of dusty folded paper documents in rolls from inside a square tin box before he pulled a wooden object from a dusty white cloth. He lighted a candle by

FIGURE 9.1 *The author in conversation with the Shaykh of the local Qur'anic school, al-Baraka village, Tata Province (photo by author).*

the door of the little chamber, pointed to the dusty slate and noted "This is my most valuable historical and personal document." After a moment of silence as if waiting for signs of admiration to show on my face, he continued, "this might seem to be a less valuable Qur'anic tablet to you or others, but for me it reminds me of hundreds of black African slaves in this region. This tablet is a symbol of social resilience against discrimination." At first, I could not see the link between the wooden object and racial discrimination. Yet at the same time I was intrigued by his words. I asked if I could take a photograph of him holding his treasured wooden object. He refused. "We do not reproduce images of Qur'anic text. We embody it by drinking for instance the ink used to write God's sacred words," he said. During the weeks following this conversation, I tried to gather more data about the phenomenon of slaves and Qur'anic learning in Tagmout, Akka, Tissint, Tizounine, and other villages along the line of the trans-Saharan trading routes; and while my investigation led me nowhere, I shifted my attention to Ziri's story about the history of the tablet and its origins, which I recount in the pages below.

By the late 1940s and with the growing centralization of administration and bureaucracy after Moroccan independence in 1956 (Ensel 1999), descendants of *Haratine* and blacks (also known locally as *ismgan* meaning "black" in Tamazight), who relied on their former masters to survive through hard daily labor and traditional subsistence farming, began to either migrate to urban cities and sometimes Europe or seek modern education (Ennaji and Pascon 1988; Aadri 1984; Al-Susi 1966; Ensel 1999; Benachir 2003). Feeling that their religious and economic hold on the traditional social hierarchy was in danger, largely because of their dwindling spiritual prestige, local *shurfa* tried to limit these economic and social transformations brought about by colonial modernization policies, but with little success. The signs of a new social and economic order were already there, and the shifts from traditional Islamic learning to modern education only accelerated the rate of change. Individuals and families who could not abide by the old rules of the traditional systems were asked to leave the home of their former masters. Some did and never returned, joining a growing labor force in Casablanca and Agadir. Others realizing that their economic subsistence was still tied to these powerful religious families, remained under their protection. They could not take the risk of economic uncertainty and chose the certainty of being fed and housed in the large compound of their masters.

Tidir, a descendant of a slave family from Timbuktu, was an example of those affected by the crumbling traditional social and economic order. I was first informed about her during a discussion about female household servants with an informant, and I was intrigued by her name. Tidir, an Amazigh name, was rarely given to black women of slave ancestry. My indigenous ethnographic instinct proved right when Ziri informed me weeks later that Tidir was the only surviving female descendant of Bakki, the protagonist we will meet in our tablet story. Just a few miles from the historical market of slaves in Tissint, where her late grandmother Tamu (diminutive of Fatima) and father Bakki (diminutive for Mbarek, also referred to by his dark-skinned color as Akawel) were sold, Tidir lived alone in the last stage of her life. Unlike her father Bakki, Tidir was never able to get married, mostly because of her socially derided slave ancestry. Ziri met Tidir when he worked as a daily laborer in the village of Tissint in the 1950s, not far from the building of a religious brotherhood (*zawiya*) of M'Ghimima where her father memorized the Qur'an. The *zawiya* served as a site of both social activities and religious education (Eickelman 1972–73, 1983; Awad 1992). Ziri made it a habit to visit with Tidir sometimes three times a week after his daily prayers. Tidir lived alone after she lost her eyesight and stopped working in the complex of the *zawiya*. He brought her food whenever he could until he relocated to the village of Tagmout after marrying into a local family. A few months later, he learnt of her death. In his oral account of Tidir's father story, Ziri seemed as if he was talking about a family member.

During the nineteenth century, hundreds of slaves were brought from Timbuktu with trans-Saharan trading caravans (Schroeter 1992; Sikainga 1998, 2011; Michaux-Bellaire 1910; Jackson 1809; Foucauld 1888). They were sold and exchanged in resting towns and entrepots such as Tindouf, Tizounine, Iligh and Akka (Figure 9.2). Tissint was one of the last markets where slaves captured from sub-Saharan and West African villages in Mali and Senegal were exchanged and bartered for salt and other products including cloth and even palm dates. Bakki was one them. He was born to Tamu and a local Sharifian man in Tindouf. A few months after his birth he was sold as a baby with his mother to another family in the slave market of Tissint, who gifted them to the religious brotherhood of M'Ghimima in the early decades of the twentieth century. His new master patron was a graduate of the Nasiriyya religious brotherhood based in Tamghrut and one of the most respected scholars of M'Ghimima. Unlike the founder of the brotherhood of M'Ghimima who came from a different patron, some of his descendants were trained in other religious brotherhoods such as the Nasiriyya that was founded in the seventeenth century (Gutelius 2002). Largely funded by revenues from farming and trans-Saharan trade, the Nasiriyya was able to expand its membership to other religious brotherhoods largely because of its relaxed rules, such as making it non-obligatory to carry a rosary (*tasbih*) and simpler rules of prescribed *dhikr* prayers. The Nasiriyya had great social and political relationships with the Derkawa and Tijaniya religious brotherhoods throughout southeastern Morocco (Bodin 1918).

After the new owners of Bakki and his mother arrived in the region of Tissint, they lived with their master for a short period. It was a tradition to donate animals and sometimes slaves to religious brotherhoods, especially when there was a need for labor. As a follower of M'Ghimima the villager opted to offer Bakki and his mother to the *zawiya* during the annual religious festival. When he was gifted, Bakki bore the name Ganga, the original

FIGURE 9.2 *An informant and a descendant of a generation of slaves from Senegal, Akka (photo by author).*

black African name his mother called him by until she died. Rumor had it that it was the name of her father who died protecting her from the men who stole and later sold her in Tindouf. Even though Tamu was given an Islamic name after she was sold to her new master in Tindouf and became part of his harem, her first owner did not accept her son as a legitimate

Muslim largely because of his disdained skin color (Lapanne-Joinville 1950, 1952). As a new member of the religious brotherhood of M'Ghimima, the patron shaykh chose to free Tamu and Bakki, accept them as Muslims and allow them to be part of the household. It is in this environment where the story of the tablet began for Bakki, then a descendant of a liberated mother who was raised in the M'Ghimima *zawiya* surrounded by religious discussions led by scholars trained in many Islamic schools throughout the Anti-Atlas. As a man, Bakki was allowed to marry Fatna, the daughter of another freed slave; they gave birth to six children of which only Tidir survived.

In 1956, a few weeks after Moroccan independence, Tidir died in her crumbling home overlooking the cemetery of M'Ghimima and its dry river. A few months before she became sick, she gave Ziri the tablet folded in a white piece of cloth noting that it was given to her by Bakki, her father, days before his death. Over the weeks and whenever they met, Ziri learned about Bakki and how he became a well-known *hafiz* despite facing social rejection within and outside the religious brotherhood of M'Ghimima. Using his biographic narrative as a Qur'anic memorizer (*hafiz*) in southeastern Morocco, I trace Qur'anic learning through the different uses of the tablet as a material object indexing religious and social meanings. The tablet marks the different rituals and religious contexts in which it is used as well as the trajectory it undergoes in such rituals. Accordingly, Qur'anic memory cannot be understood without the indices of the tablet.

Time and place: Bakki speaks

During my historical and anthropological work in southeastern Morocco, I was overwhelmed by the number of documents and historical archives that private families have preserved for decades. Yet, while historical records and archives provide rich accounts of noble families—legal cases, political disputes, droughts, water, and other subjects—the voices of women, Jews, and slaves were relatively absent and marginal (McDougall 1998). In order to deal with this archival challenge, I relied on oral histories from different generations and social groups. This approach allowed me to fill the void in family and private archives regarding marginal social actors and groups, especially slaves and blacks. Henceforth, and using my interviews with Ziri about Bakki and Tamu, I will take you back to the early decades of the twentieth century as I retell the story of Bakki and his tablet by imagining his voice as a student of traditional Islamic learning.

My name is Bakki. Like many slaves we had a few names at our disposal. Most female slaves were called Mbarka (McDougall 1998). Only a few like my mother were allowed names like Fatma (the Prophet's daughter's name) or Yamna (the Prophet's mother's name). Even when masters who had the decency to give their freed subjects Islamic names, social and tribal rules forced them to give them diminutive names and sometimes added adjectives to signal that we they are still at the bottom of the social ladder. I have always been known by the name Bakki Akawel. Bakki was short name for Mubarak (blessed) and Akawel was a local Berber term for "dark-skinned." Therefore, while I might have been blessed with Islam and Islamic learning as I grew up, my dark skin was an external marker that society used to remind me of my historical origin, *bilad al-Sudan*, the "the lands of the Blacks."

By the second half of the twentieth century, extreme heat and drought destroyed most of the harvest. Wells dried up. Then the locust arrived, devastating what remained of the crops. The drought soon turned into famine, killing many villagers including my mother. I was about eight years old. Passed down through the years, local oral history has it that the village of M'Ghimima and its *zawiya* was established by descendants of Shaykh Sidi Abdellah ben Abdel Wahab, who served as imam of al-Ghamama mosque in Medina, in the Arabian Peninsula. After they settled in the oasis outside Tissint, they christened the village M'Ghimima after the Medina mosque, meaning, the cloudy place (Figure 9.3). The village earned a sacred aura among communities near and far, and its people had been protected wherever they landed. In this semi-arid region of Morocco, subsistence farming was a mode of life and economic survival. There was no surplus of crops and livestock. Families cultivated a variety of seasonal vegetables such as fava beans, carrots, parsnips, and dates in small plots shaded by thick clusters of palm-trees. During the annual religious

FIGURE 9.3 *Zawiya M'Ghimima (photo by author).*

festival, followers of the brotherhood and their families from far and nearby villages bring olive oil, honey, dates, goats, camels and sheep as donations to the *zawiya*.

Memorizing the Qur'an as liberation

As I came of age, I realized the religious importance of the family I had lived with as a servant; at the same time, I knew that my social horizon was limited given my status as a freed slave. Still I was not seen by members of the religious household as a regular slave (*'abd*). I knew that the male patron had a soft spot for me. It was probably because I had no parents. Therefore, I was given a lot of freedom in the compound of the *zawiya*. I could go to the farming fields to bring mint, vegetables or alfalfa; I fetched drinking water for the *zawiya*, and many times I was permitted to sit and listen to the shaykh of the *zawiya*, and occasionally visiting scholars, as they lectured students. My first official encounter with the Qur'an was at the age of eleven. Since I was of slave ancestry and, unlike many children of M'Ghimima and other neighboring villages, I never attended the local Qur'anic school of the *zawiya* even though I lived inside (Plate 25). Nevertheless, on a daily basis my eyes and ears were exposed to children cleaning their tablets and mechanically reading sections of the sacred Qur'an in front of the shaykh. Yet, by the age of eight the sound became familiar to me and I was already becoming a Qur'anic reciter. I slept on a mattress in an empty room close to the mosque (*timzguida*) of the *zawiya*. On a daily basis I could hear Qur'anic recitations.

One winter night, I was so cold I could not go to sleep; I started reciting *surat al-Fatiha* to forget the cold, unaware that the shaykh who stayed up after the last prayer could hear my faint distant voice. The next morning, I was summoned to his morning circle. The shaykh began reading verses from short Qur'anic chapters (surahs) and ordered me to complete the sections from where he stopped. He tested my memorization a few times to the surprise of the children and advanced students who were present in the circle. Then, he let me go to fetch water for the *zawiya* from the nearby well as I did every morning. After lunch and before the afternoon seminar started the shaykh asked me to join him in the mosque. After kissing his right hand, the shaykh ordered me to sit down which I did immediately without looking at him. "Only a blessed soul could memorize the sacred word like you did," he noted. Then paused repeating a few prayers before he continued, "Allah will not forgive me if I stand between you and carrying his words. You must be a good soul for the sacred letter to be engraved in your memory without any effort and therefore I am accepting you starting from this date to be my student. You will learn the word of God and you will transmit it to a future generation." He proceeded to give me a recently made tablet. I kissed his hand and sweating from a mixed feeling of fear and happiness I speedily strode out of the mosque to my corner in the household.

In just a few hours, news spread in the village and neighboring hamlets and towns about the orphan slave who knew the Qur'an by heart. Some saw it as an omen; others thought of it as a miracle of the *zawiya*. Some claimed that a jinn wrongly gave me the *baraka* of the Qur'an by mistake at night instead of the youngest son of my patron. Others professed that I licked the Qur'anic writings of my master's son tablet. A few noted that while I was dark-skinned and I would not naturally be able to have the gift of the sacred book, I was also in reality a *sharif* born into the wrong skin to a family of nobility in Tindouf.

Tablets, ink, and pens

My first initiation as a *talib* (student disciple) began with the wooden object (*lawha*, locally known as *luha*). Outside the mosque and not far from the shrine of one of the descendants of the founder of the *zawiya*, a group of children sat on the dusty ground in a line against the eastern wall of the *zawiya*. Barefoot and donning long black and white wool garments known as *djelbas*, we scrubbed off our wooden tablets with a mixture of clay (*salsal*) and water and put them in the sun to dry. We then polished their surfaces with a piece of soft palm tree brush until they shone. Afterwards, we went inside a section in the mosque known as the *msid*, laid them on our mattresses and drew straight lines with pieces of reed. The tablet looked clean and ready for writing. At that moment I realized that the tablet was a part and an extension of my body. It needed to be cleaned with water before we put the name of God on it just like my body needed to be cleansed before every prayer. For years I had been able to recite religious prayers and sections of the Qur'an with ease, but going through the practical experience of having my personal tablet and taking care of it was a new moment for me. I felt content and satisfied but also a heavy weight of responsibility. For the first time I saw people looking at me; I am no longer a marginal servant: I have a tablet. I wondered what my mother would think. She would be part of me; I am about to begin the journey of a hafiz. I had a sacred object that could lead me to higher status if I took care of it and embodied what it represented. I paused and promised my mother to do well.

Unlike the rest of the boys, I could not write but I knew every consonant and vowel. I had to learn writing. I was quick to learn how to prepare the tablet for writing. On a Friday afternoon before the *'asr* prayer my teacher asked me to repeat after him the *basmala* phrase ("In the name of Allah, the Merciful the Compassionate"). He wrote the phrase on my tablet and began teaching me the Arabic letters. While others recited the verses and sections of the Qur'an on their own or under the supervision of students older than them, I spent a few weeks learning how to write letters. By the end of the second week and after the Friday prayer and our communal barley couscous, I was informed by the shaykh that I was ready to write the first chapter (*surah*) of the Qur'an, the *Fatiha*. I was set to begin the following morning. Before the sunset prayer a group of older students (*talaba*, sing. *talib*) were tasked to make the ink, known as *smagh*. I joined them. While some fetched firewood; others made a fire under an acacia tree just a few steps from the cemetery. The lead student held a large bundle of sheep wool as another one prepared a clay pot on the fire. I slowly threw more wood on the fire. As the pot heated, a student gently placed the wool inside it and as it began to carbonize another one added water until we had a dark liquid. We poured small portions of the black fluid in little jars that belonged to each *talib* and added water to make it slightly runny. I finally had my own jar of *smagh* and my tablet.

It took us less than an hour to make the ink and we were able to return before the sunset prayer giving me more time to acquire the final object required for my first writing initiation: a pen (*qalam*). Pens made out of reed were key to Qur'an writing on a tablet or any other legal document on paper, wood, or leather. Pens were intimate and personal objects just like tablets: they were rarely given away. When personally used, pens were offered as gifts, the occasion was always special. Not just anyone can make a reed pen or use those of others. I remembered that my shaykh never lost sight of his pen, usually folded in a small leather bag gifted to him by a merchant from Timbuktu during one of his trips to the annual market of Tissint. At a corner in the mosque not far from the *mihrab* where the shaykh sat, gray prayer beads in his right hand counting his *tasbih*, a local scribe sat with his feet tucked under his legs on a red and orange carpet. A bundle of long reeds was set by his side. Using a sharp knife, the scribe worked on making new pens for me and other students. With dexterity, he cut through the sides and then the nib of the reed pen until it became flat and squared on the writing point, making it suitable for writing. He made about a dozen pens, prayed the last prayer and left before we gathered for our communal dinner. By the end of the day I had my tablet, jar of ink, and my pen. Having watched parents in the *zawiya* over the years bring their children these three essential objects before they begin the process of Qur'anic learning, I had mine made for me by the shaykh. I am ready to be a student-disciple (*murid*).

Learning and graduation

My first recitation practice was characterized by different feelings. I was overwhelmed by the fear of failure; I was overconcerned by misspelling and misreading. After breakfast, I sat down in front of my shaykh, now teacher and spiritual guide, wearing my clean djellaba that was gifted to me by a member of the household. It had patches all over, but in those days, having a piece of cloth over your skin was a luxury for many. The shaykh smiled as he took my tablet. I interpreted his beaming face as a sign of encouragement and approval. It felt strange that after years of living in the margins of the compound of the *zawiya* I felt at its center.

Holding my tablet with one hand and dipping his own pen in the jar of *smagh*, he started to write the last surah of the Qur'an titled *an-Nas* (Mankind). I was told that we learn the Qur'an in the Maghribi tradition by first hearing the words from the mouth of the shaykh directly and starting from the shortest surahs of the Qur'an. My teacher handed me back my tablet and commanded me to repeat after him, correcting and praising my pronunciation at different occasions. After sensing my relative comfort with the text, he released me and I spent the rest of the morning reading the surah over and over on my tablet. After I memorized the text, and before lunch, I recited sentence by sentence my first text in front of the teacher who checked my pronunciation of every word based on the reading style (*qira'at Warsh 'an Naafi'*) of Imam Warsh. Although I learnt the Arabic letters and how to copy Qur'anic text just a few weeks after my first introduction to writing, it took almost a month before I was permitted to use my pen. On a daily basis, the shaykh and sometimes one of his advanced students wrote on my slate sections of the surah. They read it first, I repeated a few times and then I was asked to learn it by heart on my own. By the time I learnt all the vowels and the different consonants, I was allowed to write by myself using my own pen. I remembered my excitement when I wrote the first phrase of my verse dictated by my shaykh. I felt liberated and empowered by writing the word of God.

After three years of Qur'anic memorization I graduated with the blessing of my teacher. Before a ceremony was held to celebrate our journey in the *zawiya*, the shaykh gathered us around in the mosque and gave a final lecture about the importance of tablet, pen, and reading and how the Qur'an is built on respecting them. He reminded us that the first word of revelation was read (*iqra'*) and that the Qur'an was meant to be read and recited in a voice that respected its sacredness. At the same time, he stressed to us the importance of writing it in a beautiful script reminding us of the importance of the verse "Nun. By the pen and that which they write with," and how a whole chapter in the Qur'an is titled *al-Qalam* (The Pen). Finally, he encouraged us to continue to preserve it by memorizing and teaching it to a generation of children in M'Ghimima and beyond so that it would remain "Inscribed in a preserved tablet" (Qur'an 85:22) (Plate 26).

On the first Friday after we completed the writing and reading of the whole Qur'an on the wooden slates, the *zawiya* invited families and villagers from neighboring villages to celebrate our achievement in an event known in Berber as *tamghran* (Qur'an's wedding). We were dressed in beautiful white djellabas made for us by the *zawiya*. We took turns riding a horse in the street of M'Ghimima each holding his tablet. As we passed each home, women ululated with joy and men congratulated us for our hard work. At the end of the ceremony, my teacher called me to the *masjid* and congratulated me like his own son. He then informed me that he would send me to continue my higher Islamic studies with his students in the *zawiya* of Imi n'Tatelt, where I spent a few years learning the sciences of Qur'an and Hadith. By the late 1930s, I was sent to serve the *zawiya* in villages around the Anti-Atlas.

After serving the *zawiya* for years, Bakki became one of its major ambassadors bringing donations from other Anti-Atlas communities and encouraging children, including some descendants of black families, to follow his example. His travels took him a few times to Algerian oases and Mauritania. In the late 1930s he travelled to Madina, where he visited the tomb of the patron master of the M'Ghimima *zawiya*. He performed the hajj ritual and returned back to southeastern Morocco with a caravan of pilgrims and merchants from Mali. In 1945, during a religious tour to gather barley and wheat for the *zawiya*, Bakki died of a snake bite.

Tablets and Qur'anic education today

When a family does not send its child to the Qur'anic school at an early age, as a local southeastern Moroccan proverb goes, it will lead him to hell after death. For centuries the Qur'anic school was primarily an institution of education meant to prepare children to be moral and responsible social actors through oral and written training provided by Islamic teachers (Eickelman 1985, 1978; Boum 2008). It is for this reason that *zawiya*s throughout southern Morocco were able to attract students from villages and towns. However, only a few children attended Qur'anic schools and were able to succeed and move through all the different stages of learning like Bakki. Families needed child manual labor to work the land and take care of their animals. They rarely sent one of their male children.

Mentorship of religious scholars allowed generations of students to establish themselves in other North African regions. At the center of Qur'anic learning were teachers, locally known as *fqih* (scholar of Islamic jurisprudence), *talb* (scholar of Qur'anic recitation), imam (prayer leader), and *'alim* (scholar) (Figure 9.4). While these names are usually exchangeable, they have different meanings in the Islamic educational hierarchy of Morocco. They still share the common trait of expertise in Qur'anic memorization although not every *fqih*, imam, *talb* or *'alim* can be a *qari'*, meaning an expert in the different variants of Qur'anic recitation (*qira'at*) (Spratt and Wagner 1986). While Bakki grew up and came of age in a period when Qur'anic teachers were regarded with respect and had a special social privilege, by the 1930s, after the nationalization of Islamic universities and madrasas, Islamic education gradually began to lose its status to French modern schools. (Eickelman 1978). The clash between the modern French-education teacher and traditional scholar and shaykh, came to the surface during the first decade after independence. As the government encouraged and sometimes ordered parents to send their children to its expanding network of modern schools, many parents challenged its decision and opted to keep their children in local Qur'anic schools.

FIGURE 9.4 *Imam of the local mosque of Tagadirt, Akka (photo by author).*

In 1968, King Hassan II responded to this growing educational issue by announcing "Operation Qur'anic School." Aware of the broader religious and political implications of Qur'anic schools, the government recognized early Qur'anic education as a key background to elementary schooling. Using the radio and television, Hassan II announced that "Operation Qur'anic School" would allow "parents not to have to concern themselves too much with the basic education of their children" for a period of two years. By putting Qur'anic schools and their teachers under government supervision, Hassan II expanded his national control over the religious domain while gaining the respect of families who valued the traditional religious system of education. Hassan II drew on the traditional role of the shaykh and his moral authority noting that this new campaign "diminishes the danger of juvenile delinquencies . . . . It is vital that someone look after [the child's] upbringing between the age of five and that of starting school [at seven], especially when his father and mother both have to work away from home" (Hassan II 1968). Nevertheless, despite this initiative by the monarchy and the state to valorize the role of the *fqih*, the social significance of the Qur'anic school slowly declined and was replaced by the prestige of modern literacy and education. In this context the tablet has slowly been marginalized by the chalk and blackboard, and today by digital tablets.

While tablets are still central objects in the traditional Qur'anic schools throughout Morocco and many parts of Africa, some teachers have long since begun to rely on white chalk and blackboard instead of individual tablets, ink, and reed pens. It was a convenient shift which allowed the teacher and the students to erase mistakes without having to wash the tablet and dry it in the sun before using it again. Nevertheless, many religious scholars objected to these modern slates seeing them as un-Islamic, and preferring the traditional *luha* as an authentic object of Qur'anic learning. By the late 1960s and early 1970s, pupils began to use modern school slates and have access to white and colored chalk, allowing teachers to use the classroom master blackboard and slates at the same time for individual and group pedagogical sessions. Children are no longer restricted by the psychological and pedagogical limits of the traditional tablet. In the early decades of the twentieth century, Bakki could not use his tablet in ways outside the rules set by his shaykh. His tablet was an extension of his shaykh; he used his tablet to write what his teacher commanded. The modern school slate allowed the new generation of children to imagine other spaces of writing and learning the Qur'an. Meanwhile the traditional tablet has been appropriated by calligraphers such as Nouri Riyadi, mentioned in the chapter's beginning, and in the tourism industry. This new generation of descendants of *shurfa* and slaves have few encounters with traditional tablets. Today the majority of this generation learn a few surahs of the Qur'an in the modern education system. Their focus has shifted from being an imam or shaykh to becoming a doctor, teacher, policeman, or government employee.

Unlike Bakki, descendants of slaves and black families largely choose the modern system of education instead of the Qur'anic school. The economic and social dependency of their great grandparents and parents is disrupted by their access to schools or migration to urban centers. Bakki found liberation through Qur'anic education, allowing him to achieve success and social prestige despite his slave background. After independence descendants of the slave and black population achieved their own version of upward mobility through modern education. In the 1960s, my brother Lahoucine finished his traditional Islamic education by memorizing the Qur'an at an early age (Boum 2008). It was a moment of family pride. Faraji, my illiterate father, believed that he was divinely blessed and that he should continue his traditional Islamic training in Tamgrut to become a local *fqih*. After pressure from local authorities my father relinquished his dream of having an imam and a source of religious pride and capital in the family. Lahoucine joined the local primary school and went on to become a regional superintendent of secondary Arabic education with a doctorate in Arabic linguistics. A generation of descendants of *Haratine*, including me, followed these steps to become primary, secondary, high school, and sometimes university teachers. Like Bakki all of them went through the Qur'anic school and held the traditional tablet; unlike Bakki they had to shift to new modes of learning sanctioned and authorized by the post-colonial state, like the school slate and now digital tablet.

PART FOUR

Circulatory Systems

CHAPTER TEN

Coins and Fish: Sovereignty, Economy, and Religion in the Islamicate Indian Ocean

Roxani Eleni Margariti

Introduction

Though diminutive in size, coins encapsulate economic trends, political ambitions, and cultural traditions of their times, including religious thought and practices. The goal of this essay is to present a particular series of Islamic coins issued in the Rasulid kingdom of Yemen in the eighth century of the Hijri calendar (fourteenth century CE), and to examine them as carriers of messages about politics and religion, instruments of economy, and material objects of everyday life in the hands of the minters who made them and users who circulated them. This examination uncovers the interconnected ways in which economy, political and religious discourse, materiality, and piety shaped the lives of these and other numismatic artifacts of the premodern Islamic world, as they circulated within and beyond the borders of the Muslim polity within which they were issued. Insightful for the nature of money in general is Keith Hart's definition of it as "the product of social organization both from the top down ('states') and from the bottom up ('markets')" and thus "both a *token* of authority and a *commodity* with a price" (Hart 1986: 637). For coins in particular, the "conceit" of tracing their "social lives" (Appadurai 1986) unveils value systems intersecting with economies and materiality. Studies of Yemeni Rasulid coinage more specifically must draw from a now rich and diverse literature on Islamic numismatics and the monetary histories of the medieval Islamic world.[1] In what sense may these and other sets of coins be described as 'Islamic'?[2] Though not religious objects, the inscriptions and even the images these coins bore implicated them directly in Muslim religious belief and practice; while serving as tools of trade, translating economic value, and circulating between Muslims and non-Muslims alike, they also participated in specific religious economies and had their role in the construction of Islamically ethical comportment in the marketplace. In other words, these coins participated in "the web of relations" that concretized for Muslims "what really mattered to them" as Muslims, including "the world as it ought to be."[3]

Chronologically, the coins of our case-study belong to what historian Marshall Hodgson defines as the Middle Periods in the history of the Islamicate world, characterized by "the constantly expanding, linguistically and culturally international society ruled by many governments," and the consolidation and expansion of Muslim communities, notably in Sub-Saharan and East Africa and the littoral and insular Indian Ocean world and South-East Asia (Hodgson 1974, vol. 2: 3–11). In terms of political power and the Islamic construction of sovereignty, this time span is cleft by the Mongol conquests of the mid-thirteenth century; the first half saw the rise of the institution of the sultanate, promoted mostly by Turkic military elites, while in the second half the final dissolution of the caliphate in Baghdad by the Mongols furthered the reconfiguration of the caliphate's meaning and rhetorical deployment. In economic terms, this same period witnessed the progressive integration of economies across the Indian Ocean and the Mediterranean, circulation of people and things across and beyond Muslim-ruled territories, and significantly for our focus on coins, expanding monetization. Because of the nature of its polity and the country's position at a pivotal, crucially maritime, crossroads of the interregional system, Rasulid Yemen and its coins exemplify ecological, economic, and political features of this transregional system and thus offer a particularly salient case study.

Like the Rasulid Yemeni coins, coins from a variety of places, times and polities in the expanding, increasingly monetized and progressively fragmented Muslim-ruled lands that stretched from the Atlantic to Eastern Indian Ocean, appear in written sources and in the material record, and offer themselves as primary evidence of the ways that Muslims and others interacted, discursively and materially. With reference to medieval Islamic coins, David Wasserstein, noted the "family resemblance among them," to argue that their "symbolic language" made them "boundary markers in the symbolic universe of Islam" (Wasserstein 1992: 305, 318). In a survey of coinage issued from the rise of Islam to the onset of modernity, Michael Bates observes that "an Islamic coin is a miniature dated document: its issuers speak to us directly in their own words, telling us who they were, where and when they governed, and what they believed" (Bates 1982: 3). As Stefan Heidemann puts it, early Islamic coins served as a "published bulletin of state;" moreover, the exemplary Islamic coins of the seventh century CE "are among the oldest surviving text carriers of the Qur'an" (Heidemann 2010: 162–3). In time, the stamping of inscribed coins, *sikka*, juxtaposed the basic tenets of God's unity and the nature of Muhammad's mission, with the names and titles of real and symbolic sovereigns, and as such was one of the two recognized prerogatives of Muslim political leaders. *Sikka* along with *khutba* (the invocation of the ruler's name in the congregational Friday prayer) came to advertise royal rule and the sovereign's commitment to preserve Islamic belief with divine sanction.

The coins' materiality and visual design, however, complicates their discursive role as carriers of Islamic messages about divine and earthly sovereignty, as do the paths and modes of their circulation within and beyond Arabic-reading realms. In spite of a general practice of aniconism, several series of coins issued in the name of Muslim sovereigns in the Middle Periods, including the set that we will examine below, bore figural representations. These raise, along with so many other types of material culture, the question of the status of images in Islam. Islamic coins thus provide an excellent case for arguing that Islamic approaches to images are best described as substantively ambiguous, with images prescriptively avoided in some cases and enthusiastically deployed in others.[4] While doing so, they also provoke us to imagine how both figural images and the Arabic script itself were deployed by their makers and received by their users. Islamic coins circulated and changed countless hands, often across all kinds of borders, both geographic and conceptual, including political borders and denominational lines of belonging of the subjects that used them. They thus invite us to examine the multiple layers of their manufacture, use and reception, and to ponder the meaning of communal and individual identity boundaries in the everyday lives of their users. We discover that as quotidian circulatory objects, coins functioned at multiple registers at once, and served variably the multiple purposes and axes of belonging of their diverse users.[5]

Coins, kings, and caliphs: *sikka* and sovereignty

In the course of the fourteenth century, the mint of the city of Aden—at the time the single most important port town of the Rasulid kingdom of Yemen and a major maritime hub of the western Indian Ocean—produced a series of silver coins, or *dirhams*, featuring images of fish. In the earliest and better-known design, exemplified by the silver issue of the fifth Rasulid sultan al-Mujahid Ali b. Dawud (1322–63 CE), the "field," or main surface, of one side of the coin displays two fishes within an octalobe or hexalobe outline, arranged as if swimming head to tail in a circle around a central dot and surrounded by inscriptions (Figure 10.1a-b). In a different design, featured on the coins of al-Mujahid's successor, al-Afdal al-Abbas b. Ali (1363–76 CE), a single, very neatly designed fish nests on top of or below an inner circle that frames the field bearing the inscriptions (Figure 10.2a-b). The coins issued under the next two Rasulid sovereigns, al-Ashraf Ismail b. al-Abbas (1377–1400 CE) and al-Nasir Ahmad b. Ismail (1400–24 CE) return to the two-fish design filling the field, though in some examples the fish now look different (Figure 10.3).[6] An exceptional coin of the former, al-Malik al-Ashraf, from the city of Zabid, also pictures fish but of a different kind still: a wreath of tiny stylized fish framing the field (Figure 10.4). Overall, the motif develops through time, a topic that we will revisit in this essay.

FIGURE 10.1 *Dirham with the two swimming-fish motif, struck in Aden in the name of sultan 'Ali al-Mujahid, 736AH/1335–1336CE. New York, American Numismatic Society, 1998.22.39.*

FIGURE 10.2 *Dirham with single fish, struck in Aden in the name of al-Afdal al-'Abbas, 770AH/1368–1369CE. New York, American Numismatic Society, 1998.22.59.*

FIGURE 10.3 *Dirham with two swimming-fish motif, struck in Aden in the name of al-Ashraf, 791AH/1389CE. Note the difference with al-Mujāhid's issues, Fig. 10.1. Copenhagen, The David Collection, DK C268. Photography by Pernille Klemp.*

FIGURE 10.4 *Exceptional dirham struck in Zabid featuring wreath of tiny fish. Collection of the author. Photography courtesy of Steven Album Rare Coins.*

Importantly, the opposite face of all these coins is purely epigraphic: both the field and the margin bear inscriptions. The legends across both faces constitute variations on a well-established general model for Islamic coinage, and convey the point of view of their engravers and the sovereigns dictating their epigraphic discourse. Arranged in the field and continuing in the margin of the purely epigraphical side of the coin, the legend states the foundational Muslim doctrine, the *kalima*, with a standard introduction (*basmala*) and extension: "in the name of God/ there is no god but God/ Muhammad is the messenger of God/he sent him with righteous guidance (and) the true religion" (*bism Allāh al-raḥmān al-raḥīm lā ilah illā Allāh, Muhammad rasūl Allāh, arsalahu bi'l-huda* [*wa-*]*dīn al-ḥaqq*). The extension completes the phrase and proclaims the nature of Muhammad's prophethood; it is then followed by the naming of the first four caliphs of Islam "the imams, Abu Bakr, Umar, Uthman, Ali."

This side, identified as the obverse, or "heads" side of the coin,[7] is the face of the coin that literate users were possibly inclined to read first. Describing an early Rasulid coin, seventeenth-century Yemeni chronicler Yahya b. al-Husayn records for his readers the full text of the coin's inscriptions starting with the *basmala* and *kalima*, i.e. what in the pictorial dirhams remained the purely epigraphical face of the coin, and calls the side with the sovereign's titles the coin's "back side" (*ẓāhiruhu*).[8] A certain primacy, then, attaches to the side of the coin that displays the declaration of Muslim belief: faith in the absolute oneness of God, reverence for God's prophet and his divinely guided message of religious truth, respect for the first four successors of the prophet Muhammad as sovereigns of the *umma*. This side of the coin would evoke a standard reception by Muslims who read it, proclaiming as it does basic elements of Muslim doctrine; significantly, the invocation of the four "rightly guided caliphs" as recognized by Sunnis, in contradistinction with Shi'i dogma that asserts the sovereign primacy of Ali, appeals to a sensibility that we can call assertively Sunni.

Conversely, the fish side of the coin, identified here as the reverse or "tails," bears messages that synergize with the declarations of the obverse, and simultaneously are more specific to the time and place where the coins were produced. The legends here give the year of minting and the toponym of the mint, and record the full name and titulature of the reigning Rasulid sovereign, prefaced by the titular compound, *al-sulṭān al-malik,* which had become standard both in Mamluk Egypt and in Rasulid Yemen.[9] The coin also memorializes another authority: that of the last Abbasid caliph, whose sensational death in 1258 when Baghdad fell to the Mongols changed conceptions of Islamic political sovereignty forever. Inscribing his epithet *al-Musta'ṣim billāh* and designating him as commander of the faithful (*amīr al-mu'minīn*), links local power with global charismatic authority.

What do these titles say about the Rasulids' self-presentation and projections of power to subjects and dynastic peers, both Muslim and non-Muslim? Originally a clan of Turcomen soldiers who came to South Arabia as military functionaries for the dynasty of Salah al-Din b. Ayyub, the Rasulids ruled Yemen from 1229 to 1454 and presided over an expansive state straddling the crossroads of transregional commerce between the Indian Ocean and the Mediterranean (Smith 1974; Varisco 1993: 13–24; Vallet 2010). The title "sultan" had become the norm for Sunni potentates in the waning years of the so-called "Shi'i Century" and through the antagonisms of the Crusades. Theoretically, it was the Abbasid caliph who conferred the title. In reality, the military elites who bore it, like the Rasulids and the Mamluks, dictated its investiture while maintaining the fiction of caliphal legitimization and the symbolic power of association with the Abbasid caliphate through an invocation of the caliph's name. The Rasulids' and the Mamluks' mode of pursuing *sikka*—which as noted earlier denotes the prerogative of sovereignty to have coins struck in the name of the ruler and inscribed with particular dynastic appellations—has a number of commonalities in the expressions of faith as well as the titulature that these coins display. As Turkic successors of the Ayyubids, upholders of Sunni orthodoxy and rulers over largely Arabic-speaking multi-confessional realms, both Mamluks and Rasulids legitimized their rule through messages about the connection of religious orthodoxy and sultanic sovereignty on those miniature flags that were their coins. At the same time, these two dynasties competed with each other, and the invocation of different Abbasid caliphs on their coinage reflects independent and even rival claims to divinely sanctioned authority; reading between those tightly packed lines, we can deduce from the inscriptions of this coinage both specificities and universalities of explicitly Islamic rule.

Dinars and dirhams: economy, materiality, and values of precious metal coins

While text and titles constitute our first recourse for identifying coins and their historical contexts, most of their original users would probably have related first to the material and visual aspects of coins rather than to the text itself. To mint a coin, minters placed a small chunk of blank metal alloy on a fixed engraved mold (the lower, pile, or anvil die) and struck it with a hand-held equivalent (the upper or trussel die).[10] The resulting artifact, which people held in their hands or placed in purses along with other coins, had a distinct look, texture, and feel. At a basic level, a coin's materiality begins with its size, weight, and the metal content of its alloy, what numismatists call "fineness."

Islamic coinage of the medieval period was a tri-metallic system, with gold and silver coins (dinars and dirhams) universally recognized and circulating widely thanks to their intrinsic value, and copper coins constituting primarily fiduciary or token money of more limited and localized circulation. While there was an officially recognized equivalency between dinars and dirhams, in reality marketplaces were dominated by one or the other, depending on supply chains and trading networks. Silver dirhams were the most commonly issued denomination during Rasulid rule. Although Yemen had famous silver mines since pre-Islamic times, and some of them were productive into Rasulid times, silver was also imported into

Yemen and probably also derived from older dirhams, melted down to strike new ones, especially with each new sovereign's accession to power.[11] Overall, Rasulid silver coins were light and thin, but quite fine (that is made of an alloy with a higher percentage of silver and a lower percentage of copper); they were lighter and thinner, but for the most part finer, than Egyptian dirhams, which circulated concurrently in Yemeni and transregional marketplaces (Vallet 2010: 229–32).

Serving their users as money, namely as "a store of value; a unit of value; and a medium of exchange" (Schultz 2010: 342), coins featured in the debates over morality in the marketplace and the assessment of dealings as legal and ethical. Because their value was tied to their precious metal content, and had little of the contingency of fiduciary or token currency (represented by copper), a general consensus arose among Muslim thinkers early on that gold and silver coins constituted legally admissible currency, a proper medium for major economic transactions, namely taxes, payments, and partnerships (Udovitch 1970: 51–6).[12] An extreme expression of this notion—going as far as to deny the validity of copper coinage by emphasizing the divine sanction for gold and silver currency—appears in a fascinating treatise by the fifteenth-century Egyptian savant al-Maqrizi, who argued that "it has always been God's custom towards his creatures, in all corners of the earth and among every nation, that the currency that has been used to determine prices of goods and costs of labor consists only of gold and silver" (Allouche 1994: 55).[13]

What was the range of transactions facilitated specifically by Rasulid silver dirhams? Money, with its power to abstract and to embody value, played an important role in tax payments and domestic and international trade. According to a fifteenth-century administrative treatise that provides a wealth of information about Rasulid fiscal organization, in the period when the fish dirhams were still being struck, a person who qualified as poor or was otherwise entitled to tax deductions, could settle their reduced tax dues on imported dates, shark meat, or three strips of goat-wool, with one of these thin silver coins (Smith 2007: 41–2, 82–3). In a story meant to extol a sovereign's righteous benevolence while describing fiscal policy and monetary reform, the preeminent chronicler of the Rasulid dynasty al-Khazraji relates that the Rasulid sultan al-Mujāhid introduced a new kind of dirham and demanded that all taxes be collected using this new unit. This coincided with a downturn in revenues for farmers, driving many of them to tax flight, and leading to the ruin of agricultural lands; the monarch, "who was a lover of the peasants and interested in their affairs," established a new, more favorable system for assessing the peasants' taxes, and the abandoned vales returned to cultivation (1907: 52–4).[14] In both examples, silver coins play a major role, and their utility as units and measures of value is clear; what is not specified is whether "physical coins" were involved, an important question of monetary and economic history. While peasants may not have paid their taxes in specie, but rather in kind, the awareness of the specific unit of value embodied in the silver dirham determined their relationship with the state and evaluated it as righteous or corrupt.

Payments with physical money—as opposed to payment in kind or with credit—certainly took place, especially in Yemen's regional and transregional markets where several different kinds of coinage circulated. Simultaneous use of different issues of varying fineness or quality is attested by the presence of money assayers (*naqqād*, pl. *naqqādūn*) and money changers (*ṣarrāf*, pl. *ṣarrāfūn*) who theoretically guaranteed fairness in the marketplace. The full extent of physical coin circulation in this and other premodern contexts remains elusive because of the biases of narrative sources and the archaeological record. Yet, in the case of the Rasulid dirhams of the fourteenth century we are fortunate to have a witness in a hoard found on the northwestern coast of India, the so-called "Broach hoard." Buried somewhere in Gujarat, probably shortly after the date of the last issue in the 1390s, the hoard contained 448 gold pieces from Venice, Genoa, Mamluk Egypt, Ilkhanid Iran, and the Delhi Sultanate, as well as some 1200 silver issues, the majority Mamluk and Rasulid dirhams (Digby 1980: 129–38).[15] While this hoard maps the expansive networks of transregional trade between the Indian Ocean and the Mediterranean systems over a long period of time, the particular combination of Mamluk and Rasulid silver issues within it reflects the concurrent use of these two distinct sets of Islamic denominations in the market places across the Arabian seaboards.[16]

Finally, there are a range of other values attached to precious metals themselves. The Qur'an militates against hoarding gold and silver but, as Barry Flood has demonstrated, for exegetes and jurists the proscription was tied to a condemnation of idolatry and an "economy of unbelief," as well as to the notion of a proper deployment of precious metals to facilitate human transactions "through circulation" (Flood 2009: 35–7). On a different register, gold and silver were 'the two ancient gems and liquid rocks' (*al-jawharatayn al-'atiqatayn wa'l-ḥajaratayn al-mā'i'atayn*) in the formulation of tenth-century Yemeni savant al-Hamdani, who attests to the long tradition of mining, metallurgy, and metalsmithing in Yemen, but also suggests the astrological significance that silver and gold carried.[17] Medieval Islamic science associated seven metals with the so-called seven main "planets," the celestial bodies located in distinct concentric spheres, centered upon Earth and exerting important influence on human lives (Dunlop 1957).[18] Silver, in particular, was linked to the moon, an eminently influential planet, whose phases determined the Islamic calendar, and whose multiple symbolism featured in the iconography of a variety of objects (Carboni 1997: 4, 11; Dunlop 1957: 36–7). While it is hard to establish that makers and users were individually cognizant of the Qur'anic, juridical, chemical, alchemical, and astrological meanings attached to silver, a "social life of things" approach to the coins brings into view the full range of these associations with the order of the universe.

Fish and other images: the visual messages of coins

Our examination of the fourteenth-century Rasulid dirhams has thus far focused on the features responsible for that "family resemblance" of all Islamic coins. The figural elements accompanying the Rasulid sovereigns' names in the set under consideration here may be a somewhat more surprising and even "anomalous" feature in Islamic numismatic output, but they are equally full of meaning.

The first pictorial motifs to appear on Rasulid coins were those on issues struck in the name of the sultan al-Mujahid, whose long and adventurous rule began in 1322, and whose monetary reform took effect some fourteen years later. While two- and then one-fish motifs appear for the next century or so almost exclusively on the coins of the port city of Aden (with the one exception from the city of Zabid on the Tihama coastal plain), other devices—a seated cross-legged figure, a rider on a horse, two birds fighting, a single bird, a lion or baboon, a star, a set of three swords, and a cup—feature on the coin series of the other Rasulid mints. Starting with the first systematic study of Rasulid mints by Heinrich Nützel in the nineteenth century, scholars have noted the exceptionality of the Rasulid coin designs, remarkable for the range of motifs, the absence of close precedents in coin types from elsewhere, and the systematic association of set motifs with particular mints (Prideaux 1883–5: 9–10; Nützel and Kinzelbach [1891] 1987: 31–32; D'Ottone 2015: 93–4; 2020: 224). These scholars have also acknowledged other contexts in which Muslims minted coins with pictorial devices, and thus have highlighted a broader phenomenon.

The visuality of the "mainstream" of Islamic coins undoubtedly hinges on the iconic quality of the word. But when they do bear images, coins demand additional exploration of cultural symbols, ruler self-representation and expectations, and transcultural dynamics. As Michael Bates and Robert Darley-Doran put it in an essay on the art of Islamic coinage, "Muslim religious thinkers have practically nothing to say about appropriate coin design—and there are many exceptional Muslim coins with images, *both as a result of non-Muslim influence and arising from the use of indigenous motifs*" (my emphasis added: Bates and Darley-Doran 1985: 352). Figural designs appear early in the history of Islamic coinage, and in some of the most fascinating moments of Muslim becoming. Spanning nearly a century in the later Middle Period of Islamic history, the Adeni Rasulid pictorial issues thus command our attention and raise questions: why fish, and, more broadly, what purposes did images serve?

Three principal methods—not mutually exclusive—help answer these questions: comparative examination of the appearance of figural images in related coinages; art historical research on the specific motifs' origins and possible paths of transmission and translation; and search of meaning in local contexts. Following the first method, we find motifs in a heraldic capacity, as blazons associated with particular sovereigns or other potentates and expressive of hierarchy, genealogy, or power. As Paul Balog has argued, the Mamluks appear to have consistently used images—fleur-de-lis designs, rosettes, stars and animals, especially the lion—as blazons (Balog 1964). Given Rasulid and Mamluk close diplomatic, economic, and cultural ties, Mamluk heraldry may illuminate modes of representation of Muslim rulership in which the Rasulids, too, partook. However, the heraldry interpretation of Rasulid coin motifs is precluded by the consistent association of Rasulid figural designs not with particular rulers but instead with particular mints: cities where the coins were struck; in other words, with the local context.

Turning to the visual cultures to which Rasulid Yemen was intimately connected, we find the fish motif current in both the Mamluk and the Ilkhanid realms.[19] In Egypt and the Levant, swimming-fish motifs appear in a variety of fourteenth-century media, from textiles to pottery, and metal objects (Sardi 2016: 254–63). Ilkhanid visual production exhibits similar pictorial interests. Excavating the artistic and cultural significance of these figures on Mamluk textiles, one scholar has linked the Mamluk fish designs with equivalents on Ilkhanid Mongol artefacts, and has suggested that that these possible prototypes may have been carrying astrological meanings and/or transferring across Eurasia the Chinese use of the fish symbol to denote the concepts of plenty and prosperity (Sardi 2016).[20] In the local context of Rasulid Yemen, a zodiacal reading, with the fish standing for the sign of Pisces, appears likely. Rasulid princes' interests in astronomy (*'ilm al-nujūm*) and its sister science of astrology (*'ilm aḥkām al-nujūm*) is attested in their own writings and the artistic works they patronized and consumed. Telling of both the Mamluk-Rasulid connection and the astrological symbolism of fish motifs, is a magnificent brass tray incised and inlaid with silver and bitumen, and bearing the full name and royal epithets of the sultan al-Mu'ayyad, the immediate predecessor of al-Mujahid, and a full depiction of the zodiac (Plate 27); made in Mamluk Egypt but commissioned for or by the Rasulid sovereign, it reveals intertwined paths of patronage and visual production (Carboni 1997: 14). A coin series linking the Rasulid sovereign's name with a zodiacal sign may similarly reflect astrological interests and shared culture.[21]

Several factors, however, leave space for additional, complementary readings. Rasulid sources do not explicitly link coin imagery with the zodiac and astrology, and Rasulid coin motifs do not neatly correspond to the range of zodiac signs. More importantly, the development of the fish design on the Adeni coins takes place locally and points to its local resonance. Together with the motif's juxtaposition with the inscribed titles of the Rasulid sultans, the reading of these coins in their local and regional context of manufacture and circulation points decidedly "seawards." Aden, a vital hub of transregional trade, featured the only Rasulid mint located directly on the seashore.[22] In this context, the choice of the fish motif appears as a nod to the importance of the maritime economy so vital for the life of the kingdom.

But what of Islam? In a pioneering, if factually and stylistically outdated, global history of fishing cultures, the author declares that "Mahometan tradition abounds in fish lore of the oddest kind" (Radcliffe 1921: 438–40). Arguing for what he calls the Muslims' "liberty of ichthyophagy," the author points to the exclusion of fishing and fish consumption from the Qur'anic injunction against killing game while on pilgrimage.[23] In spite of the overtly orientalist phraseology and attitude, the emphasis on Muslim lore about fish and on legally sanctioned pescatarian dietary practices offers a corrective to the notion of Islam as a thalassophobic religion of the desert.[24] More capaciously, the fish motifs on the Rasulid Adeni coins resonate with the Qur'anic trope of the sea as a stand-in for God's pact, whereby he made all of creation subservient to humans: "And it is He who made the sea subservient so that you may eat fresh meat from it and extract from it ornaments that you may wear. And you see the ships plowing it so that you may seek of His bounty, and perhaps you may give thanks" (Q16:14). Oceanic space as an avenue of transportation and as a source of valuable resources thus constitutes a gift from God and a sign of his munificence. Moreover, as medieval Muslim travel and biographical literature attests, the dangers of oceanic travel were mitigated by divine providence, saintly intercession, and miracles.[25] Such miracles and the repeated Qur'anic reference to the sea's bounty, may well have been on the mind of the *naqqāsh al-sikka* who designed Aden's fish dirhams and made them one version of the Rasulid state's banners that were its coins, as well as an instrument in the hands of subjects who lived from the sea.

Conclusion

The Rasulid dirhams examined here were specific products of the political and economic milieu of late medieval Yemen, representatives of the exceptional status of the port city where they were minted, and unusual carriers of images. Yet, they also shared with many other types of Islamic coins both physical characteristics and discursive, material, and notional roles. They combined statements of divine Islamic sovereignty and worldly dynastic authority. Their universal messages were carried primarily through the words inscribed on them; at the same time, both words and images localized those messages. Abstracting and embodying value, they acted as crucial instruments of local and far-flung economies; they mediated relationships between Muslim states, rulers, and subjects, and facilitated transactions across multifarious borders, linking medieval Muslims with each other and with people of different faiths across the transregional juncture of the Indian Ocean.

CHAPTER ELEVEN

The Aljibe del Rey in Granada

D. Fairchild Ruggles

At the top of Granada's historic Albaicín quarter stands the Carmen del Aljibe del Rey (House of the King's Cistern) (Figure 11.1). The residential buildings with walled gardens (a type known in Spain as a *carmen*) that occupy the site today have replaced a much earlier eleventh-century palace of the Zirid king Badis. But under the floor of the *carmen*, the original Zirid water cistern still remains in an excellent state of preservation, along with the canal that serves it and the wellhead through which the public was granted access to the water.[1]

The cistern and its contents may seem an unusual kind of object for a book on the materiality and circulation of objects in the Islamic world. The cistern is more appropriately a work of architecture, not a circulating object, and while the water that it contained did circulate in interesting ways, it lacked many of the properties of a material thing. The question of whether water qualifies as an object reveals a series of assumptions about material things, and for this scholar, provokes the question of whether we can bring to bear on water the kind of methodology inculcated in those of us who are art and architectural historians. Some of the most basic techniques that art history uses to analyze its subjects are formal analysis, categorization of style, identification of authorship and patronage, historical context, and the way that the recipients use and understand the object. These are not the only questions art historians ask, and the list does not begin to acknowledge theoretical frameworks of analysis that challenge the premises of such interrogation. But as a set of basic inquiries, they serve to trouble the status of water as a proper object of study.

First, water lacks form. Without a vessel to contain it, water washes away and disappears, so that, even when present, it can be hard to see. We do not typically see moisture in the soil (although it is there, and farmers know to look for it), and while we notice clouds, we do not otherwise recognize the

FIGURE 11.1 *Aljibe del Rey (photo by author).*

water that evaporates into the air. Lacking form, water also lacks style, by which I mean the expressive way that a thing communicates. To illustrate this point: we can recognize hydraulic technologies as functional types belonging to specific places and historical periods, but the water propelled by a waterwheel or traveling along an aqueduct has no expressive style, because one drop of water looks exactly like another.

Likewise, water eludes the methodology of the art historian because it is not made: it has no architectural designer, no author, no patron. The architect or artisan may create the vessel that holds the water, but the water itself is not created, except by God, as expressed in the Qur'an: "God sends down water from above to give life to earth" (Sura al-Nahl 65; see also 21:30, 23:18, 24:45).

A corollary to this is that water is not a historical phenomenon. There is no moment when it comes into being, except Creation itself, and with this we are on theological rather than historical territory. While we can date the central Patio de la Acequia in the Generalife Palace (Granada) to the reign of the Nasrid sultan Muhammad III (1302–8), we cannot date the water that flows into its central channel (Plate 28). The water was not made in the moment that the Sultan ordered the garden built in the fourteenth century, nor does it come into being when it comes into view in the palace. Rather, it flows into the Patio de la Acequia from a garden on the palace's upper terrace, where it traverses the courtyard floor, having dropped vigorously into that garden from the channels carried down the balustrade of a water stairway, the source for which lies beyond the walls of the palace proper. We can trace the route of the water from the Generalife Palace to mountain sources fed by rain and snow that fell months ago (Plate 29). Although the constructed channels that carried the water date to the period when they were first dug, the water itself belongs to a timeless cycle of rainfall and evaporation.

And yet, despite all of the ways that water eludes characterization as an "object," it is precisely its unrelenting materiality that keeps us from placing it in a framework defined as either religious or secular. The fact that the Qur'an and Hadith contain so many references to water, together with water's role in the rituals of ablution and bathing, would suggest that in principle and in practice water is a profoundly important element of Islam as a religion. Yet, water does not have a dedicated form or markings, in the sense of prayer beads or a manuscript that can be clearly linked to a cultural or religious purpose. Perhaps for this reason, water cannot be said to have a cultural or religious identity; such identity can only be projected onto it. In the case of Granada, even though much of the water was supplied to the public via mosques, and although we know that the city was ruled by Muslim rulers, and although we have some idea of which communities lived in which quarters, we do not know the religion of the consumers of the water. In this sense, the material allows us to reframe the question because, instead of falling neatly into a religious or secular category, the materiality of water reveals these to be specious categories. Water simply is.[2]

Yet, having put forth the argument that water lacks the basic qualities of objecthood that might express an Islamic purpose or meaning, I now wish to test the argument by tracing the journey of one drop of water as it melts from snowfall in the Sierra Nevada mountains and travels from there to its destination in the Aljibe del Rey in Granada.

Granada was a mere village when the Taifa king Zawi b. Ziri (r. 403–10/1013–19) established the Zirid dynasty in al-Andalus, soon after the fall of the Amirids of Cordoba. In the ninth century, Granada had been the seat of resistance of a group of *muwallad*s (converts to Islam), led by Ibn Hafsun of Bobastro, protesting their second-class treatment. That community of *muwallad*s dwelled on the hilltop of the quarter known now as the Albaicín and known then as the Hisn Gharnata (Orihuela and Vílchez 1991: 15–20). When the revolt was crushed, Granada's vitality waned. Zawi b. Ziri chose Granada as his capital in 400/1009-10, because of its easily defended high position with views of the surrounding territory in all directions, and he built a fortress called the Qasabat Gharnata, later known as the al-Qasba al-Qadima (Ibn al-Khatib 2010: 101). From *The Tibyan* of Abd Allah b. Buluggin is this passage:

> Their eyes lighted on a beautiful plain full of rivers and trees. All the land around was watered by the Genil, which has its source in the Sierra Nevada (*Jabal Shulayr*). They were quick to perceive that from its central

> position the mountain on which the city of Granada now stands commanded the surrounding country. In front lay the Vega (*al-fahs*) . . .
>
> Abd Allah b. Buluggin 1986: 48 [ms. 21–2]

Ziri's nephew Habus also built (or rebuilt) a fortress on the hill on the west side of the Darro River, and the city grew in importance under Badis (429–65/1038–73), son of Habus, who built himself a palace on the topmost part of the hill. That hill is at the center of the quarter now known as the Albaicín. The Sabika hill where the Alhambra was erected later had some minor construction, but it was insignificant until the Almoravid period (1090–1147) when the two hills became the bases for opposing political groups and each was developed to serve as home base.[3] The Sabika rose dramatically in importance when the Nasrid rulers (1238–1492) chose it for their seat of government and embellished it with the palaces that together comprise the Alhambra and Generalife.

While the Albaicín's elevation protected its urban settlers in turbulent times, the site had one serious disadvantage: there was no immediate source of water.[4] Less than 3 mm of rain falls in Granada's hot dry summers, with slightly more generous precipitation of 47 mm per month in the winter.[5] But even in periods of relative abundance, the city's hilly topography is such that the water runs quickly downhill and drains into the River Darro and River Genil (Figure 11.2). Therefore, to obtain a reliable water supply, Badis ordered that a canal—*acequia* in Spanish, derived from the Arabic *saqiya*—should be built to draw water from the Fuente de Alfacar, a natural source about 10 kilometers distant and 920 meters above sea level, and to bring it to his settlement on the Albaicín Hill, a drop of about 200 meters. This was the Acequia Aynadamar (from *ayn al-dama*ʿ, meaning spring of tears) (Figure 11.3). The supervisor was Mu'ammal (d. 492/1099), vizier to Badis, his successor, and the Almoravid Yusuf b. Tashfin (r. in Granada *c.*1071–1106) (Lafuente 1845: 131; Abd Allah b. Buluggin 1986: 137–8, 140–3).

Our drop of water falls as snow on the mountains high above the city, the Sierra de la Alfaguera (from *al-fawwara*, meaning fountain), where it melts and is collected at the Fuente de Alfacar, and flows along the Acequia de Aynadamar. As at the Generalife Palace, the water flows endlessly in a natural cycle of precipitation and evaporation that has no beginning. But once the rain or snow has fallen to earth, is the water owned? A diagram dated sometime between 1617 and 1747 shows the course of the canal as it made its way from Alfacar to Granada (Orihuela and García 2008: 144) (Plate 30). In the countryside, hundreds of small farms drew water from it, before it reached the city walls of the Albaicín, where it was allocated to individual residences. Although the Zirid king built and paid for the earliest version of the canal—fulfilling his role as beneficent ruler—the farmers and urban residents who received the water were surely taxed in some way for the service. The water was not free, and yet neither was it owned as it flowed through the canal. In addition to irrigating agricultural holdings, the canal also provided a source of

FIGURE 11.2 *Model (from the Alhambra) showing site topography and rivers (photo by author).*

FIGURE 11.3 *The Acequia de Aynadamar (photo by Javier Martín, public domain).*

energy for mills that ground the grain produced by those farms, which by the fourteenth century, according to Ibn al-Khatib (713–76/1313–75), numbered 130 (Ibn al-Khatib 2010: 105). His estimate may have been inflated, but whatever the correct number, the fact remains that millers do not want to keep the water that propels their mills; to the contrary, they need a water source that rushes quickly through their mills, providing a dynamic energy source to power them. In this sense, the millers and farmer had a right (earned through both taxation and inherited as a tradition) to the use of the water at whatever stage in the hydraulic cycle that it reached them, but it did not belong to those recipients, or to the Zirid king, except insofar as he represented the state's custodianship (Trillo 2002: xlv–xlvi).

The Aynadamar canal was not the only source of water for Granada. The Acequia al-Cadi, and possibly the Acequia al-Kubra, were begun slightly later in the same eleventh century, per an order of the Zirid king Abd Allah, according to Ibn al-Khatib (Ibn al-Khatib 2010: 167). The Acequia al-Kubra, which drew its water from the Genil River, is visible running parallel to it on a map drawn by Ambrosio de Vico (d. 1623) sometime between 1590–5 (Figure 11.4).[6] The Acequia al-Cadi, which is not well documented in the Arabic sources, was added in the eleventh century or later, but certainly before the Almohad arrival in the mid-twelfth century.

Our single water drop could have reached the city via one of these canals, or via the Acequia de Axares, a canal built to serve the lower part of the

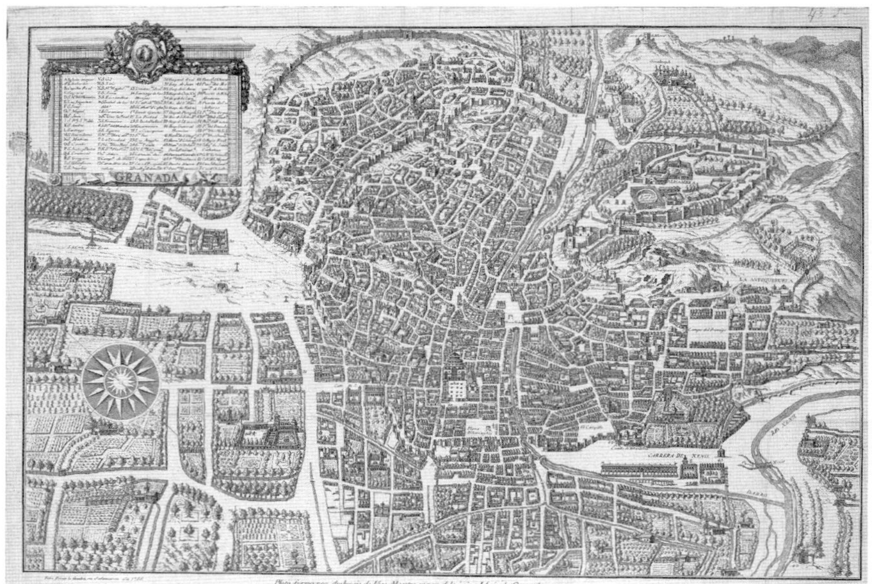

FIGURE 11.4 *Map of Granada, drawn by Ambrosio de Vico, engraved in 1795 by Felix Prieto (public domain).*

Albaicín as the city grew (Plate 31) (Orihuela and Vílchez 1991: 30). Unlike the Aynadamar, the Axares canal drew its water from the Darro River at a point far upstream. Since all of the water flowing into Granada originated in mountain snowmelt, whether carried in streams or artificial canals, our water drop could have taken this path to reach Granada. As the Axares neared Granada, it split into two branches, one maintaining the name Acequia de Axares (known as Acequia de San Juan after 1492), and the other becoming the Acequia de Romayla (known as the Acequia of Santa Ana after 1492). These initially ran parallel to the Darro on its west bank, but at about the halfway point, the Romayla crossed the river via a bridge.

The Axares canal ran toward the neighborhood draped along the lower skirt of the Albaicín, providing water to the residences there as well as the quarter's public baths, which date from the eleventh or twelfth century.[7] Tracing this alternative path for our water drop, it could therefore have come from the snowcapped peaks of the Sierra, to the Darro as it emerged from the mountains, into and along the course of the canal, until it reached the bathhouse in Granada.

On the east side of the Darro River, stood the Alhambra on the Sabika Hill. The site did not acquire any significant buildings until it became the royal seat in the thirteenth century under the Nasrids, which is why it has not figured in the hydraulic story so far. But when the Nasrids settled there in 1238, the sultan Muhammad I ordered the construction of the Acequia Real (Royal Canal) to supply all the needs of the palace complex (Ibn Idhari 1954: 125). The Acequia Real flowed from the Darro and, like the Acequia de Axares, drew water from it at a point far upstream (Plate 31) (García 2016: 355–82; 2013: 27–30, 148–403). The water channels of the Acequia Real, and additional canals that branch from it, such as the Acequia del Tercio and Acequia de los Dos Tercios, still flow today and are protected as natural heritage. Anyone who has visited the Generalife Palace has walked along this canal (or one of its branches) as it courses through the appropriately named Patio de la Acequia. From there, the water had to cross the ravine that separates the Alhambra from the Generalife via an aqueduct that is still visible, although no longer used (Figure 11.5). Stored in a water tower (seen behind the aqueduct's single span), it could be drawn upon to irrigate the many gardens, pools, and baths of the Alhambra's cluster of palaces.

However, the drop of water that we are tracing did not travel along the Acequia Real. It came via the Acequia de Aynadamar, a crucially important distinction when we consider its destination. The dependence on water in Granada, combined with its hilly topography, led to a city divided by the hydraulic networks. The Aynadamar originates in a spring in the Alfacar, but the other canals came from upstream draw points in the Darro or Genil rivers. The topography of the two hills required that two different sources of water be tapped, which led to the development of distinct hydraulic networks, which in turn led to a concomitant split in city administration. From the eleventh century, two cities had developed: the Qasaba Gharnata,

FIGURE 11.5 *Aqueduct connecting the Generalife to the Alhambra (image credit: AdriPozuelo, public domain).*

as the Albaicín was known, and the Qasaba al-Hamra', known today as the Alhambra. The distinction in administration was reflected in the two congregational mosques, one serving the people of the Albaicín, standing more or less where the Church of San Salvador is today, and the other serving the Nasrid palaces on the Sabika hill. This is an example of the powerful effect that a material resource, such as water, may have on the organization of human society.

A key function of government is to levy taxes to ensure cost-sharing and to provide a system of justice. Therefore, once our drop of water was channelized into the Aynadamar, a new set of issues arose pertaining to the rights of usage. The acquisition of sufficient quantities of water had been solved by manipulating natural conditions through strategies of engineering, but thereafter the challenge was how to apportion it fairly, so that the cost of maintenance was equitably assessed and the benefit of receiving water was equitably distributed. The formlessness of our drop of water becomes important here. The water could be owned only insofar as it could be contained in a well, canal or pail, and yet while it flowed through canals and into containment basins, it was something upon which claims could be made and, consequently, a complex set of socio-political mechanisms had to be developed to manage those claims.

A fair system for the distribution of water was especially important in dry areas where agriculture depended on irrigation. In Granada, the Aynadamar canal served the farms of the Viznar region (outside the city) during the day, and was allocated to fill the cisterns within the city during the night, with the result that the urban dwellers had to be vigilant to ensure that the farmers did not take more than their share.[8] The reverse was less of a problem, since the city consumers received their water only after it had flowed past the farmers' draw points. The stakeholders in such systems were cast in relationships according to their place in the spatial flow: if a stakeholder upstream took more than the stipulated share or polluted the water in some way, the downstream farm or urban consumer would feel the impact. Because the distribution of water could cause tension, it had to be managed, usually using a system of measurement based on time or volume.

Systems that calculated units of time include sundials, which could be as crude as a stick erected in the ground or something more scientific such as sundials, marble fragments of which still exist in the collections of the Alhambra and the Archaeological Museum of Cordoba. These instrument plates, etched with lines to measure the sun's shadow, were probably more useful in the calculation of the times for prayer and fasting, and indeed one of the Cordoba sundials, which dates to the eleventh century, distinguished clearly between hours of the day indicated with straight lines, and hours for prayer indicated with zigzag lines (Barcelo and Labarta 1988: 231–47; Berggren 2001: 1–14; *Les Andalousies* 2000: 245, no. 249). Another system for allocating water might use a container, such as a bowl with a hole in its base, set within a much larger bowl of water. As the smaller bowl filled slowly with water and sank, it provided a measurement of a uniform unit of time: not in the abstract quantity of minutes and hours, but experienced as one observable bowl of time. By making time palpable, the bowl translated the abstraction into something material that could then be exchanged as a commodity, as occurred in Granada by the Nasrid period (Trillo 2005: 163–83; see also Garrido Atienza [1902] 2002).

Alternatively, water can be measured in terms of its volume, through mechanisms that allocate the flow into distinct streams. In Timimun, Algeria, the system began as a single stream that was then separated by means of a diverter into sixteen equal units of flow as it flowed out of a rectangular basin (Plate 32). But over time, mergers occurred, perhaps as a consequence of the sale of land parcels, or perhaps marriage between two families with adjacent landholdings, so that instead of sixteen equal irrigation canals emerging from the diverter box, there are now ten canals of unequal capacity. This system has precisely the same logic as any modern "share" in a company. The water diverter does not dictate social relations, but it clearly shows social and economic networks mapped materially. To ensure that stakeholders adhered to the rules of apportionment, a system of adjudication was necessary. Records do not exist for Granada's courts prior to 1492. But in the decades following the conquest, a water court was established in the city to handle disputes over water rights; and through the edicts, or *Ordenanzas*, issued by this administrative body, the canals were kept clean and water flowed to the lands and institutions that had traditional claims upon the water. The *Ordananzas* indicate that regulatory practices in the post-conquest period continued on the basis of the previous, legitimating claims "because that is how it was done in the times of the Moors" (*Ordenanzas que los muy Ilustres, muy magníficos Señores de Granada mandaron guardar, para la buena gobernación de su república, impressas año de 1552,* folio 215v, in Orihuela and Vílchez 1991: 30). A remnant of this kind of justice system still exists in Valencia. The Water Tribunal, which dates from the tenth century, still convenes to render decisions about the fair allocation of water for the city of Valencia and its surrounding plains (Glick 1970; Guillén y Rodríguez de Cepeda 1921). Such a court must have been a useful way to regulate relationships between urban and rural water consumers, both of which would have wished to defend their rights to water that was due to them. But within the city, Granada was unique in having a network of urban cisterns that provided water freely for the public good (Orihuela and Vílchez 1991).

There are twenty-eight cisterns in Granada, dating from the eleventh through the fifteenth centuries, twenty-seven of them in the Albaicín. While such cisterns lie below ground and are generally overlooked, they become visible through their stone and ceramic wellheads or, as in the streets of Granada, through the arched openings in small brick kiosks or cut into the walls of buildings. Revealing the presence of an entire water network, these window-like openings are the places where the invisible subterranean system of water distribution materializes on the city surface. As one walks through the streets of the Albaicín, the wells appear on every plaza and next to many churches, the churches having replaced the Zirid and Nasrid mosques after the conquest of 1492.

One of the oldest cisterns is the eleventh-century Aljibe de San José which served the former Masjid al-Murabitin, the minaret of which still stands in good condition (Figure 11.6). The mosque was destroyed in 1517 and

FIGURE 11.6 *San José minaret and aljibe opening (on the lower left) (photo by author).*

replaced by the Church of San José, but the cistern continued to function as an appendage of the church. Similarly, the thirteenth-century Aljibe de San Miguel Bajo belonged to a mosque of unknown name that was demolished in 1528 and replaced by the Church of San Miguel Bajo, and the same transition was imposed on at least half the cisterns in the Albaicín (Orihuela and Vílchez 1991: 88, 92; Trillo 2007: 321).[9] The mosques provided the water as a public service in these cases, either in the form of a well in the mosque's courtyard or through an adjacent ablution facility (Orihuela and Vílchez 1991: 52–3). But in other cases, a wealthy patron may have provided the water free of charge, thereby fulfilling the hadith which reported the Prophet as commending the charity of filling another person's bucket with water (Bukhari n.d., no. 304, no. 891, and no. 1182). The Aljibe del Rey (known in Arabic sources as *al-jubb al-qadim*, or "the old well") is such an example of a privately owned well, and, for the purposes of tracing the path of our water drop, let us imagine that it arrived here rather than one of the many other cisterns served by the same canal.

The Aljibe del Rey was built on the command of the eleventh-century Zirid king Badis to serve his hilltop palace and the surrounding neighborhood. The current residential buildings of the Carmen del Aljibe del Rey, with their walled gardens and orchard, belong to a much later period, but if we walk into the *carmen*'s enclosed courtyard, we find ourselves standing on a floor that forms the roof of the palace's original subterranean Zirid water cistern (Figure 11.7). The enormous cistern was filled in two ways: by the Aynadamar canal, and via an impluvium, a classic Mediterranean architectural typology consisting of inward sloping roofs that guide rainfall into the courtyard to drain into the tank beneath the courtyard floor. The cistern (10.63 m long × 11.37m wide × 3.82 m deep) is a significant work of subterranean architecture, spanned by four parallel barrel vaults resting on nine sturdy free-standing pillars and six engaged pillars (Figure 11.8). Its lime-coated interior held 300 cubic meters of water and was the largest of the cisterns in Granada (Orihuela and Vílchez 1991: 62). Unlike the buildings and gardens above, which were designed for the sensory display of wealth and pleasure, this cavernous container was not meant to be seen, and yet, it had a profound material impact on the palace's inhabitants.

The historic diagram (see Plate 30) shows that the houses of the Albaicín were linked along the fan-like lines of the hydraulic network. While none of the original Zirid houses for which the network was initially developed still exist, the system's connections can still be observed in the single-span aqueduct that springs from the rear wall of the Carmen of the Aljibe del Rey, carrying the Aynadamar waters from that palace across the narrow street and into the walled garden of another Islamic palace, the Dar al-Horra, built in the fourteenth century for Nasrid patrons (Figure 11.9). In this oldest part of Granada, the eleventh-century residences were eventually replaced by newer houses in later centuries, but streets, property lines, and canals would not have changed significantly over time. Therefore, the network mapped in the seventeenth-century diagram reflected not only the water system of its own day, but also that of the earlier centuries.

In tracking the path of our single drop of water, I would like to imagine that it did not flow into the Dar al-Horra (or whatever structure preceded it), but was deposited in the Aljibe del Rey. The eleventh-century residents of the palace would have extracted water from the great subterranean tank via a wellhead positioned somewhere in the courtyard floor, in a manner similar to any other large household with its own internal cistern. Additionally, the same cistern provided water to the public, through its exterior face. As the

FIGURE 11.7 *Courtyard in the Carmen del Ajibe del Rey (photo by Constantinos Raptis).*

largest and possibly oldest of the cisterns in the Albaicín, it was also the only well from which water was sold, perhaps because, as a private source, it was not subject to norms of charity, unlike mosques (Trillo 2012: 151–74, 168). Thus, it provided water to the residents of the palace, to the neighborhood, and to vendors who would deliver it to houses not served by a well. The brick frame of the Aljibe del Rey was restored in 1985, and the openings to all the cisterns in the Albaicín were blocked with metal plates over a century

FIGURE 11.8 *Aljibe del Rey, cistern interior (photo credit: Constantinos Raptis).*

FIGURE 11.9 *Aqueduct linking the Carmen del Aljibe del Rey (on the right) to the Dar al-Horra (the rear wall of which is on the left) (image by author).*

ago to prevent outbreaks of disease—specifically cholera—spread by the dirty pails lowered into the water, as described in *The Lancet* in 1903 (Granada 1903: 427), yet the sill of the cistern provides a record of human use. Visible—indeed palpable—on the interior edge of the stone sill are the grooves made by the friction of ropes, as buckets were lowered into the cistern, day after day, through the centuries (Figure 11.10).

With its enormous capacity, the Aljibe del Rey stood out as the largest cistern in Granada. However, in other respects, it was ordinary, one of the many canal-fed underground reservoirs that survive from the period of Muslim rule and from which households fetched their water. Indeed, Granada owes its existence to this water network, which is why the story of its circulation matters. While with an object of art or manuscript there might be multiple users and readers, we know that the population of people who might ever touch a book or handle a precious ivory was restricted: only the literate, only the wealthy. These are the objects, heavily invested with the maker's intentions, for which we can talk about form, artistic style, historic moment of creation, and author and patron.

Our single drop of water lacks these attributes of "thingness." However, by choosing it as our object we are compelled to look at its material agency in connecting every living person in Granada, past and present, Muslim and Jew, from the eleventh-century Zirid king who built his palace on the Albaicín Hill and brought water to it from afar, to the Nasrid sultans building their palaces on the opposite hill from the mid-twelfth century until

FIGURE 11.10 *Interior face of the Aljibe del Rey. (Photo by author).*

1492, and that linked these powerful patrons to the servants and slaves who were sent to get water from the neighborhood well. The connections occur through the shared space of the city, across time from the eleventh century to the fifteenth, and between social classes. The grooves that we see in the stone of the cistern are the record of generations of nameless individuals—most likely women—who came to the well to fill the jars for the household they served (Ruggles 2020), and as the narrator of this story, the destination that I choose for our water drop is one of these jars. Each person, in dropping her pail over the sill and hoisting it up, eroded the stone a tiny bit, and in that way eased the rope's path for future users.

The water transported to the Aljibe del Rey did not have form, except insofar as it conformed to the dimensions of the thing that contained it. The water held in the vessel was not made by an author or patron, except perhaps a divine creator, and yet it cannot be identified as "Islamic" or "Muslim." It did not have the kind of intentional or expressive meaning that we read from complex symbolic signs, like a niche lit with a lamp or an architectural inscription. Yet, the water that flowed into and through Granada made hilltops habitable for the mighty and provided a basic sustenance for the ordinary, and in this sense its material presence was deeply meaningful. Water was the thing on which everything else depended.

CHAPTER TWELVE

Zamzam Water: Environmentality and Decolonizing Material Islam

Anna M. Gade

Here is a small glass vial of water that is claimed to be from the well of Zamzam in Makkah (Figure 12.1). It may be worn or hung as a decoration, and it has the Qur'an's Throne Verse (*ayat al-kursi*, Qur'an 2:255) inscribed on an acrylic insert within the container.[1] The top of the capsule shows the Name of God, Allah, engraved multiple times. I bought it on the Internet.[2] The tiny sealed bottle represents a Muslim tradition of submerging written scripture into water for aesthetic effect, and this is also a feature of some religious practices of Muslims. The artifact could thus be said to be an example of *zamzamiyya*: vessels that contain Zamzam's water (Flood 2014; Porter 2013). This object, however, was made to be carried and worn. It has an opening at one end in which to insert a cord or chain. The pendant's primary material is not human-made, and as a symbol the clear water inside represents water as a resource itself. This ecological property renders this case study of a vial of Zamzam's water to be an intervention in understanding scales of "environmentality" in material Islam.[3]

The mere description of this object expresses questions about the nature of the water it contains, from both environmental and religious perspectives. For example, the vial holds water that is religiously stipulated for drinking but that cannot be drunk. Instead, it is embodied as decoration, possibly talismanic since it is combined with the Qur'an's protective, written word that is fixedly dipped into it. It also represents the global circulation of the water of Zamzam through pilgrimage and devotion, and potentially

FIGURE 12.1 *Vial of* zamzam *water. Collection of the author (photo by C. Ryan Perkins).*

commerce. Since Zamzam's water cannot be bought or sold in quantity according to law, the smallness of this artifact indicates not just its portability and its sealed im-potability, but also its scarcity. Furthermore, because it is a luxury object and it appears to be a souvenir, as jewelry it signifies the property of preciousness all the more.

An acknowledgment of the full "environmentality" of this water, whether in this form or through any other of its global flows, however, requires more than a formal analysis of things or the various modes of Zamzam water's circulation (e.g., Appadurai 1990). To be able to explain any instance of Zamzam's water in religious or environmental terms calls for fundamental change in the scope and scale of theory used for the study of material Islam. These adaptations challenge structures and erasures from the colonial era. As such, they are long overdue in the field of religious studies, including its more recent sub-field, material religion.

There is already a great deal of environmental and religious science (*'ulum*) about water in the authoritative sources of Islam. Water, as with all its many states and cycles, is among the primary *ayat* (signs) of God in the Qur'an. As the Qur'an states, humans themselves are constituted by this "object" (25:54), which the text also explains in more than a hundred of its verses to be the environmental resource upon which life depends. All of this is, explicitly, a "sign" of God and this is among His mercies that are continuously emphasized throughout the Qur'an. The text depicts water in many forms on this earth, from oceans to rain, as well as the transformed environments of the world to come; rivers flow in the Garden (heaven), and waters boil in the Fire (hell). Characteristically, the Qur'an also prescribes moral, intellectual, and ritual responses to these descriptions, such as to be thankful. Many hadith mention water, primarily in terms of resource use and management.

Recent Muslim environmentalists promote related principles and practices of water conservation, like *hima* and *harim*, that have been documented since the time of the Prophet Muhammad. There are copious jurisprudential rulings on water in all schools of *fiqh*, both transactional and ritual (such as the controversy over 5 Al-Ma'idah 6[4]), and much of this could be called "environmental law." This includes, for example, the notion that there is a human right (*haqq*) to water. On a religious order of reality that is referentially symbolic, water can also indicate the really "real." Sufis have long expressed truths like these through their teachings and practices, such as water-as-purification, waters "of" and "as" life, bodies of water as a common metaphor for experiential knowledge, and so forth.

Zamzam's religious myths and rituals are not of a diminished order of materiality when compared to circumstances that are overtly "environmental." On the contrary, religious realities redouble "real" environmental properties, as Zamzam's water continually functions as a symbol of itself as a resource. In research, I have found that religious environmentalists attempt to tangibly operationalize water as simultaneously being both a "resource" as well as a "symbol" within messages of environmental outreach, such as in Islamic environmental education in Indonesia (Gade 2019b).

"Water in Islam" is a long-established sub-field of religion and ecology, at times touching on some of the environmental dimensions already indicated, above (Foltz et al. 2003; Izzi Dien 2000). In the emerging fields of environmental humanities, including religious studies, religious water is also a familiar theme. For example, consider the cutting edge of a global movement of environmental activism in the form of community rights called "rights of nature" that posits rivers' environmental personhood (Gade 2019a). Recent work in religious studies on water highlights classic interpretive themes such as purity and pollution, while also identifying what environmental studies now knows as "wicked water problems."

For environmental studies, which includes environmental humanities, it goes without saying that water studies are foundational, and also a rapidly growing area of focus. This is the case whether examined in terms of resource or disaster management, biological and physical sciences like limnology and hydrology, marine science and atmospheric study, and much more. Classical Muslim sources on "the environment" date back over a thousand years, having water as a theoretical and empirical foundation, and from these the modern sciences of environmental studies like chemistry and biology later originated. Medieval Muslim manuscripts define "environment" (*ma'ysh*, for example), as a scientifically ecological or geographical term, as being spaces that can support diverse forms of life because of the presence of a supply of water, such as by not being parched, or having the capacity to sustain biotic habitats with an abundance of fresh water.[5] In the narrative of Hajar that is the origin story for Zamzam's well and water, for example, her banishment was expressly ordered by the Prophet Ibrahim (some say this was by the will of God), to a landscape where water was said not to be available.

Recognizing dimensions of environmentality like these has major implications for the field of material religion. This also answers everyday questions about how to "scale" where this water begins, and where, and when, and what will be the end of water? Such morphologies of scale are meant here in both geographical and phenomenological senses. "Scale" even has a semantic significance here in connection to the assessment or measure of justice, as featured prominently in the Qur'an with respect to *mizan*, (lit. "scales" or "balance"). Zamzam water's particularized materiality singles it out as special, unique water, and also a symbol of more. This renders it a representation of environmental realities within a religious field, both in this world and in the landscapes of the world to come. Furthermore, it is also a manifestation of themes in an environmental field, as a natural resource.

This artifact signifies characteristics of what is a phenomenal and idealized object, Zamzam water, but more fundamentally it indicates the environmental dimensions of theorizing material Islam from the perspective of the academic study of religion. Traversing fluidly through Zamzam water's geographic, geological, social, and metaphorical flows, of which this object represents only my personal share, environmental and religious themes render Zamzam water a model for how to scale the environmentality of material religion. Furthermore, from classical sources to planetary futures, the process of singling out "some" water also implies simultaneously a natural replenishment of resources as well as their sustainable limits. It is not just that the little vial of water that Amazon.com sent to my door is at a boundary of what can be called "Zamzam," but Zamzam water, and maybe water itself, is at the boundary of what are the current scales for theorizing material Islam in decolonial frames. Surprisingly, this is not so much an effect of its religious properties but by nature of its environmental ones.

Zamzam, material religion, and measures of scale

In environmental studies, leveraging cultural and religious symbolism (one's own and others') is a predominant mechanism by which committed environmentalists attempt to activate engagement and education as tangible initiatives. Meanwhile, in recent years, scholars of environmental humanities like Bruno Latour have re-emphasized that myth and symbol are the only way to apprehend the material, political, epistemic, and moral dimensions of environmental presents and futures (Latour 2017). However, this paper takes the geographical idea of "scale"—also a concern of Latour's, cultural geographers, and as was developed in Anglophone ecocriticism by Morton (Morton 2013)—rather than the humanistic view of "symbol" as the primary intervention to be made in material religion in light of environmentality. By implication, this intentionally bypasses two central concerns of post-Protestant theory of both religion and environment cast in terms of the Euro-American concept of Nature: "experience" (as in the romantic and phenomenological traditions) and "biocentrism" (e.g., Bennett 2010; Wilson 1996).

The academic study of symbol has found a semi-autonomous historical trajectory through each of the humanistic sub-fields of environmental humanities, across disciplines from history to music studies and ecocriticism. Old Christian themes like "the sacred" and "the sublime" are a part of each one of these stories, potentially to re-emerge at any affective, ethical, or ontological turn. In religious studies, a crudely comprehensive theory of symbolism, such as that which defined the field in its anthropological modes up until the 1990s, may now be considered passé. Nevertheless, new frontiers in environmental humanities now call for a review of the nineteenth- and twentieth-century inheritances of "symbol" in order to reassess the familiar overlay of the concrete and the imaginal, and in light of the scalar propositions of environmentality.

Outdated notions of symbol, whose academic remnants are still preserved in the field of material religion, are now breaking down under the ethical burden conveyed by new concerns of environmental humanities. This collapse is occurring through more than decolonizing critique. An inherited naive phenomenology, exemplified by Latour's object-oriented approach to "things" as in *We Have Never Been Modern* (1993), remains characteristic of Anthropocene studies (e.g., Mitman et al. 2018, and also as here, this is still the dominant approach in material religion, e.g., Gade 2015). These can come up short on methodology if not also theory.

In methodologies of environmental studies as well as classical Islamic theory, environmental phenomena occupy a continuum from the scientifically physical, biological, and palpably virtual, to the meaningful, imagined, and experienced—human and non-human. This represents a leading edge of humanistic fields when it comes to twenty-first-century notions such as catastrophic climate futures and the Anthropocene. Religious studies, too, operates on commensurate multi-dimensional scales that can process an environmental load, and has "value-added" capacity for analysis that is ethical, ontological, and existential. An adjustment needs to be made to recalibrate theory of symbol and scale in order for the field of material religion to address environmentality including, as in Agrawal's work, matters of postcolonial power and governance.

Material religion needs to recover its theory of morphology, i.e., understanding scale, as both taxonomy and process. In fact, the field of religious studies has already long had robust theory to scale environmentality, which could for its redesign now draw on the templates of classical Muslim theory (such as that of Ibn Sina), once decolonized from European inheritances. The charge of Christian crypto-theology, such as has been commonly leveled at Micrea Eliade's work *The Sacred and the Profane*, applies just as readily to the entire field of Anglophone material religion as it would to a selected single work. However, it was also a single work by Mircea Eliade, *Patterns in Comparative Religion*, that did in fact anticipate the ontological turn beyond "symbol" to "scale" with its phenomenology of the transformative process that was expressed through a model for categorical relations: hierophany ("any manifestation of the sacred, in whatever form").[6]

As Jonathan Z. Smith would later say in 1999, at the opening to his lecture series commemorating *Patterns* at the University of Chicago Divinity School, "[*Patterns*] is a work that can be thought with or against, but never thought around or away" (Smith 2000: 315). Many of the demonstrations given in Eliade's book are instances of environmental resources: rocks, trees, etc. An entire chapter of *Patterns* is devoted to various examples of water, relating to his overall explanation of how objects are selected, chosen or singled out of a class, a process determinative of normative status (Eliade 1996: 188–215).

Eliade's "morphology of the sacred" for religious studies models the essential matter of "scaling" the environmentality of water commensurately to material religion. The shock of the book for students comes in the final chapter of *Patterns*, in which Eliade makes a case for rejecting "symbol" as the primary theoretical lens for the study of religion, not in an evolutionary sense (as did the *Religionswissenschaft* of F. Max Müller and others previously), but now to reconcile with the history of religions' grounding in empirical, phenomenal, and material manifestations.

The main claim of Smith's first lecture on Eliade's *Patterns* is that Eliade himself was inspired by natural science, namely the biological morphology of Goethe, for his project. Eliade's very first line of *Patterns* indicates this, appearing with an embedded reference to a famous quote by the mathematician Poincaré: "Modern science has restored a principle which was seriously endangered by some of the confusions of the nineteenth century: 'It is the *scale* that makes the phenomenon'" (Eliade 1966: xvii, his italics). Eliade's claim that the morphology of a religious phenomenon must be treated with the same order of accuracy and precision as a scientific one is, as a matter of scale (and not without some irony), a first critical intervention to bring material Islam into view within religious studies.

Decolonization is called for in the field of material religion in order to overcome erasures, such as Eliade's very own systemic omission of Islam. For this to happen, the supremacy of the Christianized grounds on which theories like that of "the sacred," "presence," or "enchantment"—on which Eliade and others rely for epistemic universalization, and as still prevails in the current field of material religion—must be categorically reassessed as well. This overall project, one of the aims of this volume as a whole, is further explored theoretically in this paper's conclusion. To return now to the case at hand, however, here a more descriptive intervention follows by way of representing Zamzam's water from the perspectives of historical Muslims in terms of scales of myth, ritual, and symbol.

The Hajj pilgrimage (and included in this discussion, *'umrah*) is an authoritative system through which Muslim sources answer questions about Zamzam water and its religious and environmental scales of influence locally, globally, and even universally across space and time. The annual Hajj, like the daily worship called *salat*, orients Muslims worldwide around a single place, the Haram at Makkah, which is the site of the Zamzam well. Hajj is one of the obligatory and rewarded actions of religious worship (*'ibadat*) known as the "five pillars of Islam," and it is to be undertaken on the jurisprudential basis of its stipulation. However, Hajj is largely comprised of symbolic enactments. During much of the multi-day itinerary across the landscape, the actions that are necessary and sufficient to render pilgrimage valid act out or commemorate occurrences of the sacred past, such as events known from the story of the Prophet Ibrahim and his family, as well as events in the future (as in standing like on the Day of Judgment at the plain of 'Arafat). Finally, these actions also follow sunnah, the model of the Prophet Muhammad, in carrying out Islamic Hajj.

Zamzam's water is implicated mythically and ritually in all of the scales of these prophetic dimensions as they relate to actual geographic sites of the Hajj. Zamzam, as both a water source and the water itself, is integral to the stories of Hajj, and is also foundational to more than one of the stipulated actions of Hajj. Pilgrims drink from the water of Zamzam on arrival, as sunnah. In addition, after the initial circumambulation of the Ka'bah, pilgrims perform *sa'y*, running, between two hills known as Safa and Marwa in commemoration of the mother of the Prophet Isma'il, Hajar, seeking water for her child after her abandonment in the desert. According to the story, when Hajar was running, the well of Zamzam sprung up as her son's heel struck the ground. This account does not appear in the Qur'an, nor is there any mention of Zamzam in the text (however, the story does appear in Gen. 21 of the Hebrew Bible). The expression, "Safa and Marwa," does appear in the Qur'an, but not as hills or mountains, but rather as potential foci of ritual circumambulation (2:158). There is further information in tradition that Hajar began to dig a pool so that the water would form in a well, said to be the same source from which pilgrims would later drink. Today, the site of the original well is completely closed off.

The extraction of the resource itself also indicates scales of the environmentality of Zamzam's water. For centuries after the Islamic origins of Hajj, the water source for Zamzam was adjacent to the Ka'bah, at about 21 meters away. There is now a marker for this place set in the tile of the *mataf* area, where pilgrims circle the Ka'bah. Hajar and Isma'il are also said to be buried at the Ka'bah, and such sites like Maqam Ibrahim (the place at which it is said his feet were planted as the Ka'bah rose up), all mark the precinct's landscape, just as does the nearby space of the two hills, Safa and Marwa. The site of extraction for Zamzam's water, however, moved in 2010 to a new, modern facility. All the water coming from under Makkah is from the same aquifer, called Wadi Ibrahim. Therefore the waters of "Zamzam," that for the last decade have been piped in to the Haram, are still drawn from the same water table as was the water from the traditional closed-off well at the Ka'bah, now all to be viewed within the greater scale of a total water catchment area that is about 60 square kilometers in area (Plate 33).

At the time of the change in location for Zamzam water's extraction, a filtration system was installed. Operating at maximum, the system pumps between 11 and 19 liters per second. The water is now piped into the Masjid Al-Haram from a part of town known as Kudai, about 4 kilometers away. Even though the site of extraction has changed, the water is still considered to be "Zamzam," and it is provided to pilgrims in the sacred precinct area through public fountains and in tanks and bottles, and is consumed in many hundreds of thousands of single-use plastic cups each day. About 700,000 liters is dispensed per day in the Grand Mosque (the Haram around the Ka'bah), increasing to 2 million liters per day in the pilgrimage season. Authorities state that they collect about a hundred samples of Zamzam water there each day in order to test for bacteria and impurities (Kingdom of Saudi Arabia, 2015).

How Zamzam's water is measured out for widespread provision to pilgrims up "to scale" during Hajj season, or, as in the case of the artifact here, bottled and sold in miniature, casts it in terms of questions of "authenticity," "access," and "availability." These coalesce around three major themes of inquiry about the resource's origin, distribution, and sustainability. The pendant considered here represents all of these, singling out some of Zamzam's water for circulation, embodiment, and display; the water enclosed in this capsule is a priceless resource that represents its own scaled environmentality as material religion.

Authenticity: is the water good? / what is it good for?

Zamzam water, being not just any water, has special properties, speaking both religiously and environmentally. The first set of everyday questions about Zamzam water are about its authenticity with respect to these criteria. These are relevant with respect to Zamzam's purported and even miraculous medicinal properties or public health risk, depending on the one who asks, or answers. These claims are part of Islamic religious truths as well as representing scientific and chemical results. The answers to the question about how it is considered to be good (or not) are grounded in the water's origin in a unique place. For example, environmental questions about the water's properties arise from the hydrogeological conditions of the region of extraction. Religious questions about Zamzam's good and beneficial properties treat the water as geographically hyper-real, that is, having supranatural capacities that exceed that of other water because it has come from the right place. Related questions commonly heard today are similarly focused on origination, but consider the reverse of "goodness" from a chemical standpoint, asking: can the water be harmful because of its precise origins in a place? Still further questions are about the properties of a given sample if it is not authentic, i.e., fake, or "any good" at all.

Among the most common questions about Zamzam water are: is it good?; and, what is it good for? The water in this vial poses one set of answers to these questions, although perhaps not the standard ones. At one side of a spectrum of goodness, there is the oft-cited hadith reporting that the Prophet Muhammad stated that Zamzam's water "is good for whatever it is good for" (Ibn Majah, *Sunan*, Book 25, Hadith 181).[7] Other traditions add healing properties to Zamzam's purported benefits. This is supported by some reports about companions of the Prophet which are considered reliable, such as the one that relates that A'ishah would collect Zamzam water to carry back home with her, and that Ibn 'Abbas would keep it in his house to offer to guests. Later generations, it is said, would bring children to the well, presumably for their health. There has been some question about whether the water would still have such healing properties if transported away from the Ka'bah, but the hadith of A'ishah taking it away seems to settle that question for many. Today, Zamzam water is popularly included, along with honey and olive oil, as a medicinal element, such as would be related in Prophetic medical sciences: *al-tibb al-nabawi*. It is prized by pilgrims on Hajj and '*umrah*. They may take some away with them to carry back home, even though Zamzam water's commercial sale, export, and import are now expressly prohibited by law in Saudi Arabia and many other nations.

Scientifically, there is a unique chemical composition of this water. This aspect of environmentality leads to questions about whether Zamzam water is good, or even if it is safe to ingest from a health standpoint. The well of Zamzam, past and present, is not very deep, extending only about 30 meters underground. The water flows through sedimentary rock, and therefore it has a relatively high mineral concentration, and it is also slightly alkaline. According to researchers, unfiltered it has around 800 mg/L of dissolved solids, and nitrate levels exceed the standard recommended limit of 10 mg/L by several times. It is also exceptionally high in radionuclides, well over WHO's limits for U, Th, K-40, and Cs-137 (however, it is also ingested only in extremely small quantities). While some say that all this helps make these the best, most healthy, and healing waters on the planet, a report from the BBC showing high levels of arsenic (Lynn 2011), and subsequent statements issued by British agencies have caused renewed international controversy in recent years. However, since then there have also been official statements that Zamzam's water is safe to consume, including public messaging about there being an Internet livestream that provides transparency about extraction, filtration, and bottling at the new well site.

A unique chemical signature can be used to test accurately for counterfeit water, reliably verifying authenticity. This underscores further concerns about risk from a public health standpoint, such as those about the possibility of there being "bad," false, and unsafe water getting passed off as being the real thing. Claiming that illegitimate bottled water sold as "Zamzam" poses a health hazard is also a way to discourage its fabrication and distribution all over the world. With this widespread international discourse, questions of authenticity and efficacy slide into classical anthropological questions of purity and pollution, as well as environmental health benefit and harm. As a matter of authenticity, the water is seen to be chemically and religiously singular at every scale. This means that the material religion of Zamzam's water may be socially and scientifically assessed as otherworldly, as being good or bad, and environmentally it must continually be managed as a shared resource.

Accessibility: can you get it, and how?

Pilgrims are supposed to drink at Zamzam, for both the greater and lesser pilgrimages. Controlled access is provided at sites in the sacred precinct of the Haram, and also at the extraction and bottling location across the city. Outside of Saudi Arabia, however, access is less clearly defined, although it is also strictly regulated. Commercial export of Zamzam water has been prohibited by the state. Pilgrims can only purchase and take it out of Saudi Arabia in a fairly small amount, five liters, on their own. Its accessibility is therefore restricted and scaled down overall. Like many environmental and religious resources, it is considered to be so valuable, it cannot have any monetized or commercial value ascribed to it.

With these questions of access, the morphology of non-expansion and prohibited circulation contrast with other treatments of water and holy water in the field of material religion. There is a lot of fake water out there, as indicated by frequent news reports of criminal Zamzam arrests from all over the world, including smuggling, as in a recent seizure in Malaysia (Bernama 2019). This fact emphasizes the degree of the resource's restriction, however, over and above any plentitude in deceptive reproduction. This contrasts with foundational theory of material religion about the circulation of site-specific and holy water as well as other pilgrimage objects, such as the study of the manufacture of Lourdes water in the Roman Catholic USA (McDannell 1995).[8] Today's modern circulation of Zamzam water, even on the Internet where I got mine, amplifies the rare value of the water, and the limits on its distributive diffusion.

Given its great value, it is paradoxical that Zamzam water is prohibited as a commodity; this comes unexpectedly from the perspective of environmental humanities. A principle of neoliberal conservation theory and practice is the intentional ascription of new registers of value to natural objects, such as through systems of rights or property, or even market-driven commoditization (like eco-tourism). The tenet that Zamzam water is "not for sale" helps to keep the place-based scale and the global impact of this water, and its well, materially and ritually grounded in, and under, the landscape at Makkah.

Prohibitions on transactions about water also have precedence in Islam, so considerations of the free access to Zamzam's water (meaning, it may not be accessed so freely) are not surprising. *Fiqh* rulings and principles limit the private ownership of the resource of water in many contexts; for example, the "right to thirst" (*haqq al-shirb*) is a basis for an unrestricted access to water under some circumstances. By precedent in many regions, inherited water rights (such as for irrigation) may not be bought or sold. A sound hadith on the authority of Abu Huraira that is often cited in this regard, is: "Three things cannot be denied to anyone: water, pasture and fire." A weaker but better-known version of the report found in the same collection (Ibn Majah, *Sunan*, Book 16, Hadith 38) begins, "Humanity is partners in three things," and some other variants include a phrase that stipulates that these things can neither be bought nor sold.

Accessibility and economy scale the environmentality of Zamzam water in the religious register. That it is supposedly not possible to obtain the water in quantity through commercial transaction shows just how its unique authenticity is linked to an environmental landscape. On a scale that is wider than this, except through a ritual mechanism of pilgrimage by which a pilgrim may acquire more for circulation, accessibility is measured by drops, like those in the vial presented here. Such a minimized scale of magnitude always conveys the suggestion that privileged access may dry up or disappear.

Availability: is there, was there, and will there be enough?

The vial exhibited here represents its own rarity in the water's origin and circulation, and also perhaps the possibility that—like the rain that falls from the sky, an occurrence about which there is much in the Qur'an and sunnah—this water may be restricted to a vanishing droplet through natural causes. Furthermore, the environmentality of the perceived sustainability of this resource carries over from this world into the next across religious and phenomenal scales. These themes recur throughout the myths and rituals of Zamzam, as well as in Muslims' questions about its availability now and in the future.

The theme of loss and re-discovery echoes back in stories about Zamzam in the mythic past to ancient times before the appearance of the Islamic ritual framework. Philologically, the name "*zamzam*" indicated both a water source as well as a possible pre-Islamic sanctuary under the Ka'bah (the "well of the Ka'bah," which may have held ritual objects in pre-Islamic times). According to narratives in Islamic traditions, it was then "made to be forgotten" after the time of Hajar due to a curse set on the tribe of Jurhum for having violated the sanctity of the Ka'bah. As it is related by Islamic traditions, like standard *Sirah* literature and histories like that of Al-Tabari, Zamzam was subsequently rediscovered by the grandfather of the Prophet Muhammad, 'Abd Al-Muttalib, after first having seen it in a dream. The biographies by Ibn Hisham and Ibn Ishaq recount that "Abd Al-Muttalib had four dreams, each revealing different names for the site. In the fourth dream, he heard, 'Dig Zamzam! Dig Zamzam! It never runs dry and it is not found wanting (*la tudhammahu*)'" (Hawting 1980: 44–5).

Whether Zamzam would last in the past is a question answered by myth: in fact, these accounts evidence that it did not always, as it was continually rediscovered. In the environmental present, Zamzam is fed entirely by rainwater that seeps into the aquifer under Makkah. The Saudi Geological Survey has put large-scale efforts into the management of the Wadi Ibrahim Aquifer, including establishing the Zamzam Studies and Research Center (ZSRC) which monitors Zamzam's water supply. There is an annual dip in the aquifer's level in Hajj week as well as during Ramadan; in addition, the development of the area is causing worry about degraded run-off and adequate replenishment of the aquifer through seepage in the catchment area. In response, there are at least two current projects to ensure the sustainability of the well water in connection with the greater Wadi Ibrahim Environmental Management System (WIEMS). These projects include rainwater harvesting and land use management, such as the ambitious Jabal Omar Development Project (JODP) that is designed to offset the impact of high-rise developments in order to protect groundwater levels, especially during times of high use.

With Zamzam's sustainability dependent upon rain, there are also more distant questions about whether it can last in regard to projected climate futures. The potential for near long-term depletion through human use is addressed by the management of the Saudi environmental agencies, but the possibility of the shift in future climatic patterns depends on acts of God, that is rain, even under anthropogenic conditions like humans' greenhouse gas emissions. Sustainability in this register is at another scale of environmentality for theorizing material religion because of the potential for irrecoverable loss and disappearance in the Anthropocene's scales of "deep time" (as in the discussion in Davies 2016).

For the field of material religion to embrace environmental realities like these requires grappling with how environmental humanities increasingly measures phenomena, seen and unseen, against ineffable and unknown horizons. These certainties exceed rationalized environmental frames, such as extinction of species, the elimination of life-supporting climate conditions, and the disappearance of resources like fresh water. As Timothy Morton and others express it, the environmental thought that cannot be un-thunk (Morton 2012) presents a scale beyond the human even, and the planetary (Latour 2018). This incorporates an existential horizon of annihilation to which a relational interspecies ontology (e.g., Haraway 2016) is the usual prescribed response. In this mode, the field of classical religious studies has apocalyptic analytical language ready-made for environmental crisis, an apparatus that is more systematic for apprehending crises than are the folk emotion-words (like "hope") that are otherwise commonly promoted in environmental humanities. However, this case of Muslim water shows that even this is not enough of a conceptual expansion to apprehend the scales of environmentality that are in effect.

The availability of Zamzam's water is a register of the no-analog conditions of the future. Unlike conventional, everyday discussions of disastrous planetary futures in environmental humanities, a Muslim religious understanding of earth time has already accepted the unavoidable end of water, and the very earthly abode itself. Qur'anic theory of eschatology, the ends of the world, allows for a horizon on the scale of relations beyond ecological destruction, and this is also in the same register that current post-Christian theories seek in their newly existential key. The environmental and religious horizon of materiality, such as in projected landscapes in worlds to come, may be radically altered as the consequences of the present through both environmentality and eschatology. About a fifth of the Qur'an's content vividly depicts "signs" (*ayat*) of environmental change in the soteriological present, as well as in the future transformed landscapes of consequential worlds to come, in which ultimate environmental justice is to become manifest on an apocalyptic scale.

Conclusion: the environmentality of material Islam

In 2010, when the site of the well of Zamzam was being moved across the city of Makkah to the location of the present pump site, a rumor circulated in the city. The story was that there was an unspoken plan in the works to divert Zamzam's piped water back through the affluent residential settlement along the hillside in order that it would flow through the area of rich people's homes before reaching the sacred precinct. According to the gossip, just when the alleged project was started, Zamzam would not flow. It was as if the water itself was apparently resisting the inequity and injustice, or another force blocked it from flowing across the landscape.

Analysis in this paper has stopped short of claiming any autonomous moral or environmental agency for Zamzam's water (Merchant 2015).

Water is clearly a "creature" (*makhluq*) and also "Muslim" from a Qur'anic standpoint, and many kinds of non-living substances including "the earth" (*al-ard*) itself do acquire expressive voice on Judgment Day (Gade 2019b). However, at no point has this examination implied any instance of biocentric extensionism, as frequently popularized within the Anglophone tradition of environmental ethics, nor any sense of environmental personhood, as often applies in cases of Indigenous "traditional ecological knowledge" (Berkes 2012).

A story like that of Zamzam water refusing to enter the wrong neighborhood for the right reasons instead here shows how water studies, such as hydrogeology, connects to human conditions of power and justice at a level of environmentality (Yusoff 2018). The environmentality of material religion links human and nonhuman scales, including scales of environmental justice, against horizons of scarce and diminishing resources. For the study of material religion looking forward, environmentality produces new morphologies and new horizons. Work in critical Black studies, Kathryn Yusoff's *A Billion Black Anthropocenes or None*, analyzes the racist structures of geology, the field in which the concept of the "Anthropocene" was born. Considering how Yusoff's work applies to hydrogeology in the present case underscores that environmentality for material Islam means questioning the position of colonialized theory from religious studies within the environmental humanities. This would include the post-Christian theology of "the sacred," and its aestheticized companion "the sublime," as well as their secularized and Marxian variants.

Post-Christian theory about other-directed affect still dominates discussion of global material religion in Americanists' terms. Such writings tend to double in prestige as overall "theory of religion," like Thomas Tweed on geographic circulations and domesticated Christianized sentiments (Tweed 2008, owing much to Appadurai), writings on material religion in terms of Roman Catholic presences (Orsi 2018 and elsewhere), and enchantment (Morgan 2018, and many others). Marxian analysis still opts for a Benjamin-esque version of these special feelings with "the aura," and even Marx's own notion of "commodity fetishism" was originally expressed through a religious rhetoric of experience.

Parochializing this heritage marks a step toward regarding Indigenous and Islamic sources as a basis for new theory in material religion that can express scales of environmentality as belonging empirically within the real world. When material Islam is cast as "material religion" primarily on Muslim terms, including the deep and systematic rigor of Sufi theories of experience, it may then develop secondary, diverse, and ancillary European-heritage extensions that disrupt and re-inscribe the historical process of colonization. As demonstrated by this very analysis, this may lead to the subsidiary or comparative inclusion of Christianized theoretical investments, even up to and including perplexing notions like "manifestations of the divine." Furthermore, robust Islamic epistemological frames (as always potentially relative to the Qur'an insofar as they are religious) additionally go beyond this to express empirically the morphologies that may grasp environmental relations and scientific processes, morals and ethics of environmental justice, and the futures of creatures inhabiting this world and the worlds to come.

As this object's symbolization points to itself, to the resource that is water, it simultaneously scales the environmentality of material religion to ultimate concerns, like that substance upon which all biological existence depends. This singling out of "some" water from the rest (as special water, from Zamzam) clarifies issues about the abundance and availability of resources, and answers questions about the end of water according to spatial and existential boundaries. One need not be a sophisticated mystic, an expert environmental scientist or ethicist, or even a very good mother to understand that the end of water is the end of life. The ultimacy of themes of access and authenticity, disappearance and recovery, and plentitude and scarcity of these waters acts as a "religious" theorization of environmental materiality in Islam.

Themes of religious authenticity, access, and availability likewise have here pointed to the scalar dimensions of "environmental" measures of material Islam, beginning in an everyday and immediate sense and leading up to planetary futures. This materiality of religion arises tangibly through the referential and reflective modes of these phenomena. As the converse of the usual consequential logic of environmental studies, here it is also the case that "imagining" resources, their use, and sustainability is not epiphenomenal, but, as shown in the case of Zamzam, this may alter the "real" horizons of ontology, extraction, and transaction.

A point on which to begin, and on which now to end, is that this is real water, coming from the desert. Across material and symbolic dimensions (as profound meditation, ritual practice, specialized physical science, or as by my own token), questions and answers revolve around the mysteries of water itself: plentiful, like rain from the sky, yet exceedingly rare, and it may disappear. If this environmentality is to be the moral of a story about Zamzam and its waters, then this surely must be part of the power of this charm here. The Qur'an's chapter, Al-Mulk, ends with the final verse that conveys this question, with no answer, with this meaning in English: "Say: 'Don't you see? If your stream were lost some morning [lit. into the earth underground], who could then supply you with clear-flowing water?'" (67:30).

CONTRIBUTORS

Anna Bigelow, Associate Professor, Department of Religious Studies
Stanford University, USA

Anna Bigelow's work focuses on holy places shared by Muslims and non-Muslims in South Asia and the Mediterranean. She is the author of *Sharing the Sacred: Practicing Pluralism in Muslim North India* (2010), a study of a Muslim majority community in Indian Punjab and the shared sacred and civic spaces in that community. Bigelow's current projects include a comparative study of shared sacred sites in India and Turkey and a study of the circulation of material objects at Sufi shrines.

Aomar Boum, Associate Professor, Department of Anthropology
University of California, Los Angeles, USA

A historical anthropologist, Aomar Boum is interested in the place of religious and ethnic minorities such as Jews, Baha'is, Shias, and Christian in post-independence Middle Eastern and North African nation states. He is the author of *Memories of Absence: How Muslims Remember Jews in Morocco* (2013). He is also the co-author of *The Historical Dictionary of Morocco* (with Thomas K. Park), *The Holocaust and North Africa* (with Sarah A. Stein, 2019), and *The Historical Dictionary of the Arab Uprisings* (with Mohamed Daadaoui, 2020).

Joyce Burkhalter Flueckiger, Professor, Department of Religion
Emory University, Atlanta, USA

Joyce Burkhalter Flueckiger specializes in South Asian religions, gender, performance studies, and anthropology of religion. She is the author of *Material Acts in Everyday Hindu Worlds* (2020), *Everyday Hinduism* (2015), *When the World Becomes Female: Guise of a South Indian Goddess* (2013), *In Amma's Healing Room: Gender and Vernacular Islam in South India* (2006), and *Gender and Genre in the Folklore of Middle India* (1996).

Anna M. Gade, Vilas Distinguished Achievement Professor and Associate Dean for Research and Education, Gaylord Nelson Institute for Environmental Studies
University of Wisconsin at Madison, USA

Anna M. Gade teaches courses in the environmental humanities. Her PhD is in the History of Religions, specializing in Islam. She has previously authored two major books on the Qur'an. She has grounded original research in ethnographic field study in the region of island, peninsular, and mainland Southeast Asia for more than twenty-five years. Her most recent single-authored book is *Muslim Environmentalisms: Religious and Social Foundations* (2019).

Christiane Gruber, Professor, History of Art Department
University of Michigan, Ann Arbor, USA

Christiane Gruber's scholarly work explores figural representation, depictions of the Prophet Muhammad, and ascension texts and images in Islamic traditions, about which she has written three books and edited half a dozen volumes. She also pursues research in Islamic book arts, codicology, and paleography as well as modern and contemporary visual and material culture. Her most recent publications include her monograph *The Praiseworthy One: The Prophet Muhammad in Islamic Texts and Images*, and her edited volume *The Image Debate: Figural Representation in Islam and Across the World*, both published in 2019.

Michael Muhammad Knight, Assistant Professor of Religion and Cultural Studies
University of Central Florida, USA

Michael Muhammad Knight is the author of twelve books, including *The Five Percenters: Islam, Hip Hop, and the Gods of New York* (2007), and *Why I am a Five Percenter* (2011). His forthcoming monograph, *Metaphysical Africa,* examines the Ansaru Allah Community, also known as the Nubian Islamic Hebrews.

Ousman Murzik Kobo, Associate Professor, History Department
Ohio State University, USA

Ousman Murzik Kobo earned his PhD in History from the University of Wisconsin-Madison. His research and teaching interests include twentieth-century West African social and religious history; contemporary Islamic history; Islamic mysticism; Islam and European colonialism in Africa; Muslim ecumenical leadership in post-independent West Africa; and the social history of West African migrants in the United States. He has also published widely on topics ranging from Islamic education during the twentieth century, Muslim leadership in post-independent West Africa, and the politics of migration and citizenship in contemporary Africa. His book, *Unveiling Modernity in West African Islamic Reforms, 1950–2000* (2012), documents and compares the histories of contemporary Islamic reforms in Ghana and Burkina Faso in the contexts of Muslims' pursuit and localization of ideas of modernity inherited from colonial rule and postcolonial discourses.

Scott Kugle, Professor, Department of Middle Eastern and South Asian Studies
Emory University, Atlanta, USA

Scott Kugle's fields of expertise include Sufism, Islamic ethics, and issues of gender and sexuality. He is the author of seven books, including *Sufis and Saint's Bodies: Corporeality and Sacred Power in Islam*, and *When Sun Meets Moon: Eros, Ecstasy and Gender in Urdu Poetry*. He conducts research in India and Pakistan, on topics like meditation practices and sacred music, while his research languages are Arabic, Urdu, and Persian.

Roxani Eleni Margariti, Associate Professor, Department of Middle Eastern and South Asian Studies
Emory University, Atlanta, USA

Roxani Eleni Margariti's research interests include the social and economic history of the Middle East and the Indian Ocean, maritime history and material culture, and the reception of Islamic monuments in Greece. She is the author of *Aden and the Indian Ocean Trade: 150 Years in the Life of a Medieval Arabian Port* (2007). Her current book project, *Insular Crossroads: The Dahlak Archipelago, Red Sea Islands, and Indian Ocean History*, examines the biography of a Muslim island polity in medieval and early modern times.

Richard McGregor, Associate Professor of Religion and Islamic Studies
Vanderbilt University, Nashville, USA

Richard McGregor's primary field of research is medieval Egypt and Syria, with a focus on public religious practice, ritual, and Sufism. He is the author of two monographs, co-editor of two collected volumes and one translation. His most recent book, *Islam and the Devotional Object: Seeing Religion in Egypt and Syria* appears with Cambridge University Press, in 2020. His current projects include a new translation of the biography of Muhammad.

D. Fairchild Ruggles, Debra L. Mitchell Chair, Department of Landscape Architecture
University of Illinois, Urbana-Champaign, USA

D. Fairchild Ruggles also holds appointments in Art History, Architecture, Medieval Studies, Spanish and Portuguese, and Gender and Women's Studies. In addition to books on Islamic art, cultural heritage, landscape history and theory, and the arts patronage of women in Islam and South Asia, she has written short films on Islamic art for the NEH Muslim Journeys Bookshelf. Her newest book is *Tree of Pearls* (2020). She currently serves as art and architecture field editor for the *Encyclopaedia of Islam*.

Mark Soileau, Associate Professor in Anthropology
Hacettepe University, Ankara, Turkey

Mark Soileau's research interests focus on the rituals and cultural memory of Sufi groups in Turkey. He is the author of *Humanist Mystics: Nationalism and the Commemoration of Saints in Turkey* (2018).

Kayla Renée Wheeler, Assistant Professor of Critical Ethnic Studies and Black Studies
Xavier University, Cincinnati, USA

Currently, Kayla Renée Wheeler is writing a book on contemporary Black Muslim dress practices in the United States. The book explores how, for Black Muslim women, fashion acts as a site of intra-religious and intra-racial dialogue over what it means to be Black, Muslim, and a woman in the United States. She is the curator of the Black Islam Syllabus, which highlights the histories and contributions of Black Muslims. She is also the author of *Mapping Malcolm's Boston: Exploring the City that Made Malcolm X*, which traces Malcolm X's life in Boston from 1940 to 1953.

NOTES

Introduction

1 Quoted in Chittick (1989: 246).

2 Quotations from the Qur'an in this introduction are from Asad (2008).

3 From Book 1, 612 of the Book of Miscellany (*Kitāb al muqadamāt*) of the *Saḥiḥ Muslim*: "ʿAbdullah bin Masʿūd (May Allah be pleased with him) reported: The Prophet (peace be upon him) said, 'He who has, in his heart, an ant's weight of arrogance will not enter Jannah.' Someone said: 'A man likes to wear beautiful clothes and shoes?' Messenger of Allah (Peace be upon him) said, 'Allah is Beautiful, He loves beauty. Arrogance means ridiculing and rejecting the Truth and despising people.'"

4 The repeated phrasing "Pre-text, Text, and Con-text" in Ahmed's 2016 study *What is Islam?* points out that no phenomenon we might denote as Muslim or Islamic exists outside of its history, moment, and the broader circumstances in which it unfolds. See a full discussion of Ahmed's "Con-text" in Knight, in this volume (Chapter 4: 72).

5 As an inanimate analogue to Foucault's bio-power, thing-power is particularly productive as a concept for material religion as filtered through Deleuze and Guattari's notion of the assemblage (Deleuze and Guattari 1987).

6 I am grateful to Omid Safi for his insights on this point.

Chapter 2

* Unless otherwise noted, all English translations are the author's

1 When he was in Paris, Nasir al-Din Shah also visited the Panthéon, which he describes as a "cemetery for men of eminence" (Nasir al-Din Shah 1874: 252).

2 This carpet attempts to show a dynastic tree with the "Great Men" visual model; other Iranian carpets, however, depict the "tree of nations": see Kurzman (2005).

3 On the use of photography in Qajar painting, see *inter alia* Stein (2013); and Roxburgh (2014, 2017); and on the "Europeanizing" or "Frankish" painterly style (*farangi-saz*) in Persian painting, see most especially Canby (1996); and Diba (1989).

4 I wish to thank Gwendolyn Collaço and Ünver Rüstem for their help identifying French travelogues and Ottoman costume albums containing images similar to the banner-wielding "Young Muhammad." I also extend my gratitude to Joanne Bloom, Photographic Resources Librarian, for providing me with a high-resolution image of the print in the Fine Arts Library at Harvard University.

5 This infamous Lord of Baltimore fled England in order to avoid accusations of abduction and rape, and salacious rumors had it that he kept a personal harem in the Ottoman capital.

6 For a photograph of the "great men" of the first Iranian *majlis*, see Kasravi (2006, last plate (unpaginated)).

7 Buisson was a deist and his dictionary elaborates on secular morality and non-dogmatic spirituality: see Gillig (2014: 121, 126).

8 On the Bidari lodge, see Vaziri (1991); and Sabatiennes (1977: 440), in which the author describes the lodge as a "school for parliamentary democracy" in Iran.

Chapter 3

* Unless otherwise noted, all translations are by the author

1 My thanks to Christiane Gruber, Jonathan Parkes Allen, and Torsten Wollina for help at various points during the writing of this chapter.

2 For easy comparison see www.al-tafsir.com.

Chapter 4

1 I frame this discussion in terms of "Nation of Islam tradition" rather than "the Nation of Islam," to describe the diversity of communities and thinkers who draw from the Nation's texts, practices, and history, rather than center a single organization. The Nation of Islam tradition includes not one but multiple communities referring to themselves as the "Nation of Islam," as well as the "post-Nation" community led by Warith Deen Mohammed, and the Five Percenters, who draw from *The Supreme Wisdom Lessons* but are not (usually) affiliated with the Nation or self-identifying as Muslims.

2 Referring to the excerpt as 10:14 draws from the citational practices of the Five Percenters. The "10" means that this excerpt appears as the tenth item ("degree") in the lesson. The "14" identifies the excerpt as coming from the *Lost Found Muslim Lesson No.1*, which Five Percenters refer to as the "1–14" or "1 to 14." *The Supreme Wisdom Lessons* are not "officially" published, and Nation Muslims and Five Percenters generally oppose their public dissemination. Numerous independent websites and self-publishers, however, have made the *Lessons* accessible. The *Lessons* were also reproduced in the FBI files on figures such as Elijah Muhammad and Master Fard Muhammad, aka W.D. Fard. Wallace D. Fard, FBI file (25-206067), Chicago, 2/21/1957.

3 See also *Shabazz v. Lokey*, et al. (2018) which was filed by a Nation of Islam member incarcerated at the same prison whose copies of the *Lessons* were confiscated. Virginia DOCS regarded the *Lessons* as the "foundational text for the Nation of Gods and Earths" and claimed that the *Lessons* "advocate violence" while failing to recognize that the same texts were foundational for the Nation of Islam, which Virginia DOCS recognized as a legally protected religious community.

4 To summarize: the majority of Five Percenters today, particularly those who also use the name "Nation of Gods and Earths" for their community, reject the

suggestion that Five Percenters are Muslims or make claims upon Islam "as a religion" (though Islam receives an alternative meaning in Five Percenter discourses as a "way of life"). However, there have also been Five Percenters who identified as Muslims, including the elder First Born Prince Allah (d. 2001) and a group known as the "Allah Team" that advocated a view of Five Percenters as an extension of the Nation of Islam rather than a separate and entirely self-defined community. Five Percenter literature also makes occasional claims upon larger Islamic tradition, citing figures such as Ibn al-'Arabi, al-Hallaj, Bullhe Shah, and the Isma'ili caliph al-Hakim as evidence of "classical Islam" offering portals into theomorphic humanity. While it would be generally inaccurate to think of Five Percenters as self-identifying Muslims, the borders remain perforated.

Chapter 5

* Unless otherwise noted, all translations are by the author.

1 Even in decentralized societies such as the Igbo, bead necklaces represent power, wealth and social influences. Here too, the colors and the material from which the beads were made help to identify social position within society.

2 Although the correct Arabic word for the Muslim prayer beads is *misbah*, the word *tasbih* and *tasbah* have remained dominant in West Africa.

3 There are some notable variations in which the three elements are recited together for a total of thirty-three times, but the standard in West Africa is to recite them individually as explained above. An often-cited hadith involves the narration of Abu Huraira, who reported that the Prophet instructed them to recite "Subhan-al-lah", "Alhamdu lillah", and "Allahu Akbar" together thirty-three times. See Al Tirmidhi, Book 43, Hadith 44 (https://sunnah.com/tirmidhi/48/44) (accessed December 12, 2020).

4 Sufism, Islam's esoteric tradition, is widespread throughout Shi'i and Sunni Islam. Sufis engage in extra spiritual exercises and discipline, in search of inner understanding of the Divine. Each Sufi order, also described as Sufi "paths" (*tariqa*), has its own unique liturgies and hierarchies. In addition to *dhikr* in search of spiritual illumination, they also venerate their spiritual leaders and the Prophet Muhammad. In its popular expressions, Sufi followers expect their spiritual indulgences and the love of God, the Prophet Muhammad and their own Shaykhs, living or deceased, to yield mystical blessings (*baraka*) and to distinguish them spiritually from ordinary Muslims.

5 The term Salafiyya refers to the doctrine in Islam that claims to practice Islam as it existed at the time of Muhammad and the *Salaf*, the early generation of his followers. They insist on returning Islam to its "pristine" form because, from their perspective, Islam has strayed from its original path and has acquired unacceptable innovations and accretions in the process.

6 In his *Majmu'a al-Fataawa*, Ibn Taymiyya offers a ruling on *tasbih* that seems to have shaped Salafi discourse regarding its permissibility. Although in general, Salafis tend to dismiss the use of *tasbih* as an impermissible innovation (*bid'a*), a careful reading of Ibn Taymiyya's ruling on the subject suggests that he based his arguments on the user's *niyaat* (intention). Recognizing that some individuals used dates and stones to count their *dhikr*

during the time of the Prophet Muhammad, and he did not categorically prohibit the practice, Ibn Taymiyya condemned those who use it ostentatiously to show off piety, while recognizing its value to those who employ it as an assistive instrument with good intention. See https://central-mosque.com/index.php/Practises/is-using-masbahah-prayer-beadsdhikr-beads-bidah.html (accessed November 1, 2019), citing Ibn Taymiyyah, 1991, vol 22: 506.

7 For the history of the Tijaniyya *tariqa*, see among others, Wright (2015), Robinson and Triaud (2000), Ryan (2000), Abu-Nasr (1965), and Adnani (2007).

8 For West African pilgrims during the precolonial period, see Van Duc (1995).

9 According to Rudiger Seessman (Seessman 1998), Shaykh Salma originated from what became French Sudan, now Mali. He began his career as an anti-colonial preacher, and therefore migrated from every territory that came under colonial rule.

10 I reformulated the narrative into a poetic style based on their pauses in the narrative. Interview with El Hadji Adam Zeigha Ouedraogo and his brother El Hadji Saidou Ouédraogo at Rahmatoulaye, May 2, 2002. Also interview with Sawadogo Salifou at Ouagadougou, February 24, 2002.

11 Saydou Nourou Tall was the grandson of Shaykh Umar Tall, the erstwhile enemy of the French, whose death in 1864 was blamed on French support of Umar Tall's adversaries.

12 The colonial records mentioned that he instructed the youth not to obey their parents who had not embraced Islam and forbade them from attending their funerals.

13 The history of the Yakouby branch of the Hamwiyya, as Sean Hanretta has analyzed eloquently, provides further evidence in support of the argument that the association of Hamwiyya with violence was only true in the fantasies of a few French colonial administrators; there is no sufficient evidence even in the colonial archives to support that allegation.

Chapter 6

* Unless otherwise noted, all translations are by the author

1 In her earlier work, Emma Tarlo assumes that clothing which makes Muslims identifiable refers implicitly to women's clothing. Later publications perpetuate this assumption, as in Lewis 2015.

2 Sultan Muhammad II (ruled from 1378 to 1397) of the Bahmani Dynasty invited Hafiz to move from his home in Shiraz to the Deccan (to Bidar near present-day Hyderabad); see Eaton 2008: 61; and Browne 2000: 285-9.

3 Amir Khurd (Sayyid Muhammad Mubarak Kirmani) died in 1369, and his book is the earliest collection of biographies of Chishti Sufis.

4 In Arabic, this proverb is *tark ul-dunya ra's kulli 'ibada*.

5 The article, Bashir 2014, follows the impulses of his book, *Sufi Bodies* 2013, which paid more attention to clothing symbolism than did my book, *Sufis and Saints' Bodies* 2007.

6 This is how the author's own Chishti teacher explained the symbolism of a four-cornered cap: *tark-e dunya, tark-e akhira, tark-e ʿuqba*, and *tark-e tark*.

7 Ruzbihan reportedly grabbed the hem of the robe of the beautiful youth and said, "In whatever form you come and in whatever form you display yourself to the loving eye, I will still recognize you behind it!" A similar story is attributed to Bayazid Bistami, who reportedly saw God in the form of a handsome youth.

8 In the discourses of Nizam al-Din Awliya, a saint or *wali* has two dimensions of power: *wilayat* or intimacy, which is the special love between him and God that comes from renouncing the world and everything other than God; and *walayat* or authority, which is the relationship he has with other people in worldly interactions.

9 The editor of Saʿdi's collected poems, Muhammad ʿAli Faroghi, records this ghazal taken from Amir ʿAli Khan Sudi's *tazkira* entitled "Mirʾat al-Khayal" where it is ascribed to Saʿdi; it begins, *bi-rubud dilam dar chamani sarv-ravani*.

10 Translated here are couplets 1-5 and the final couplet from the ghazal; it begins *an sarv-e naz been keh che khush mi-ravad bi-rah*.

11 This ghazal by Bahadur Shah Zafar begins *Buti sar kashi kafiri kaj-kulahi*.

12 Those whose colors tend toward yellow, gold, or orange likely belong to the Nizami branch of the Chishti Order, while those whose colors tend toward ochre, maroon, or brown likely belong to the Sabiri branch: see Ernst and Lawrence 2002.

Chapter 7

* Unless otherwise noted, all translations are by the author

1 From the poem beginning *Dün gece seyrim içinde / Ben dedem Ali'yi gördüm* (Gölpınarlı 1963: 114).

2 These concepts are mentioned in the first chapter of a work called *Makâlât* (see *Makâlât* 2009), though they are not therein referred to as doors, and they have subsequently been greatly elaborated.

3 *The Travels of Ibn Battuta* (1962: 420-1). The traveler reports the name of the lamp in Arabic as *bisus*, which would be the Persian *pihsuz*: "fat-burner." See also Melikian-Chirvani 1985.

4 This poem, beginning "*Gönüller ruşen olur / Gaziler Dergahı'nda . . .*", is included in the privately distributed songbook used by the Gaziler Bektashi community in Ankara.

5 From the poem beginning "*Derdim çoktur kangısına yanayım . . .*" (Gölpınarlı 1963: 188-9).

6 For an account of the Bektashi *sofra* meal that follows *aynü'l-cem* rituals, see Soileau 2012.

7 There is variation among different Bektashi communities in details of the *aynü'l-cem* and the words spoken during it. The description given here is a composite based on several Ottoman-era manuscript manuals, some of which have been published in recent years, such as *Bektaşî Erkânnâmesi* (*Bektaşî*

Erkânnâmesi 2006), and in Noyan 2010. Also consulted was a privately distributed ritual manual followed by contemporary urban Bektashis in Turkey.

Chapter 8

1 I was in Hyderabad, at Osmania University, to conduct a workshop on folklore fieldwork methodologies, for which we planned to conduct research with Muslim women. I knew that under a green flag was a Muslim ritual site and, to meet our Muslim neighbors, I walked across the street from our guesthouse to the home above which this flag was flying. I returned to conduct long-term fieldwork with Amma for two months between 1990 and 1991 and again for nine months between 1994 and 1995. That research culminated in my book *In Amma's Healing Room: Gender and Vernacular Islam in South India* (2006). I have returned to Hyderabad for shorter visits almost every year since 1995, during which time I spend time with Amma's family. It is on these visits that I observed and spoke with Amma's daughter-in-law, Lateefa, and Amma's grandson, Akber, about their healing practice.

2 Specifically, Amma used the word *shaytani* (lit., of the devil), but the word is used to refer to, more generically, negative forces.

3 See, for example, "Is Taweez (AMULET) Allowed in Islam?" (2008) and "Wearing Amulets" (n.d.).

4 Jane Bennett observes "an actant [agent] never really acts alone. Its efficacy or agency always depends on the collaboration, cooperation, or interactive interference of many bodies and forces" (Bennett 2010: 21).

5 While Amma sat at her healing table up to ten hours a day, Akber works full-time at a local college and only sits at the healing table on weekends and during some evening hours.

6 Geert Mommersteeg observes it is writing that distinguishes Islamic amulets from West African indigenous ones (Mommersteeg 1990: 66).

7 Abba told me that he had been part of the British Army and thus had learned "roman [script] only," and had not had the opportunity to learn Arabic script. Amma was educated through sixth grade in Urdu, thus knows the script.

8 I thank Scott Kugle for identifying the source of these seeds to be the maulsari tree.

9 This ritual has its own materiality—the cloth spread and seeds—but these are secondary to the orally recited words of God.

10 This redistribution of words (the names of Allah, the *kalima*, etc.) can also be found in decorative Islamic calligraphy.

11 As she aged, I noticed Amma no longer asked for patients' mothers' names, but used Hava (Eve) as the mother's name for everyone. She explained that, yes, as her eyesight was weakening, it was easier (required less individualized calculation) to simply use the name of the mother of all humans: Hava.

12 For example, to a patient who came in with the complaint of headaches and received the diagnosis of zero, Amma declared, "There's nothing wrong. You

just need glasses!" She proceeded to give him the name of a local optometrist, but also wrote a general protective *taviz*.

13 My mother's name is Ramoth (a place name in the Hebrew Bible), which Amma heard and wrote in Urdu as Rehmat (blessing).

14 See Zadeh (2009) for discussion of these questions of purity and pollution around handling or wearing of amulets containing words of the Qur'an in early Islamic jurisprudence.

Chapter 10

1 The densest documentation and scholarly output of the literature on Islamic numismatics and monetary histories relates to Egypt; for model synthetic works that expertly and lucidly describe the role of money in medieval Islamicate economies and societies and provides key references, see Schultz 2010; 1998.

2 Marshall Hodgson famously coined the term "Islamicate" to describe the cultural production of Muslim-led societies as opposed to the purely religious phenomena emanating from core "Islamic" beliefs (Hodgson 1974, vol. 1: 58–60). In an influential statement about the analytical category of Islam and religion in general, Shahab Ahmed took issue with Hodgson's distinction, and pointed to major interstices of culture where the distinction breaks down. A coin with a representation of the Mughal emperor holding a wine cup is one of the objects Ahmed highlighted to make his case, so emblematic of the issue that it also features on the book's dust cover (Ahmed 2016: 71–2).

3 The quoted text draws from comments made by David Morgan on material religion in response to the workshop that brought this volume into being.

4 A related point is made by Ahmed 2016: 50–1, n.129.

5 I draw the notion of "axes of belonging" from Alka Patel's study of architecture across denominational lines in medieval Gujarat (Patel 2004: 19–20). For some of these ideas about different sets of medieval Islamic coins circulating with merchants of different faiths in the Western Indian Ocean, see Margariti 2014: 201–3.

6 See Nützel and Kinzelbach [1891] 1987: 50, 52, 60, 64. This work, originally published in 1891 and translated into English a century later, remains a standard reference for Rasulid coinage. The list here does not pretend to be exhaustive. The "fish dirhams" await a future comprehensive study. See also Album 1998: 58.

7 On the identification of the obverse and reverse, heads or tails, of the coin in numismatics in general, and in Islamic numismatics in particular—where for technical reasons there is no strong consensus for identifying obverse and reverse—see Album 1998: 11; and Bacharach 2006: 11–3; cf. Balog 1964.

8 This point is made by Album 1998: 11, (note 17). The Arabic prooftext is supplied by Nützel [1891] 1987: 30–1.

9 For deployment of the title sultan along with the reference to the caliph, see Balog 1964.

10 The engraving of the molds was a job for specialized craftsmen, the *naqqāshūn al-sikka*.

11 On mining activity, famous mines, and reopening of old mines in Yemen, see Dunlop 1957: 42; Peli and Tereygeol 2007: 187–200; and Vallet 2010: 344–5. D'Ottone 2020: 227, n.72 discusses the melting down of old "demonetized" coins.

12 Jurists were aware of, and sensitive to, the various roles played by coins of all three metals in the marketplace, and some accommodation took place; on this see also, Schultz 2003: 170–1.

13 For an analysis of Maqrizi's money talk, that connects Maqrizi's ideas to the Shafi'i legal school's conservative approach to economic partnerships, see Schultz 2003.

14 It has been assumed, though not entirely securely, that this episode really refers to the introduction of the pictorial dirhams of which the fish dirhams are a set. For the latest take on the question of al-Mujahid's reform and the coins resulting from it, see D'Ottone 2020: 218–24.

15 Of the 1200 dirhams, 217 are identified as Rasulid, a proportion that has important implications for the balance of trade between Egypt, Arabia, and the western Indian coast.

16 On overlapping zones of coin circulation in earlier periods, see Flood 2009: 38–40; Margariti 2014: 203–13.

17 For an account of Hamdani's contribution to our understanding of gold and silver sources and an English translation of the main passages, see Dunlop 1957: 29–49.

18 For an early presentation of this scheme, attributed to the masters of chemistry (*arbāb al-kimiyā*) by the tenth-century polymath Al-Khwarizmi (d. ca. 387/997), see his *Mafātīḥ al-'ulūm* (Al-Khwarizmi 1895: 256–258).

19 Arianna D'Ottone makes the important related point that Rasulid coinage was open to influences from a variety of sources (D'Ottone 2015: 93–94; 2020: 224).

20 An example of the representation of the zodiacal constellation of Pisces, featuring the two swimming fish motif, occurs in a fifteenth-century Iranian manuscript of the celebrated tenth-century scholar of astronomy 'Abd al-Raḥmān al-Ṣūfī; see Carboni 1997: 38–9.

21 The most systematic and impressive zodiacal program appears on the coins of the Mughal emperor Jahangir, the first coin in the series displaying Pisces through a swimming fish design not unlike our much earlier Rasulid Adeni examples (Carboni 1997: 26–7).

22 This point is also made on the label of one of the Adeni fish dirhams by the curators of the online collection of the David Museum of Copenhagen.

23 Radcliffe is clearly referring to Qur'an 5:96: It is permitted for you to catch and eat seafood—an enjoyment for you and the traveller—but hunting game is forbidden while you are in the state of consecration [for pilgrimage]. Be mindful of God to whom you will be gathered.' (Abdel Haleem 2004:77)

24 By "thalassophobic" I mean existentially fearful of, and unsuited for, engaging with the ocean. For a genealogy of the notion that Islam is "a child of the desert," inimical to maritimity, see Wick 2016: 59.

25 As conveyed by the renowned fourteenth-century traveler Ibn Battuta, the "Litany of the Sea" (*ḥizb al-baḥr*), a ritual prayer attributed to Abu'l-Ḥasan al-Shadhili, the founder of the homonymous Sufi order, reflects these themes as well as the Qur'anic tropes; see Ibn Battuta 1958 vol. 1: 24–7. For an example of a maritime miracle by a saintly figure residing in late medieval Aden, see Margariti 2007: 142. Maritime miracles and the city of Bombay form the subject of Nile Green's analysis of the religious economy of the city of Bombay (Green 2011).

Chapter 11

1 Since 2008, the Carmen del Ajibe del Rey houses the Fundación Agua Granada, which has an informative exhibition about the historical development of the water resources of Granada's Albaicín. See www.fundaciónaguagranada.es (accessed December 7, 2020).

2 On the subject of how the categories of religion and secularism have been applied to Islam, see Ahmed 2015; and Shaw 2019.

3 The Almoravids ruled from the Qasabat Gharnata, but they were opposed by a group under the direction of Abu Jafar Ahmad III, al-Mustanṣir ibn Hud Sayf al-Dawla (d. 540/1146) who occupied the Sabika Hill.

4 Antonio Orihuela Uzal and Luis García Pulido suggest that in Granada's early phase (eighth through tenth centuries), there was a walled defensible settlement (although it is not known where) and that water was lifted up from the Darro River (Orihuela Uzal and García Pulido 2008: 144–9). There is an extensive body of scholarship, almost entirely Spanish, on the subject of the growth of Granada in the Islamic period and its water supply network, beginning with the Acequia de Aynadamar. The contribution of the present paper is to show how water illuminates elements of society that would otherwise remain invisible.

5 http://www.aemet.es/es/serviciosclimaticos/datosclimatologicos/valoresclimatologicos?l=5514&k=and (accessed 17 February 2020). For comparison: Chicago gets 100 mm precipitation in a typical summer month, dropping to a monthly average of 60 mm in the winter.

6 Ambrosio de Vico's hand-drawn plan of Granada is the first plan to survive for the city. It was engraved on copper plate, with alterations, by Francisco Heylan in 1613; and reengraved in 1795 by Felix Prieto.

7 The analysis of the building material made by Navarro Palazón and Jiménez Castillo suggests the twelfth century (Navarro Palazón and Jiménez Castillo 2012: 13). But the column capitals are spolia from the Umayyad palaces in Cordoba destroyed in the civil war of 1010, which might suggest an earlier date.

8 While there are no Arabic sources that explain the distribution policy, numerous documents in the sixteenth century, following the conquest, spell out these allocations (Garrido Atienza [1902] 2002).

9 Probably more: the number is difficult to estimate since there is not an exact correlation between the location of the former mosques and the post-1492 churches.

Chapter 12

1 The verse, 2:255, begins: "God: there is no deity except for He, the Ever-Living, the Self-Subsisting. Neither slumber overtakes Him, nor sleep. His is all that is in the heavens and all that is on earth." The full verse appears frequently in Muslim visual arts, appreciated for its message of ever-vigilant divine power and protection.

2 This is the same item, from a different seller on Amazon.com: https://www.amazon.com/MuslimJewelry-Sterling-Silver-Ayatul-kursi-Pendant/dp/B00VZ8VI70 (accessed August 16, 2020).

3 "Environmentality" is a term used by Arun Agrawal in his book on political ecology in India (Agrawal 2005). The term is meant here in a somewhat different regard, which is to be "environmental" in the sense of what is considered to be the subject matter of the interdisciplinary approaches of environmental studies today, including the environmental humanities.

4 There is jurisprudential controversy over variant readings of the stipulation to "wash" or "wipe" the feet in this verse, as would be applied in the practice of ritual ablutions.

5 The word *bi'ah* is the modern term for "environment" in Arabic; however, it is not used in classical sources, nor does it feature in the Qur'an.

6 The Christianized sense of the hierophany is rejected in both religious studies and Islam on similar doctrinal grounds, the shared objection being be that it is too particularly incarnationalist (Christological or *hululi*) in a theological sense. Nevertheless, the process exemplifies the ontological "scale" that environmental humanities now seeks earnestly to develop and apply.

7 However, some jurists do say that it should not be used for *wudu'*, and this holds even if the Prophet had in fact used it for this purpose. All citations from the *Sunan* of Ibn Majah in this essay are found in https://sunnah.com/ibnmajah (accessed December 12, 2020).

8 Inspired by Stanley Tambiah on Theravada images and relics in Thailand (Tambiah 1984), art historian David Freedberg's writings on image in medieval European Christianity had combined with work like that of Church historian Peter Brown on relics long before that, as well as other studies of historical Christianities, such as by Caroline Walker Bynum and David Morgan, into what had coalesced by the 1990s as the new sub-field, "material religion." Every one of these studies points to processes of reproduction of objects and the scalar proliferation of their power, presence, or aura (Freedberg 1989; Brown 1982; Bynum 1988; Morgan 1997).

BIBLIOGRAPHY

Introduction

Ahmed, S. (2016), *What is Islam? The Importance of Being Islamic*, Princeton, NJ: Princeton University Press.

Asad, M. (2008), *The Message of the Qur'an*, London: The Book Foundation.

Asad, T. (2006), "Responses," in D. Scott and C. Hirschkind (eds.), *Powers of the Secular Modern: Talal Asad and His Interlocutors*, Stanford, CA: Stanford University Press, **pp missing.**

Bennett, J. (2010), *Vibrant Matter: A Political Ecology of Things*, Durham, NC: Duke University Press.

Bigelow, A. (2010), *Sharing the Sacred: Practicing Pluralism in Muslim North India*, New York: Oxford University Press.

Bigelow, A. (2012), "Everybody's Baba: Making Space for the Other," in G. Bowman (ed.), *Sharing the Sacra: The Politics and Pragmatics of Inter-communal Relations around Holy Places*, New York: Berghahn Books, 25–43.

Bigelow, A. (2019), "Lived Secularism: Studies in India and Turkey," *Journal of the American Academy of Religion*, 87 (3): 725–764.

Can, S. (2005), *Fundamentals of Rumi's Thought: A Mevlevi Sufi Perspective*, trans. Zeki Saritoprak, Somerset, NJ: The Light Inc.

Chittick, W. (1989), *The Sufi Path of Knowledge: Ibn al 'Arabi's Metaphysics of Imagination*, Albany, NY: State University of New York Press.

Chittick, W. (2005), *Ibn 'Arabi*, Oxford: OneWorld.

Deleuze, G. and F. Guattari (1987), *A Thousand Plateaus: Capitalism and Schizophrenia*, St. Paul, MN: University of Minnesota Press.

Elias, J. (2012), *Aisha's Cushion: Religious Art, Perception, and Practice in Islam*, Cambridge, MA: Harvard University Press.

Ernst, C. (2003), *Following Muhammad: Rethinking Islam in the Contemporary World*, Chapel Hill, NC: University of North Carolina Press.

Flood, F. B. (2006), "Image against Nature: Spolia as Apotropaia in Byzantium and the dar al-Islam," *Medieval History Journal* 9 (1): 143–166.

Flood, F. B. (2019), *Technologies de devotion dans les arts de l'Islam: Pèlerins, reliques, copies*, Paris: Hazan.

Gade, A. (2019), *Muslim Environmentalism: Religious and Social Foundations*, New York: Columbia University Press.

Green, N. (2006), "Ostrich Eggs and Peacock Feathers: Sacred Objects as Cultural Exchange between Christianity and Islam," *Al-Masaq: Journal of the Medieval Mediterranean* 18 (1): 27–78.

Gruber, C. (2019), *The Praiseworthy One: The Prophet Muhammad in Islamic Texts and Images*, Bloomington, IN: Indiana University Press.

Gruber, C. and S. Haugbolle (2013), eds. *Visual Culture in the Modern Middle East*, Bloomington, IN: Indiana University Press.

Halevi, L. (2016), "The Extricability of Things from Religion: A Salafi Perspective on Prayer Machines," *Material Religion* 12 (1): 106–7.

Halevi, L. (2019), *Modern Things on Trial: Islam's Global and Material Reformation in the Age of Rida, 1865–1935*, New York: Columbia University Press.

Henare, A., M. Holbraad, and S. Wastell (2006), eds. *Thinking through Things: Theorising Artefacts Ethnographically*, London: Routledge.

Hirschkind, C. (2006), *The Ethical Soundscape: Cassette Sermons and Islamic Counterpublics*, New York: Columbia University Press.

Houtman, D. and B. Meyer (2012), eds. *Things: Religion and the Question of Materiality*, New York: Fordham University Press.

Kasmani, O. and S. Maneval (2016), eds. *Muslim Matter: Photographs, Objects, Essays*, Berlin: Verlag.

McDannell, C. (1995), *Material Christianity*, New Haven, CT: Yale University Press.

Meyer, B. and T. Stordalen (2019), eds. *Figurations and Sensations of the Unseen in Judaism, Christianity, and Islam: Contested Desires*, London: Bloomsbury.

Mitchell, T. (2005), *What Do Pictures Want?: The Lives and Loves of Images*, Chicago: University of Chicago Press.

Morgan, D. (2010), "Materiality, Social Analysis, and the Study of Religions," in D. Morgan (ed), *Religion and Material Culture: The Matter of Belief*, London: Routledge, **pp missing.**

Muslim, A. (n.d.) *Sahih Muslim*, available online: https://sunnah.com/riyadussaliheen/1/612 (accessed March 30, 2020).

Ogunnaike, O. (2017), "The Silent Theology of Islamic Art," *Renovatio: The Journal of Zaytuna Islamic College*, December 5, 2017. Available online: https://renovatio.zaytuna.edu/article/the-silent-theology-of-islamic-art (accessed December 12, 2019).

Pinney, C. (2004), *Photos of the Gods: The Printed Image and Political Struggle in India*, London: Reaktion Books.

Promey, S. (2014), *Sensational Religion*, New Haven, CT: Yale University Press.

Chapter 1

Amatullah-Rahman, A.A. (1999), *She Stood by his Side and at Times in his Stead: The Life and Legacy of Sister Clara Muhammad, First Lady of the Nation of Islam*, Ph.D. diss., Clark Atlanta University, Atlanta, Georgia.

Bush, R. (2002), "Ethel Muhammad Sharrieff, 80," *Chicago Tribune*, December 13, available online: https://www.chicagotribune.com/news/ct-xpm-2002-12-13-0212130102-story.html (accessed February 17, 2020).

Chan-Malik, S. (2018), *Being Muslim: A Cultural History of Women of Color in American Islam*, New York: New York University Press.

Collins, P.H., (1990), *Black Feminist Thought: Knowledge, Consciousness and the Politics of Empowerment*, Abingdon, UK: Routledge.

Farrakhan, L. (1993), *A Torchlight for America*, Chicago: F.C.N. Publishing Company.

Gibson, D-M. (2012), *A History of the Nation of Islam: Race, Islam, and the Quest for Freedom*, Santa Barbara, California: Praeger.

Gibson, D-M. and J. Karim (2014), *Women of the Nation: Between Black Protest and Sunni Islam*, New York: New York University Press.

Hakim, H. and S. Muhammad (2003), "Ethel Sharieff, Daughter of Hon. Elijah Muhammad," *The Final Call*, January 1, available online: http://www.finalcall.com/artman/publish/National_News_2/Ethel_Sharieff_daughter_of_Hon_Elijah_Muhammad_325.shtml (accessed February 17, 2020).

Hassain, M. (n.d.) "The Woman in Islam," *Muhammad Speaks*, available online: http://noiwc.org/images/womaninislam1.pdf (accessed October 10, 2019).

Hassain, M. (1969a), "Woman in Islam," *Muhammad Speaks*, May 23: 30.

Hassain, M. (1969b), "Woman in Islam," *Muhammad Speaks*, August 1: 22.

Higginbotham, E.B. (1994), *Righteous Discontent: The Women's Movement in the Black Baptist Church, 1880–1920*, Cambridge, MA: Harvard University Press.

Jerome, R.M. (1989), ed. *Back Where We Belong: Selected Speeches by Minister Louis Farrakhan*, Philadelphia: PC International Press.

Karim, J. (2006), "Through Sunni Women's Eyes: Black Feminism and the Nation of Islam," *Souls: A Critical Journal of Black Politics, Culture, and Society* 8 (4): 19–30.

Mahmood, S. (2005), *Politics of Piety: The Islamic Revival and the Feminist Subject*, Princeton: Princeton University Press, 2005.

"Possessions of a Civilized Woman," (2013), in C. Shabazz (ed.), *Muslim Girl's Training*, self-published.

Mitchell, K.E., A. Martin-Hamon, and E. Anderson (2002), "A Choice of Weapons: Photographs of Gordon Parks," *Art Education* 55 (3): 25–31.

Muhammad, E. (1965), *Message to the Blackman in America*, Chicago: Muhammad Mosque of Islam No. 2.

Muhammad, Imam W.D. (1979), "The Meaning of Leadership: Part 2," *Bilalian News*, December 28, available online: http://www.newafricaradio.com/articles/12-28-79.html (accessed February 17, 2020).

Patsides, N. (2007), "Allies, Constituents or Myopic Investors: Marcus Garvey and Black Americans," *Journal of American Studies* 41 (2): 279–305.

Plate, S.B. (2015), "Introduction to Material Religions," in S. Brent Plate (ed.), *Key Terms in the Material Religion*, London and New York: Bloomsbury, pp. 1–8.

Sahib, H.A. (1951), *The Nation of Islam*, M.A. diss., University of Chicago, Chicago.

Taylor, U.Y. (1998), "As-salaam alaikum, My Sister, Peace Be Unto You: The Honorable Elijah Muhammad and the Women Who Followed Him," *Race and Society* 1 (2): 177–96.

Taylor, U.Y. (2017), *The Promise of Patriarchy: Women and the Nation of Islam*, Chapel Hill, NC: University of North Carolina Press.

Weisenfeld, J. (2017), *A New World-A Coming: Black Religion and Racial Identity During the Great Migration*, New York: New York University Press.

Chapter 2

Adib al-Mamalik ([1312] 1933), *Divan-i kamil*, ed. Vahid Dastgirdi, Tehran: Armighan.

Ahani, L., A. Yaghoubzadeh, and A. Vandshoari (2017), "A Presentation and Classification of Pictorial Carpets of Qajar Era," *Journal of History, Culture, and Art Research* 6 (2): 123–37.

Algar, H. (1970), "An Introduction to the History of Freemasonry in Iran," *Middle Eastern Studies* 6 (3): 276–96.

Bailey, J. (1982), "Of Monuments and Men: More Persian Pictorial Rugs," *Rug News* 4 (6): 12–15.

Bauman, Z. (2000), *Liquid Modernity*, Cambridge: Polity Press.

Bayat, M. (2010), "The Rowshanfekr in the Constitutional Period: An Overview," in H. Chehabi and V. Martin (eds.), *Iran's Constitutional Revolution: Popular Politics, Cultural Transformations, and Transnational Connections*, London: I.B. Tauris, 165–91.

Beck, G. (2000), "Celestial Lodge Above: The Temple of Solomon in Jerusalem as a Religious Symbol in Freemasonry," *Nova Religio: The Journal of Alternative and Emergent Religions* 4 (1): 28–51.

Bonnet, J.-C. (1998), *Naissance du Panthéon. Essai sur le culte des grands hommes*, Paris: Fayard.

Canby, S. (1996), "*Farangi Saz*: The Impact of Europe on Safavid Painting," in J. Tilden (ed.), *Silk and Stone: Arts of Asia*, London: HALI, 46–59.

Castellan, A.L. (1812), *Moeurs, usages, costumes des Othomans, et abrégé de leur histoire*, Paris: Nepveu.

Centlivres, P. and M. Centlivres-Demont (2005), "Une étrange rencontre: La photographie orientaliste de Lehnert et Landrock et l'image iranienne du Prophète Mahomet," *Etudes Photographiques* 17: 5–15.

Chelkowski, P. (1989), "Narrative Painting and Painting Recitation in Qajar Iran," *Muqarnas* 6: 98–111.

Cochrane, H. (1934), *The Shriner's Book: Following the Fez*, self-published by the author.

Dadgar, L. (2001a), *Farsh-i Iran: Majmu'a-i az Muza-yi Farsh-i Iran*, Tehran: The Carpet Museum of Iran.

Dadgar, L. (2001b), *The Indigenous Elegance of Persian Carpet: A Collection from the Carpet Museum of Iran*, Tehran: The Carpet Museum of Iran.

de Lamartine, A. (1865), *Les grands hommes de l'Orient*, Paris: A. Lacroix.

Diba, L. (1989), "Persian Painting in the Eighteenth Century: Tradition and Transmission," *Muqarnas* 6: 147–60.

Ekhtiar, M. (1994), *The Dar al-Funun: Educational Reform and Cultural Development in Qajar Iran*, Ph.D. diss., New York University, New York.

Elmarsafy, Z. (2001), "Submission, Seduction, and State Propaganda in Favart's Soliman II, ou Les trois sultanes," *French Forum* 26 (3): 13–26.

Gaonkar, D. P. (2001), *Alternative Modernities*, Durham, NC: Duke University Press.

Gillig, J.-M. (2014), *Histoire de l'école laïque en France*, Paris: L'Harmattan.

Grabar, O. and M. Natif (2003), "The Story of the Portraits of the Prophet Muhammad," *Studia Islamica* 96: 19–37.

Gruber, C. (2016), "Prophetic Products: Muhammad in Contemporary Iranian Visual Culture," *Material Religion* 12 (3): 259–93.

Gruber, C. (2019), *The Praiseworthy One: The Prophet Muhammad in Islamic Texts and Images*, Bloomington: Indiana University Press.

Gustafson, J. (n.d.), "Kerman xv. Carpet Industry," *Encyclopaedia Iranica*, XVI/3: 296–301, available online: http://www.iranicaonline.org/articles/kerman-15-carpet-industry (accessed December 14, 2020).

Helfgott, L. (1993), *Ties That Bind: A Social History of the Iranian Carpet*, Washington and London: Smithsonian Institution.

Ittig, A. (1985), "The Kirmani Book: A Study in Carpet Entrepreneurship," *Oriental Carpet and Textile Studies* 1: 111–23.

Kasravi, A. (2006), *History of the Iranian Constitution*, Costa Mesa, CA: Mazda Publishers.

Khosronejad, P. (2018), *Qajar Shiite Material Culture, Visual Studies of Modern Iran*, vol. 2, Stillwater: Oklahoma State University.

Khosronejad, P. (forthcoming), "Photographing Shiism in Qajar-Era Iran: Visual Devotion, Virtual Pilgrimage, and the Sacred Gaze," in C. Funke (ed.), *Beyond Karbala: New Approaches to Shiite Materiality*, Leiden: Brill.

Klausen, J. (2009). *The Cartoons That Shook the World*, New Haven: Yale University Press.

Kurzman, C. (2005), "Weaving Iran into the Tree of Nations," *International Journal of Middle East Studies* 37: 137–66.

Lambton, A. (1987), "Secret Societies and the Persian Revolution of 1905–6," in A. Lambton (ed.), *Qajar Persia: Eleven Studies*, London: I.B. Tauris, 301–29.

Minois, G. (2005). *Le culte des grands hommes. Des héros homériques au star system*, Paris: Audibert.

Nasir al-Din Shah (1874), *The Diary of H.M. the Shah of Persia During his Tour through Europe in A.D. 1873*, trans. James Redhouse, London: James Murray.

Onverwachte ontmoetingen. Verborgen verhalen uit eigen collective / Encounters: Hidden Stories from the Tropenmuseum's Collection (2012), Amsterdam: KIT.

Puin, E. (2008), *Islamische Plakate: Kalligraphie und Malerei im Dienste des Glaubens*, Dortmund: Verlag für Orientkunde.

Roxburgh, D. (2014), "Troubles with Perspective: Case Studies in Picture-Making from Qajar Iran," in J. Casid and A. D'Souza (eds.), *Art History in the Wake of the Global Turn*, New Haven: Yale University Press, 107–25.

Roxburgh, D. (2017), "Painting After Photography in 19th-Century Iran," in idem and M. McWilliams (eds.), *Technologies of the Image: Art in 19th-Century Iran*, New Haven: Yale University Press, 107–30.

Sabatiennes, P. (1977), "Pour une histoire de la première loge maçonnique en Iran," *Revue de l'Université de Bruxelles* 3–4: 414–42.

Sakhai, E. (1997), *The Story of Carpets*, Wakefield: Moyer Bell.

Seggerman, A. (2019), *Modernism on the Nile: Art in Egypt Between the Islamic and the Contemporary*, Chapel Hill: University of North Carolina Press.

Seyf, H. (1989), *Coffee-House Painting/ Naqqashi-ye qahva-khana'i*, Tehran: Reza 'Abbasi Museum.

Stein, D. (2013), "The Photographic Source for a Qajar Painting," in S. G. Scheiwiller (ed.), *Performing the Iranian State: Visual Culture and Representations of Iranian Identity*, London, New York, and Delhi: Anthem Press, 23–32.

Tanavoli, P. (1994), *Kings, Heroes, and Lovers: Pictorial Rugs from the Tribes and Villages of Iran*, London: Scorpion Publishing.

Tolan, J. (2010), "European Accounts of Muhammad's Life," in J. Brockopp (ed.), *The Cambridge Companion to Muhammad*, Cambridge: Cambridge University Press, 226–50.

Tolan, J. (2014), "Impostor or Lawgiver?: Muhammad through European Eyes in the 17th and 18th Centuries," in C. Gruber and A. Shalem (eds.), *The Image of the Prophet Between Ideal and Ideology: A Scholarly Investigation*, Berlin: De Gruyter, 261–72.

Tolan, J. (2019), *Faces of Muhammad: Western Perceptions of the Prophet of Islam from the Middle Ages to Today*, Princeton: Princeton University Press.

Vaziri, C. (1991), "Quelques indications sur le role des associations et loges maçonniques d'inspiration française dans la propagation de la Révolution française en Iran: le cas de la loge 'Reveil de l'Iran'," *Cahiers d'études sur la Méditerranée orientale et le monde turco-iranien* 12: 141–9.

Wahl, M. (1882), "Mahomet," in F. Buisson (ed.), *Dictionnaire de pédagogie et d'instruction primaire*, vol. 2, Paris: Librairie Hachette, 1251–2.

Wilber, D. (1979–80), "The Triumph of Bad Taste: Persian Pictorial Rugs," *HALI* 2 (3): 192–7.

Chapter 3

Ahmed, S. (2008), "Imaginary Prohibitions. Some Preliminary Remarks On The Founding Gestures Of The 'New Materialism'," *European Journal of Women's Studies* 15 (1): 23–39.

Al-Baghdadi, A. (1966), *Ta'rikh Baghdad wa Madinat al-Salam*, 14 vols, Beirut: Dar al-Kitab al-'Arabi.

Al-Bayhaqi, A. (1988), *Dala'il al-nubuwwa wa ma'rifa ahwal sahib al-shari'a*, Beirut: Dar al-Kutub al-'Ilmiyya.

Al-Maqqari, A. (1843), *The History of the Mohammedan Dynasties in Spain; Extracted from the Nafhu-t-tib min ghosn-l-andalusi-r-rattib wa Tarikh lisanu-u-din Ibni-l-Khatib*, trans. Pascual de Gayangos, 2 vols, London: Oriental Translation Fund.

Al-Maqqari, A. (1964), *Rawdat al-as al-'atira*, Rabat: al-Matba'a al-Malikiyya.

Al-Maqqari, A. (2006), *Fath al-Muta'al fi madh al-ni'al (Wasf ni'al al-Nabi)*, Beirut: Dar al-Kutub al-'Imiyya.

Al-Nabahani, Y. (2010), *Jawahir al-bihar fi fada'il al-nabi al-mukhtar*, 4 vols, Beirut: Dar al-Kutub al-'Ilmiyya.

Al-Qadiri, A. (1628), *Hadhihi sifa timthal na'l al-Nabi*, National Library of Israel, Ms. Yah. Ar. 353.

Al-Safadi, S. (1962–81), *Al-Wafi bi'l-wafayat*, 30 vols, Wiesbaden: Franz Steiner.

Al-Tirmidhi, A. (1996), *Al-Shama'il al-Muhammadiyya*, Beirut: Dar al-Kutub al-'Ilmiyya.

Al-Yunini, Q. (1954–61), *Dhayl Mir'at al-zaman*, 4 vols, Haydarabad: Matba'at Majlis Da'irat al-'Uthmaniyya.

Barad, K. (2007), *Meeting the Universe Halfway: Quantum Physics and the Entanglement of Matter and Meaning*, Durham: Duke University Press.

Bennett, J. (2010), *Vibrant Matter: A Political Ecology of Things*, Durham: Duke University Press.

Cahen, Cl. and L. Gardet (2012), "Kasb," in P. Bearman, Th. Bianquis, C.E. Bosworth, E. van Donzel and W.P. Heinrichs (eds.), *Encyclopaedia of Islam, Second Edition*, available online: http://dx.doi.org/10.1163/1573-3912_islam_COM_0457 (accessed May 10, 2020).

Deleuze, G. (1994), *Difference and Repetition*, trans. Paul R. Patton, New York: Columbia University Press.

Gruber, C. (2019), *The Praiseworthy One: The Prophet Muhammad in Islamic Texts and Images*, Bloomington IN: Indiana University Press.

Gruber, C. (2013) "The Prophet Muhammad's Footprint," in Robert Hillenbrand, A.C.S. Peacock, and F. Abdullaeve (eds.), *Ferdowsi, the Mongols and the History of Iran: Art, Literature and Culture from Early Islam to Qajar Persia*, London: I. B. Tauris, 297–307.

Hodder, I. (2012), *Entangled: An Archaeology of the Relationship Between Humans and Things*, Malden, MA: Wiley-Blackwell.

Humphreys, S. (1977), *From Saladin to the Mongols: the Ayyubids of Damascus, 1193–1260*, Albany: State University of New York Press.

Ibn al-Jawzi, A. (1976), *Al-Wafa' bi-ahwal al-Mustafa*, Riyad: al-Mu'assasa al-Sa'idiyya.

Ibn 'Arabi, M. (1854), *Al-Futuhat al-Makkiyya*, 4 vols, Cairo: Dar al-Kutub al-'Arabiyya al-Kubra.

Ibn 'Asakir, A. (2010), *Juz' timthal na'l al-Nabi*, printed on pages 47–63 after *Al-Jawahir al-Nifas fi bayan sifat al-sayyid min al-nas*, by al-Yafi'i al-Yamani, and before Abu al-'Abbas ibn al-Qass, *Juz' fi fawa'id hadith Abi 'Umayr*, Beirut: Dar al-Kutub al-'Ilmiyya.

Ibn al-Faqih, A. (1887), *Mukhtasar kitab al-buldan*, Leiden: Brill.

Ibn Kathir, I. (1998), *Al-Bidaya wa'l-nihaya*, 24 vols, Cairo: Markaz al-Buhuth wa'l-Dirasat al-'Arabiyya wa'l-Islamiyya.

Lincoln, B. (1996), "Theses on Method," *Method and Theory in the Study of Religion* 8 (3): 225–27.

McGregor, R. (2020), *Islam and the Devotional Object: Seeing Religion in Egypt and Syria*, New York: Cambridge University Press.

Meri, J. (2001), "A Late Medieval Syrian Pilgrimage Guide: Ibn al-Hawrani's *Al-Isharat Ila Amakin Al-Ziyarat* (*Guide to Pilgrimage Places*)," *Medieval Encounters* 7 (1): 3–78.

Meri, J. (2010), "Relics of Piety and Power in Medieval Islam," *Past and Present* 206 suppl. 5: 97–120.

Mouton, J-M. (1993), "De quelques reliques conserves à Damas au Moyen-Âge," *Annales Islamologiques* 27: 245–54.

Qadi 'Iyad ['Iyad ibn Musa] (2006), *Kitab al-shifa bi-ta'rif huquq al-Mustafa*, Beirut: Dar Sadir.

Stetkevych, S. (2010), *The Mantle Odes: Arabic Praise Poems to the Prophet Muhammad*, Bloomington Indiana University Press.

Talmon-Heller, D. (2007), *Islamic Piety in Medieval Syria: Mosques, Cemeteries and Sermons Under the Zangids and Ayyubids (1146–1260)*, Leiden: Brill.

Wheeler, B. (2006), *Mecca and Eden: Ritual, Relics, and Territory in Islam*, Chicago: University of Chicago Press.

Wilson, E. (2015), *Gut Feminism*, Durham: Duke University Press.

Chapter 4

"Activities of 'The Nation of Islam' or the Muslim cult of Islam, in Louisiana," [Hearing held, Nov. 27, 1962, Baton Rouge, La.] (1963), Baton Rouge: State of Louisiana, Ex Rel. Joint Legislative Committee on Un-American Activities, 236.

Ahmed, S. (2016), *What is Islam? The Importance of Being Islamic*, Princeton, NJ: Princeton University Press.

Allah, V.H. (2009), "Serving Justice," in S.U. Allah, C.A. Allah, and S. Allah (eds.), *Knowledge of Self: A Collection of Wisdom on the Science of Everything in Life*, Atlanta: Supreme Design Publishing, 168–73.

Allahs', J.G. (2014), "Ja'Mella God Allahs'," in, *The True History of Allah and His 5%*, self-published, 328–35,

"Arrest Man for Wearing Secret Order Regalia," (1919), *Chicago Defender*, July 5: 1.

"Full Text of U.S. Supreme Court Decision: Long Delay in Beginning Case Defeats White Shriners," (1929), *Chicago Defender*, July 13: 10.

"Girl Recounts Lore of Islam," (1934a), *Detroit Free Press*, April 26: 1.

"Raid Reveals Cult Practices," (1932), *Detroit Free Press*, November 23: 3.

"Suit May Disband Southern Shriners: Whites Ask Court to Stop Shriners From Wearing Pins," (1921), *Chicago Defender*, January 1: 1.

"Voodoo Catechism Says Heads of Four Devils Are Passport to Mecca," (1934b), *Detroit Free Press*, April 29: 13.

"'Zebra' Trial Ends its Ninth Month: Testimony on Black Muslim Religion Heard in Case of 4 Held in Coast Killings," (1975), *The New York Times*, November 30: 9.

Autodidact 17 (2014), "Five Percenters Outraged over Jay Z's 'Pimpin' of Their Universal Flag," *New York Amsterdam News*, April 17, available online: http://amsterdamnews.com/news/2014/apr/17/five-percenters-outraged-over-jay-zs-pimpin-their-/ (accessed May 4, 2020).

Beito, D. (2000), *From Mutual Aid to the Welfare State: Fraternal Societies and Social Services, 1890–1967*, Chapel Hill: University of North Carolina Press.

Benyon, E.D. (1937–8), "The Voodoo Cult among Negro Migrants in Detroit," *American Journal of Sociology* 43: 894–907.

Bowen P.D. (2011), "Abdul Hamid Sulaiman and the Origins of the Moorish Science Temple," *Journal of Race, Ethnicity, and Religion* 2 (13): 1–54.

Cooper v. Pate, 324 F.2d 165 (7th Cir. 1963).

Coward v. Robinson, 1:10-cv-147 (LMB/MSN) (E.D. Va. Nov. 9, 2017).

Curtis IV, E.E. (2002), "Islamizing the Black Body: Ritual and Power in Elijah Muhamamd's Nation of Islam," *Religion and American Culture* 12 (2): 167–96.

Federal Bureau of Investigation (1965), Wallace D. Fard, (File #25-20607).

Gardell, M. (1996), *In the Name of Elijah Muhammad: Louis Farrakhan and the Nation of Islam*, Durham: Duke University Press.

Gottehrer, B. (2007), *The Mayor's Man*, Charleston: Booksurge.

Knight, M.M. (2007), *The Five Percenters*, London: OneWorld.

Knight, M.M. (2019), "'I am Sorry, Mr. White Man, These are Secrets that You are Not Permitted to Learn:' The Supreme Wisdom Lessons and Problem Book," *Correspondences* 7 (1): 167–200.

Lord Jamar (2006), "I.S.L.A.M.," *The 5% Album*, Babygrande.

Magida, A. (1997), *Prophet of Rage: A Life of Louis Farrakhan and His Nation of Islam*, New York: Basic Books.

The Messenger (1919), vol. 7, np. December.

Moore, W.D. (2006), *Masonic Temples: Freemasonry, Ritual Architecture, and Masculine Archetypes*, Nashville: University of Tennessee Press.

Muhammad, E. (n.d.) *The Supreme Wisdom Lessons*, unpublished manuscript.

Muhammad, E. (2008), *The Theology of Time: The Secret of the Time. Theology of Time*, Phoenix: Secretarius MEMPS Publications.

Muhammad, K.A. (2018), "Murder the Devil-Defending the Honorable Minister Louis Farrakhan Special Edition," *YouTube*: https://www.youtube.com/watch?v=1siAgNT4GcE (accessed May 4, 2020).

Muhammad, W.D. (1975), "The Destruction of the Devil," *Muhammad Speaks*, July 11: 13.

Nance, S.J. (2002), "Respectability and Representation: The Moorish Science Temple, Morocco, and Black Public Culture in 1920s Chicago," *American Quarterly* 54 (4): 623–59.

Nas (1996), "Affirmative Action," *It Was Written*, Columbia Records.

Noel, P. (1989), "Bring Me the Head," *Village Voice*, February 2, available online: https://www.villagevoice.com/1999/02/02/bring-me-the-head/ (accessed May 4, 2020).

Ol' Dirty Bastard (1995), "Cuttin' Headz," ft. RZA, *Return to the 36 Chambers: The Dirty Version*, Elektra/WMG.

Rolinson, M.G. (2007), *Grassroots Garveyism: The Universal Negro Improvement Association in the Rural South, 1920–1927*, Chapel Hill: University of North Carolina Press.

Shabazz v. Lokey, Civil Action No. 7:14-cv-00457 (W.D. Va. Sep. 24, 2018).

Weber, M. ([1905] 2001), *The Protestant Ethic and the Spirit of Capitalism*, trans. Stephen Kalberg, Chicago and London: Fitzroy Dearborn Publishers.

Williams, Cherri (2017), *Facebook*, September 22, 2017, available online: https://www.facebook.com/photo.php?fbid=10203803417882451&set=pb.1729669791.-2207520000.0.&type=3&theater (accessed May 4, 2020).

Chapter 5

Archival Materials

All the archival materials were obtained from the National Archives of Senegal (Archives Nationale du Senegal, Dakar = ANS), where the French deposited copies of the colonial records of the French West African Federation.

ANS 2G21, HV RPA (1921).

ANS 2G30/10, HV, RPA, (1930).

ANS 2G30/10, RPA, (1930).

ANS 2G36/18 RPA, Soudan, (1936).

ANS 2G41/20, RPA, Soudan, (1941).

ANS 2G42/3 RPA, Soudan, Province of Ouahigouya, (1942).

Oral materials were obtained through interviews conducted in different cities in Burkina Faso and Ghana.

Secondary sources

Abu-Nasr, J.M. (1965), *The Tijaniyya: a Sufi Order in the Modern World*, New York: Oxford University Press.

Adnani, J. (2007), *La Tijaniyya 1781–1881: Les origines d'une confrérie religieuse au Maghreb*, Paris: Editions Marsam.

al Tirmidhi, Jami'at al-Tirmidhi. Available online at https://sunnah.com/tirmidhi (accessed December 12, 2020).

Dao, M. (1993), "Le wahhabisme à Ouagadougou de 1964 à 1988," *Islam et sociétés au sud du Sahara* 7: 223–9.

Diallo, H. (1985), "Islam et colonization au Yatenga (1897–1950)," *Le mois en Afrique*: 237–8.

Dubin, L.S. (2009), "Prayer Beads," in C. Kenney (ed.), *The History of Beads: From 100,000 B.C. to the Present*, New York: Abrams Publishing, 79–92.

Dumbe, Y. (2013), *Islamic Revivalism in Contemporary Ghana*, Södertörn University Library.

Hanretta, S. (2009), *Islam and Social Change: History of an Emancipatory Community*, Cambridge: Cambridge University Press.

Harrison, C. (1988), *France and Islam in West Africa, 1860–1960*, Cambridge: Cambridge University Press.

Henry, G. and S. Marriott (2008), *Beads of Faith: Pathways to Meditation and Spirituality Using Rosaries, Prayer Beads and Sacred Words*, London: Fons Vitae Publishing.

Herman, B.L. (2017), "On Southern Things," *Southern Cultures* 23 (3): 7–13.

Ibn Taymiyyah, *Majmu'a al-Fataawa*, vol 22, Riyadh: Dar 'Ålam al-Kutub, 1991.

Izard, M. (1970), "Introduction a l'histoire des royaumes Mossi 1," *Recherches Voltaiques* 12: 213–434.

Kobo, O. (2009), "The Development of Wahhabi Reforms in Ghana and Burkina Faso, 1960–1990: Elective Affinities between Western-Educated Muslims and Islamic Scholars," *Comparative Studies in Society and History* 51 (3): 502–32.

Kobo, O. (2012a), "Islamic Reform in Colonial Space: The Jihad of Shaykh Boubacar Sawadogo and French Islamic Policies in Burkina Faso, 1920–1946," *Journal of Islamic Studies* 32: 47–69.

Kobo, O. (2012b), *Unveiling Modernity in Twentieth Century West African Islamic Reforms*, Leiden: Brill Publishers.

Kobo, O. (2015), "Shifting Trajectories of Salafi/Ahl-Sunna Reformism in Ghana," *Islamic Africa* 6: 60–81.

Kouanda, A. (1989), *Les Yarsè: fonction commerciale, religieuse et légitimité culturelle dans le pays Moaga*, Ph.D. diss., Université de Paris I.

Robinson, D. and J.L Triaud (2000), *La Tijaniyya, une confrérie Musulmane a la conquête de l'Afrique*, Paris: Karthal.

Ryan, P.J. (2000), "The Mystical Theology of Tijānī Sufism and Its Social Significance in West Africa," *Journal of Religion in Africa* 30 (2): 208–24.

Sawadogo, B. (1998), *Confréries et pouvoirs. La tijaniyya hamawiyya en Afrique occidentale (Burkina Faso, Côte d'Ivoire, Mali, Niger)*, Ph.D. diss., Université de Provence.

Seesemann, R. (1998), "The Takfír Debate: Sources for the Study of a Contemporary Dispute Among African Sufis, Part I: The Nigerian Arena," *Sudanic Africa* 9: 39–70.

Skinner, E. (1966), "Islam in Mossi Society," in I.M. Lewis (ed.), *Islam in Tropical Africa, Studies Presented and Discussed at the Fifth International African Seminar, Ahmadu Bello University, Zaria January 1964*, London: Oxford University Press, 350–73.

Traoré, B. (1984), *Le processus d'islamisation à Bobo-Dioulasso à la fin du XIX siécle: approche socio-historique*, MA diss., Université de Ouagadougou.

Traoré, B. (2010), "A la recherche d'une voie Africaine de la laïcité. Islam et pluralism religieux au Burkina Faso," *Islam et société au sud du Sahara: diversité et habits singuliers* 28 (2): 9–54.

Triaud, J.L. (2000), "Islam in Africa under French Colonial Rule," in N. Levtzion and R.L. Pouwels (eds.), *The History of Islam in Africa*, Athens, OH: Ohio University Press, 169–87.

Van Duc, J. (1995), "L'administration coloniale française et les pèlerins de la Mecque: le cas des Voltaïque," in G. Massa and G Madiéga (eds.), *La Haute Volta coloniel, témoignages, recherches, regards*, Paris: Karthala, 249–262.

Wright, Z.V. (2015), *On the Path of the Prophet: Shaykh Ahmad Tijani and the Tariqa Muhammadiyya* (Revised Edition), Atlanta, GA: Faydah Books.

Chapter 6

Ahmed, S. (2016), *What is Islam? The Importance of Being Islamic*, Princeton, NJ: Princeton University Press.

Amir Khurd (1884), *Siyar al-Awliya*, Delhi: Matbaʿ Muhibb-e Hind.

Bashir, S. (2011), *Sufi Bodies: Religion and Society in Medieval Islam*, New York: Columbia University Press.

Bashir, S. (2014), "The World as a Hat: Symbolism and Materiality in Safavid Iran," in O. Mir-Kasimov (ed.), *Unity in Diversity: Mysticism, Messianism and the Construction of Religious Authority in Islam*, Leiden, NL: Brill, 343-65.

Browne, E. [1928] (2000), *A Literary History of Persia*, vol. 3, Delhi: GoodWord Publications.

Colby, F. (2008), *Narrating Muhammad's Night Journey: Tracing the Development of the Ibn Abbas Ascension Discourse*, Albany: SUNY Press.

De Sondy, A. (2014), *The Crisis of Islamic Masculinities*, London: Bloomsbury.

Eaton, R. (2008), *Social History of the Deccan: Eight Indian Lives*, Cambridge: Cambridge University Press.

Ernst, C. and B. Lawrence (2002), *Sufi Martyrs of Love: The Chishti Order in South Asia and Beyond*, New York: Palgrave Macmillan.

Faruqi, M.I. (1972), *Naghmat-e Samaʿ*, Karachi: Educational Press.

Flood, F.B. (2009), *Objects of Translation: Material Culture and 'Hindu-Muslim' Encounter*, Princeton: Princeton University Press.

Geczy, A. (2019), *Transorientalism in Art, Fashion and Film: Inventions of Identity*, London: Bloomsbury.

Gordon, S. (2003), ed. *Robes of Honour: Khil'at in Pre-Colonial and Colonial India*, New Delhi: Oxford University Press.

Gruber, C. (2010), *The Ilkhanid Book of Ascension: A Persian-Sunni Devotional Tale*, London: I.B. Tauris.

Kaltman, B. (2007), *Under the Heel of the Dragon: Islam, Racism, Crime, and the Uighur in China*, Athens, OH: Ohio University Press.

Kolig, E. (2012), *Conservative Islam: A Cultural Anthropology*, Lanham, MD: Lexington Books.

Kugle, S. (2007), *Sufis and Saints' Bodies: Mysticism, Corporeality, and Sacred Power in Islam*, Chapel Hill, NC: University of North Carolina Press.

Kugle, S. (forthcoming), *The Merciful Door: Living with a Sufi Teacher in India*, London: Beacon Books.

Lawrence, B. (1992), *Morals for the Heart: Conversations of Nizam al-Din Awliya*, Mahwah, NY: Paulist Press.

Lewis, R. (2015), *Muslim Fashion: Contemporary Style Cultures*, Durham, NC: Duke University Press.

Lings, M. (2003), trans. *Sufi Poems: A Medieval Anthology*, London: Islamic Texts Society.

Nakhshabi, Z. (n.d.), *Silk al-Suluk*, London, British Library, IO Islamic 651 (described in the catalogue by Ethé, entry 1838).

Nakhshabi, Z. (n.d.), *Silk al-Suluk*, trans. (into Urdu) unknown, Lahore: Nawal Kishore Press.

Patel, Y. (2018a), "'Their Fires Shall Not Be Visible': The Sense of Muslim Difference," *Material Religion* 14 (1): 1-29.

Patel, Y. (2018b), "'Whoever Imitates a People Becomes One of the Them': A Hadith and its Interpreters," *Islamic Law and Society* 25: 359-426.

Pernau, M. (2010), "Shifting Globalities—Changing Headgear: The Indian Muslims Between Turban, Hat and Fez," in U. Freitag and A. van Oppen (eds.), *Translocality: The Study of Globalizing Processes from a Southern Perspective*, Leiden, NL: Brill, 249-67.

Ritter, H. (2003), *The Ocean of the Soul: Man, the World, and God in the Stories of Farid al-Din 'Attar*, trans. John O'Kane, Leiden, NL: Brill.

Rizvi, S. A. A. (1978), *History of Sufism in India,* vol. 1, Delhi: Munshiram Manoharlal.

Rumi, J. (2004), *Masnavi-yi Ma'navi*, book 1, trans. Jawid Mojaddedi, New York: Oxford University Press.

Rumi, J. (2017), *Masnavi-yi Ma'navi*, book 4, trans. Jawid Mojaddedi, New York: Oxford University Press.

Sa'di, M. (1955), *Kulliyat*, ed. Mohamed Ali Faroghi, Tehran: Intisharat-e Qaqnus.

Schneider, J. (2006), "Cloth and Clothing," in C. Tilley, W. Keane, S. Küchler, M. Rowlands, and P. Spyer (eds.), *Handbook of Material Culture*, London: Sage Publications, 203-20.

Sharma, S. (2006), *Amir Khusraw: The Poet of Sultans and Saints*, Oxford: Oneworld.

Tarlo, E. (1996), *Clothing Matters: Dress and Identity in India*, Chicago: University of Chicago Press.

Tarlo, E. (2010), *Visibly Muslim: Fashion, Politics, Faith*, Oxford: Berg Publishers.

Tarlo, E. and A. Moors (2013), eds. *Islamic Fashion and Anti-Fashion: New Perspectives from Europe and North America*, London: Bloomsbury.

Chapter 7

Atalay, B. (1921), *Bektaşilik ve Edebiyatı*, Istanbul: Matba'a-ı Amire.

The Travels of Ibn Battuta, A.D. 1325-1354, vol. 2 (1962), trans. H.A.R. Gibb, Cambridge: University Press for the Hakluyt Society.

Bektaşî Erkânnâmesi: 1313 Tarihli bir Erkânnâme Metni (2006), eds. Dursun Gümüşoğlu and Rıza Yıldırım, Istanbul: Horasan Yayınları.

Velâyetnâme: Hacı Bektâş-ı Veli (2007), ed. Hamiye Duran, Ankara: Türkiye Diyanet Vakfı.

Makâlât: Hünkâr Hacı Bektâş-ı Veli (2009), eds. Ali Yılmaz, Mehmet Akkuş, and Ali Öztürk, Ankara: Türkiye Diyanet Vakfı.

Birge, J.K. (1937), *The Bektashi Order of Dervishes*, London: Luzac & Co.
Brown, P. (1981), *The Cult of the Saints: Its Rise and Function in Latin Christianity*, Chicago: University of Chicago Press.
Engelke, M. (2007), *A Problem of Presence: Beyond Scripture in an African Church*, Berkeley and Los Angeles: University of California Press.
Gölpınarlı, A. (1963), *Alevî-Bektâşî Nefesleri*, İstanbul: Remzi Kitabevi.
Jeffery, A. (2007), *The Foreign Vocabulary of the Qur'ān*, Leiden: Brill.
Kapstein, M.T. (2004), ed. *The Presence of Light: Divine Radiance and Religious Experience*, Chicago: University of Chicago Press.
Keane, W. (2008), "The Evidence of the Senses and the Materiality of Religion," *Journal of the Royal Anthropological Institute* 14 (1): 110-27.
Khan, M.B. (2013), "'Chirāgh-i Rōshan': Prophetic Light in the Isma'ili Tradition," *Islamic Studies* 52 (3-4): 327-56.
Korom, F.J. (2012), "The Presence of Absence: Using Stuff in a South Asian Sufi Movement," *AAS Working Papers in Social Anthropology* 23: 1-19.
Melikian-Chirvani, A.S. (1985), "Anatolian Candlesticks: The Eastern Element and the Konya School," *Rivista degli studi orientali* 59 (1-4): 225-66.
Meyer, B. (2012), *Mediation and the Genesis of Presence: Towards a Material Approach to Religion*, Utrecht: Universiteit Utrecht.
Morgan, D. (2010), "The Material Culture of Lived Religion: Visuality and Embodiment," in J. Vakkari (ed.), *Mind and Matter*, Helsinki: Society of Art History, 14–31.
Noyan, B. (2010), *Bütün Yönleriyle Bektâşîlik ve Alevîlik*, vol. 8, Ankara: Ardıç Yayınları.
Orsi, R.A. (2005), *Between Heaven and Earth: The Religious Worlds People Make and the Scholars Who Study Them*, Princeton: Princeton University Press.
Ruffle, K.G. (2017), "Presence in Absence: The Formation of Reliquary Shi'ism in Qutb Shahi Hyderabad," *Material Religion* 13 (3): 329-53.
Saidula, A. (2015), "*Chirogh Rawshan*: Shi'i Ceremonial Practised by the Ismaili Communities of Xinjiang China," in F. Suleman (ed.), *People of the Prophet's House: Artistic and Ritual Expressions of Shi'i Islam*, London: Azimuth Editions. 232-41.
Soileau, M. (2012), "Spreading the Sofra: Sharing and Partaking in the Bektashi Ritual Meal," *History of Religions* 52 (1): 1-30.

Chapter 8

"Wearing Amulets"(n.d.), *Islam Awareness*, https://islamawareness.net/BlackMagic/fatwa_amulets.html (accessed December 2, 2019).
Bennett, J. (2010), *Vibrant Matter: A Political Ecology of Things*, Durham: Duke University Press.
El-Tom, A.O. (1985), "Drinking the Koran: The Meaning of Koranic Verses in Berti Erasure," Africa: Journal of the International African Institute 55 (4): 414–31.
El-Tom, A. O. (1987), "Berti Qur'anic Amulets," *Journal of Religion in Africa* 17 (3): 224-44.
Flueckiger, J. B. (2006), *In Amma's Healing Room: Gender and Vernacular Islam in South India*, Bloomington: Indiana University Press.

"Is Taweez (AMULET) Allowed in Islam?" (2008), *Ahlu Sunnah wa'l Jamah*. January 26, http://ahlussunnahwaljamah.blogspot.com/2008/01/is-taweez-amulet-allowed-in-islam.html (accessed December 2, 2019).

Mattson, I. (2008), *The Story of the Qur'an: Its History and Place in Muslim Life*, Victoria, Australia: Blackwell Publishing.

Mommersteeg, G. (1990), "Allah's Words as Amulet," *Etnofoor* 3 (1): 63-76.

O'Connor, K.M. (2001), "Popular and Talismanic Uses of the Qur'an," *Encyclopaedia of the Qur'an* 4:163-82.

Popper-Giveon, A., and J.J. Ventura (2009), "Blood and Ink: Treatment Practices of Traditional Palestinian Women Healers in Israel," *Journal of Anthropological Research* 65 (1): 27-49.

The Qur'an (2004), trans. M.A.S. Abdel Haleem, New York: Oxford University Press.

Ware, R.T (2014), *The Walking Qur'an: Islamic Education, Embodied Knowledge, and History in West Africa*, Chapel Hill, NC: University of North Carolina Press.

Zadeh, T. (2009), "Touching and Ingesting: Early Debates over the Material Qur'an," *Journal of the American Oriental Society* 129 (3): 443-66.

Chapter 9

Aadri, A. (1984), *La population noire d'iligh: enquete*, **mimeographed**.

Al-Susi, M.M (1966), *Iligh qadiman was hadithan*, Rabat: al-Matba'a al-Malakiyya.

Aouad, R. (1973), *Aspects de l'esclavage marocain, 1880–1922*, MA diss., Université de Provence.

Awad, M. (1992), "Un fondateur de confrérie religieuse maghrébine: Sidi Ahmed al-Tijani (1737–1815)," *Revue Maroc Europe* 2: 233–66.

Becker, C. (2002), "'We are Real Slaves, Real Ismkhan': Memories of the Trans-Saharan Slave Trade in the Tafilalet of South-Eastern Morocco," *Journal of North African Studies* 7: 97–121.

Bellakhdar, J., A. Benabid, J. Maréchal, and J. Vittoz (1992), *Tissint, une oasis du Maroc présaharien. Monographe d'une palmeraie du Moyen Dra*, Rabat: Al Biruniya.

Benachir, B. (2003), *Négritudes du Maroc et du Maghreb*, Paris: L'Harmattan.

Berque, J. (1982), *Ulémas, fondateurs, insurgés du Maghreb. XVIIéme siècle*, Paris: Sindbad.

Bodin, M. (1918), "La zaouia de Tamegrout," *Archives Berbères* 3: 259–95.

Boum, A. (2008), "The Political Coherence of Educational Incoherence: The Consequences of Educational Specialization in a Southern Moroccan Community," *Anthropology and Education Quarterly* 39 (2): 205–23.

Boum, A. (2013), *Memories of Absence. How Muslims Remember Jews in Morocco*, Stanford: Stanford University Press.

Boum, A. and T. Park (2016), *Historical Dictionary of Morocco*, Lanham: Rowman and Littlefield.

Brigaglia, A. (2017), "Fi Lawhin Mahfuz: Towards a Phenomenological Analysis of the Quranic Tablet," in A. Brigaglia and M. Nobili (eds.), *The Arts and Crafts of Literacy: Islamic Manuscript Cultures in Sub-Saharan Africa*, **Germany**: De Gruyter, 69–102.

Eickelman, D.F. (1972–73), "Quelques aspects de l'organisation politique et économique d'une zawiya marocaine au XIXe siècle: Un essai socio-historique," *Bulletin de la Société d'Histoire du Maroc* 4–5: 37–54.

Eickelman, D.F. (1978), "The Art of Memory: Islamic Education and its Social Reproduction," *Comparative Studies in Society and History* 20: 485–516.

Eickelman, D.F. (1983), "Religion and Trade in Western Morocco," *Research in Economic Anthropology* 5: 335–48.

Eickelman, D.F. (1985), *Knowledge and Power in Morocco: The Education of a Twentieth Century Notable*, Princeton: Princeton University Press.

El Hamel, C. (2002), "'Race,' Slavery and Islam in Maghribi Mediterranean Thought: The Question of the Haratin in Morocco," *The Journal of North African Studies* 7 (3): 29–52.

El Hamel, C. (2013), *Black Morocco: A History of Slavery, Race, and Islam*, Cambridge, U.K.: Cambridge University Press.

Ennaji, M. (1998), *Serving the Master: Slavery and Society in Nineteenth-Century Morocco*, trans. S. Graebner, New York: St. Martin's Press.

Ennaji, M. and P. Pascon (1988), *Le Makhzan et le Sous al-Aqsa: La correspondence politique de la Maison d'Iligh (1821–1894)*, Paris: Editions de CNRS.

Ensel, R. (1999), *Saints and Servants in Southern Morocco*, Leiden: Brill.

Foucauld, C.D. (1888), *Reconnaissance au Maroc, 1883–1884*, Paris: Challamel.

Gutelius, D. (2002), "The Path is Easy and the Benefits Large: The Nasiriyya, Social Networks and Economic Change in Morocco, 164–1830," *The Journal of African History* 43: 27–49.

Hassan II, King of Morocco (1968), "Radio Speech Inaugurating 'Operation Quranic School,'" October 9, *Maroc Documents* no. 5: March 1969.

Ilahiane, H. (2004), *Ethnicities, Community Making and Agrarian Change: The Political Ecology of a Moroccan Oasis*, Lanham, MD: University Press of America.

Jackson, J.G. (1809), *An Account of the Empire of Marocco, and the Districts of Suse and Tafilalet*, London: W. Bulmer.

Lapanne-Joinville, J. (1950), *Note sur l'esclavage au Maroc*, Rabat: Centre des Haute Etudes d'Administration Musulmane Hassan II.

Lapanne-Joinville, J. (1952), "La reconnaissance de paternité de l'enfant issu du concubinat legal," *Revue marocaine de Droit* [**no. ?**]: 153–66.

Les Site Infos (2019), "Ibda'at isaiyya 'ala al-alwah al-Qur'aniya," *LeSiteinfo*, July 18, available online: https://www.youtube.com/watch?v=AWz43OV7lc0 (accessed April 12, 2020).

Lévi-Provençal, E. (1922), *Les historiens des Chorfa. Essai sur la littérature historique et biographique au Maroc du XVIème au Xxème*. Paris: Paul Geuthner.

McDougall, E.A. (1998), "A Sense of Self: The Life of Fatma Barka," *Canadian Journal of African Studies* 32(2): 285–315.

Michaux-Bellaire, E. (1910), "L'esclavage du Maroc," *Revue du Monde Musulman* 11: 422–7.

Naj, S. (2011), *Fils de saints contre fils d'esclaves: Les pèlerinages de la Zawya d'Imi n'Tatelt (Anti-Atlas et Maroc présaharien)*, Angers: Centre Jacques-Berque.

Schroeter, D.J. (1992), "Slave Markets and Slavery in Moroccan Urban Society," *Slavery and Abolition* 13 (1): 185–213.

Sikainga, A.A. (1998), "Slavery and Muslim Jurisprudence in Morocco," *Slavery and Abolition* 19 (2): 57–72.

Sikainga, A.A. (2011), "The Paradox of the Female Slave Body in the Islamic Legal System: The Cases of Morocco and Sudan," *Hawwa* 9: 215–33.

Spratt, J.E., and D.A. Wagner (1986), "The Making of a Fqih: The Transformation of Traditional Islamic Teachers in Modern Cultural Adaptation," in M.I. White and S. Pollak (eds.), *The Cultural Transition: Human Experience and Social Transformation in the Third World and Japan*, Boston and London: Routledge and Kegan Paul, 89–112.

Wolf, E. (1982), *Europe and the People Without History*, Berkeley: University of California Press.

Chapter 10

Ahmed, S. (2016), *What is Islam? The Importance of Being Islamic*, Princeton, NJ: Princeton University Press.

Album, S. (1998), *A Checklist of Islamic Coins,* Santa Rosa, CA: Steven Album.

Al-Khazraji (1907), *The Pearl-Strings: A History of the Resuliyy Dynasty of Yemen,* vol. 2, trans. James W. Redhouse, Leiden: Brill.

Al-Khwarizmi, Abū ʿAbdallāh Muḥammad b. Aḥmad (1895), *Mafātīḥ al-ʿulūm,* ed. G. Van Vlotten, Leiden: Brill.

Allouche, A. (1994), *Mamluk Economics: A Study and Translation of al-Maqrīzī's Ighāthah,* Salt Lake City: University of Utah Press.

Appadurai, A. (1986), *The Social Lives of Things: Commodities in Cultural Perspectives,* Cambridge: Cambridge University Press.

Bacharach, J. (2006), *Islamic History Through Coins: An Analysis and Catalogue of Tenth Century Ikhshidid Coinage*, Cairo: The American University in Cairo Press.

Balog, P. (1964), *Coinage of the Mamluk Sultans of Egypt and Syria*, New York: American Numismatic Society.

Bates, M.L. (1982), *Islamic Coins*, New York: The American Numismatic Society.

Bates, M. L. and R. E. Darley-Doran, (1985), "The Art of Islamic Coinage," in T. Falk (ed.), *Treasures of Islam,* Geneva: Musée d'art et d'histoire, 350–95.

Carboni, S. (1997), *Following the Stars: Images of the Zodiac in Islamic Art,* New York: The Metropolitan Museum of Art.

Digby, S. (1980), "The Broach Coin-Hoard as Evidence of the Import of Valuta Across the Arabian Sea During the 13th and 14th Century," *Journal of the Royal Asiatic Society of Great Britain and Ireland* 2: 129–38.

D'Ottone, A. (2015), "The Mint of Ta'izz in Rasulid Times," in **[ed?]**, *Per Enzo: Studi in Memoria Di Vicenzo Matera*, Florence: Florence University Press, 93–103.

D'Ottone, A. (2020), "The Mints of Taʿizz and Thaʿbāt in Rasulid Times: Literary Sources and Numismatic Evidence," *Rivista Italiana di Numismatica e Scienze Affini* 121: 213–69.

Dunlop, D. M. (1957), "Sources of Gold and Silver in Islam According to Al-Hamdānī (10th Century A.D.)," *Studia Islamica* 7: 29–49.

Flood, F. B. (2009), *Objects of Translation: Material Culture and Medieval "Hindu-Muslim" Encounter,* Princeton: Princeton University Press.

Green, N. (2011), *Bombay Islam: The Religious Economy of the Western Indian Ocean, 1840–1915,* New York: Cambridge University Press.

Hart, K. (1986), "Heads or Tails? Two Sides of the Coin," *Man* 21: 637–56.

Heidemann, S. (2010), "Calligraphy on Islamic Coins," in J.W. Frembgen (ed.), *The Aura of Alif: The Art of Writing in Islam*, Munich: Prestel, 161–71.

Hodgson, M. (1974), *The Venture of Islam: Conscience and History in a World Civilization,* Chicago: University of Chicago Press.

Ibn Battuta (1958), *The Travels of Ibn Battuta, A.D. 1325–1354,* trans. H. A.R. Gibb, London: Hakluyt Society.

Margariti, R.gE. (2007), *Aden and the Indian Ocean Trade: 150 Years in the Life of a Medieval Arabian Port,* Chapel Hill: University of North Carolina Press.

Margariti, R.E (2014), "Coins and Commerce: Monetization and Cross-Cultural Collaboration in the Indian Ocean (Eleventh to Thirteenth Century)," in C. Antunes, L. Halevi, and F. Trivellato (eds.), *Religion and Trade: Cross-Cultural Exchanges in World History*, Oxford: Oxford University Press, 192–215.

Nützel, H. and A. Kinzelbach ([1891] 1987), *Coins of the Rasulids,* Mainz: Verlag Donata Kinzelbach.

Peli, A. and F. Tereygeol (2007), "Al-Raḍraḍ al-Jabali: a Yemeni Silver Mine," *Proceedings of the Seminar for Arabian Studies* 37: 187–200.

Patel, A. (2004), *Building Communities in Gujarat: Architecture and Society During the Twelfth to Fourteenth Centuries,* Leiden: Brill.

Pickthall, M.M. (1930), The Meaning of the Glorious Koran, NY: A.A. Knopf.

Prideaux, W.F. (1883–85), "Coins of the Benee Rasool Dynasty of South Arabia," *Journal of the Bombay Branch of the Royal Asiatic Society* 16: 8–16.

Radcliffe, W. (1921), *Fishing from the Earliest Times,* London and Chicago: Ares Publishing.

Sardi, M. (2016), "Swimming Across the Weft: Fish Motifs on Mamluk Textiles," in A. Ohta, J.M. Rogers, and R. Wade Haddon (eds.), *Art, Trade and Culture in the Islamic World and Beyond from the Fatimids to the Mughals: Studies Presented to Doris Behrens Abouseif,* London: Ginkgo Library, 254–63.

Schultz, W. (1998), "The Monetary History of Egypt, 647–1517," in C.F. Petry (ed.), *The Cambridge History of Egypt*, Cambridge: Cambridge University Press, 318–38.

Schultz, W. (2003), "'It Has No Root Among Any Community That Believes in Revealed Religion, Nor Legal Foundation for its Implementation': Placing al-Maqrizi's Comments on Money in a Wider Context," *Mamluk Studies Review* 7: 169–81.

Schultz, W. (2010), "The Mechanisms of Commerce," in R. Irwin (ed.), *The New Cambridge History of Islam,* vol. 4: *Islamic Cultures and Societies to the End of the Eighteenth Century,* Cambridge: Cambridge University Press, 332–54.

Smith, G.R. (1974), *The Ayyubids and Early Rasulids in the Yemen,* vol. 1, London: Lusac.

Smith, G.R. (2007), *A Medieval Administrative and Fiscal Treatise from the Yemen,* Oxford: Oxford University Press.

Udovitch, A.L. (1970), *Partnership and Profit in Medieval Islam,* Princeton: Princeton University Press.

Varisco, D.M. (1993), "Texts and Pretexts: The Unity of the Rasulid Text Under al-Malik al-Muzaffar," *Revue du monde musulman et de la Mediterranée* 67: 13–24.

Vallet, E. (2010), *L'Arabie marchande: État et commerce sous les sultans Rasulides du Yémen, 626–858/1229–1454*, Paris: Publications de la Sorbonne.

Wasserstein, D.J. (1992), "Coins as Agents of Cultural Definition in Islam," *Poetics Today* 14: 303–22.

Wick, A. (2016), *The Red Sea: In Search of Lost Space*, Los Angeles, University of California Press.

Chapter 11

Abd Allah b. Buluggin (1986), *The Tibyan: Memoirs of Abd Allah b. Buluggin, Last Zirid Amir of Granada*, trans. A.T. Tibi, Leiden: Brill.

Ahmed, S. (2016), *What Is Islam? The Importance of Being Islamic*, Princeton, NJ: Princeton University Press.

"Granada: Its High Death-Rate and Contaminated Water-Supply," (1903), *The Lancet* 162 (4171): 425–7.

Les Andalousies de Damas à Cordoue: Exposition présentée à l'Institut du monde arabe du 28 novembre 2000 au 15 avril 2001, (2000) Paris: L'Institut du monde arabe.

Barceló, C. and A. Labarta (1988), "Ocho relojes de sol hispano-musulmanes," *Al-Qantara* 9: 231–47.

Berggren, J.L. (2001), "Sundials in Medieval Islamic Science and Civilization," *The Compendium* 8 (2): 1–14.

Bukhari, M. (n.d.) *Al-Adab al-Mufrad* (https://sunnah.com/adab) (accessed December 7, 2020).

García Pulido, L.J. (2013), *El Territorio de la Alhambra*, Granada: Patronato de la Alhambra y Generalife.

García Pulido, L.J. (2016), "The Mastery in Hydraulic Techniques for Water Supply at the Alhambra," *Journal of Islamic Studies* 27 (3): 355–82.

Garrido Atienza, M. ([1902] 2002), *Las Aguas del Albaicín y Alcazaba*, Granada: Universidad de Granada.

Glick, T.F. (1970), *Irrigation and Society in Medieval Valencia*, Cambridge, Mass.: Harvard University Press.

Guillén y Rodríguez de Cepeda, A. (1921), *El Tribunal de las Aguas de Valencia y los modernos Jurados de Riego*, Valencia: Imprenta Doménech.

Ibn al-Khatib (2010), *Historia de los Reyes de la Alhambra*, trans. J. M. Casciaro Ramírez and E. Molina López, Granada: Universidad de Granada.

Lafuente Alcantara, M. (1845), *Historia de Granada*, vol. 3, Granada: Imprenta y libreria de Sanz.

Orihuela Uzal, A. and L.J. García Pulido (2008), "El Suministro de agua en la Granada islámica," *Ars Mechanicae: Ingeniería Medieval en España*, s.l. Ministerio de Fomento, CEDEX-CEHOPU: 143–9.

Orihuela Uzal, A. and C. Vílchez Vílchez (1991), *Aljibes públicos de la Granada islámica*, Granada: Ayuntamiento de Granada.

Navarro Palazón, J. and P. Jiménez Castillo (2012), "El bañuelo de Granada en su contexto arquitectónico y urbanístico," *Revista el legado andalusí* 13 (45), available online: http://revista.legadoandalusi.es/n45_revista_el_legado_

andalusi/las_artes_y_los_dias/el_banuelo_de_granada_en_su_contexto_arquitectonico_y_urbanistico.html (accessed November 17, 2019).

Ruggles, D.F. (2020), "Representation, Signature and Trace in Islamic Art," in P. Patton and H. Schilb (eds), *The Lives and Afterlives of Medieval Iconography*, University Park: Penn State University Press, 57–87.

Shaw, W.M.K. (2019), *What Is "Islamic" Art? Between Religion and Perception*, Cambridge: Cambridge University Press.

Trillo San José, C. (2002), "Estudio preliminar," in M.G. Garrido Atienza, *Las Aguas del Albaicín y Alcazaba*, facsimile edition, Granada: Universidad de Granada, vii–lxxi.

Trillo San José, C. (2005), "A Social Analysis of Irrigation in Al-Andalus: Nazari Granada (13th–15th centuries)," *Journal of Medieval History* 31: 163–83.

Trillo San José, C. (2007), "Aljibes y mezquitas en Madīnat Garnāṭa (siglos XI–XV), in *Espacios de Poder y Formas Sociales en la Edad Media*, Salamanca: Ediciones Universidad de Salamanca, 315–25.

Trillo San José, C. (2012), "Entre Rey y la Comunidad: El Agua del Albaizín (Granada) en la Edad Media," *Meridies: Revista de Historia Medieval* 10: 151–74.

Chapter 12

Agrawal, A. (2005), *Environmentality: Technologies of Government and the Making of Subjects*, Durham, NC: Duke University Press.

Appadurai, A. (1990), "Disjuncture and Difference in the Global Cultural Economy," *Theory Culture Society* 7 (2–3): 295–310.

Bennett, J. (2010), *Vibrant Matter: A Political Ecology of Things*. Durham, NC: Duke University Press.

Bernama (2019), "S'gor Customs Foils Attempt to Smuggle RM2.5mil Worth of Zam Zam Water," *New Straits Times*, December 24, available online: https://www.nst.com.my/news/crime-courts/2019/12/550731/sgor-customs-foils-attempt-smuggle-rm25mil-worth-zam-zam-water (accessed February 19, 2020).

Berkes, F. (2012), *Sacred Ecology*, New York: Routledge.

Brown, P. (1982), *The Cult of the Saints: Its Rise and Function in Latin Christianity*, Chicago: University of Chicago Press.

Bynum, C.W. (1988), *Holy Feast and Holy Fast: The Religious Significance of Food to Medieval Women*, Berkeley: University of California Press.

Davies, J. (2016), *The Birth of the Anthropocene*, Berkeley: University of California Press.

Eliade, M. (1959), *The Sacred and the Profane: The Nature of Religion*, trans. Richard Trask, New York: Harcourt, Brace.

Eliade, M. ([1958] 1996), *Patterns in Comparative Religion*, trans. Rosemary Sheed, Lincoln, NE: University of Nebraska Press/Bison Books.

Flood, F.B. (2014), "Bodies and Becoming: Mimesis, Mediation and the Ingestion of the Sacred in Christianity and Islam," in *Sensational Religion: Sensory Cultures in Material Practice*, New Haven: Yale University Press, 459–93.

Foltz, R.C., F.M. Denny, and A. Baharuddin (2003), eds. *Islam and Ecology: A Bestowed Trust*, Cambridge, MA: Harvard University Press.

Freedberg, D. (1989), *The Power of Images: Studies in the History and Theory of a Response*, Chicago: University of Chicago Press.

Gade, A.M. (2015), "Emotion: Feeling 'The Consolation,'" in S. Brent Plate (ed.), *Key Terms in Material Religion*, London: Bloomsbury, 79–86.

Gade, A.M. (2019a), "Managing the Rights of Nature for Te Awa Tupua," *Edge Effects* (blog), available online: https://edgeeffects.net/te-awa-tupua/ (accessed December 12, 2020).

Gade, A.M. (2019b), *Muslim Environmentalisms: Religious and Social Foundations*, New York: Columbia University Press.

Haraway, D. (2016), *Staying with the Trouble: Making Kin in the Chthulucene*, Durham, NC: Duke University Press.

Hawting, G.R. (1980), "The Disappearance and Rediscovery of Zamzam and the 'Well of the Ka'ba'," *Bulletin of the School of Oriental and African Studies* 43 (1): 44–54.

Ibn Majah, *Sunan*, https://sunnah.com/ibnmajah (accessed December 12, 2020).

Izzi Dien, M. (2000), *The Environmental Dimensions of Islam*, Cambridge, UK: Lutterworth Press.

Kingdom of Saudi Arabia, General Presidency for the Affairs of the Grand Mosque and the Prophet's Mosque, Media and Communication (2018), "Zamzam Blessed Water," (Film, 15 minutes).

Latour, B. (1993), *We Have Never Been Modern*, trans. Catherine Porter, Cambridge, MA: Harvard University Press.

Latour, B. (2017), *Facing Gaia: Eight Lectures on the New Climatic Regime*, Boston: Polity Press.

Latour, B. (2018), *Down to Earth: Politics in the New Climatic Regime*, Medford, MA: Polity.

Lynn, G. (2011), "Contaminated 'ZamZam' Water from Mecca Sold in UK," *BBC News*, May 5, available online: https://www.bbc.com/news/uk-england-london-13267205 (accessed February 19, 2020).

McDannell, C. (1995), "Lourdes Water and American Catholicism," in *Material Christianity: Religion and Popular Culture in America*, New Haven: Yale University Press, 132–62.

Merchant, C. (2015), *Autonomous Nature: Problems of Prediction and Control from Ancient Times to the Modern Era*, New York: Routledge.

Mitman, G., M. Armiero, and R. Emmett (2018), eds. *Future Remains: A Cabinet of Curiosities for the Anthropocene*, Chicago: University of Chicago Press.

Morgan, D. (1997), *Visual Piety: A History and Theory of Popular Religious Images*, Berkeley: University of California Press.

Morgan, D. (2018), *Images at Work: The Material Culture of Enchantment*, New York: Oxford University Press.

Morton, T. (2012), *The Ecological Thought*, Cambridge, MA: Harvard University Press.

Morton, T. (2013), *Hyperobjects: Philosophy and Ecology after the End of the World*, Minneapolis: University of Minnesota Press.

Orsi, R. (2018), *History and Presence*, Cambridge, MA: Harvard University Press/Belknap.

Porter, V. and L. Saif (2013), eds. *The Hajj: Collected Essays*, London: The British Museum.

Saudi Geological Survey. n.d., "The Zamzam Studies and Researches Center (ZSRC)," available online: https://sgs.org.sa/en/activities/studies-and-research/zamzam-studies-and-research/the-zamzam-studies-and-researches-center/ (accessed February 19, 2020)

Saudi Geological Survey. n.d., "Wadi Ibrahim Environmental Management System (WIEMS)," available online: https://sgs.org.sa/en/activities/studies-and-research/zamzam-studies-and-research/projects/ (accessed February 19, 2020).

Smith, J.Z. (2000), "Acknowledgments: Morphology and History in Mircea Eliade's *Patterns in Comparative Religion* (1949–1999): Part I: The Work and Its Contexts; Part 2: the Texture of the Work," *History of Religions* 39 (4): 315–31, 332–51.

Tambiah, S. (1984), *Buddhist Saints of the Forest and the Cult of Amulets: A Study in Charisma, Hagiography, Sectarianism, and Millenial Buddhism*, Cambridge: Cambridge University Press.

Tweed, T. (2008), *Crossing and Dwelling: A Theory of Religion*, Cambridge, Mass.: Harvard University Press.

Wilson, E.O. (1996), *Biophilia*, Cambridge, MA: Harvard University Press.

Yusoff, K. (2018), *A Billion Black Anthropocenes or None*, Minneapolis: University of Minnesota Press.

INDEX

Abbasid period 53, 101, 166, 167
ablutions (wudu') 175, 183, 218 n.4, 218 n.7
Abraham/Ibrahim 46, 53, 192, 195
aesthetics 6, 23, 25, 70, 81, 85, 93, 96, 189
  ethic of 7, 95
agency 9, 60, 85, 93, 128–9, 131, 133, 140–1, 187, 201
Ahmed, Shahab 6, 11, 51, 69, 71, 72, 102, 215 n.2, 215 n.4, 217 n.2
Alevis 115, 120
Algeria 55, 87, 155, 182
Alhambra Palace 176–7, 179–81, Plate 29
Ali, Noble Drew 19–20, 70–1
  see also Moorish Science Temple
Ali ibn Abi Talib 34, 37, 47
Ali Khan Vali 34–5, 38, 43
amulet (*taviz*) 2, 3, 6, 12, 127–41, Plates 22–3
angel(s) 52, 127, 136
  Gabriel 95, 99, 139
Arabia 51, 70, 150, 166, 169
  tribes 102, 144, 200
  see also Saudi Arabia
Arabic 32, 100, 133, 139–40, 157, 163
  language 20–1, 100–1, 107, 115, 117, 131, 133, 167
  Qur'an 69, 122–3
  script 38, 99, 131, 133, 140, 141, 152, 154, 163
  sources 178, 183

Bektash, Haji 117–18, 120, 122–4
Bektashi Islam 2, 5–6, 111
Bennett, Jane 8, 9, 10, 51, 52, 193
  distributive agency 3, 129, 141
  thing power 8–11
Black Muslims (in the USA) 18, 19, 20, 23, 26, 28, 29, 30
Black nationalism 23, 29
blessing/baraka 10, 12, 37, 49, 52–4, 56, 86, 99, 105, 128, 130, 152, 154
body 22, 69, 72, 78, 79, 94, 95, 96, 97, 98, 99, 103, 128, 131, 134, 135, 139, 140, 152
  discipline 22
  hair 24, 39, 42, 52, 74, 103
Burkina Faso 12, 85–6, 90–1, 94

calligraphy (*al-khat al-islami*) 143
  calligraphers 157
candles/mum 111–14, 117–24, 145
carpet 2, 31, 35–9, 43–4, 46–7, 153, Plates 5–7
Central Asia 98, 101, 117, 119, 120
Clarence 13X (Allah) 74–8
cleanliness 5, 22–3, 29
cloth or fabric 28, 96–7,101–2, 105, 130, 131, 149, 153
  see also textiles
clothing 5, 17, 19–21, 23–8, 52–3, 55, 78, 95–7, 99, 105, 107
  bow ties 27
  cape 22, 25
  female 20, 21, 23
  garment 2, 6, 7, 17, 152
  male 95, 100, 104, 105
  modest 18–23, 25, 27–9
  robes 39, 98
  turbans 20, 32, 38–9, 41, 52, 99, 100, 105
  sartorial practice 5, 18, 19–21, 23, 25, 27, 28, 71, 107
  see also headcovering

colonialism 7, 10, 45, 51, 84–9, 93, 94, 104–5, 144, 146, 158, 190–4, 202
commodity 161, 181, 199, 202
community/Ummah 18, 21, 25–6, 29, 52, 68, 74, 76–78, 82, 87, 90–1, 102, 145, 175, 191
cosmology 13, 115, 122, 124
  Sufi 116, 118
currency 168
  coins 2, 3, 161–72
  money 12, 13, 23, 27, 53, 84, 161, 167–9
  numismatics 13, 161–2, 167, 170
  see also sikka

dervish 10, 98, 111, 120, 122, 123
dhikr (*zikr*) 82–4, 89, 93–4, 97, 107, 130, 147, 211 n.4, 211 n.6
dietary practice 13, 172

education 39, 143, 155–7, 191, 192
  access to 157
  modern 146, 157
  secular 44
  religious 143, 147, 155–7
Egypt (Cairo) 11, 54–5, 70, 93, 166, 169, 171

Farrakhan, Louis 27–8, 68
  see also Nation of Islam
first four caliphs/khalifas 166
  Ali 34, 37, 47, 166
  Abu Bakr 86, 98, 166
  Umar ibn al Khattab 36, 38–9, 45, 47, 98, 166
  Uthman 54, 98, 166
Five Percenters (Nation of Gods and Earth) 5, 68, 74–9
  women as goddesses 77
Flood, Finbarr Barry 3, 101, 169, 189, 216 n.16
freemasonry 39, 44–7, 69–73
  see also Shriner movement
Friday prayer (*jummah*) 152, 154, 164

gender 7, 8, 21, 22, 28, 84
  divinity 77
  ideologies 21, 27
  segregation 27
  theology 77
genealogy 2, 71, 76, 171
Generalife Palace 174–6, 179–80, Plates 28–9
graves *see* tomb
Gruber, Christiane 3, 8, 11, 32, 52–3, 99

Hadith 4, 49, 52, 53, 55, 56, 91, 99, 102, 143, 155, 175, 184, 191, 197, 199
  Al Tirmidhi 53, 82
  Bukhari 184
  Ibn Majah 197, 199
Hafiz (poet) 96, 212 n.2
Hafiz (memorizer of the Qur'an) 143–4, 147, 149, 151–2, 154–5, 157
Hajj 10, 155, 172, 189, 195–200
haqq (rights) 10, 191, 199
Haratine 144–6, 157
headcovering 25, 100, 105, 107
  cap 2, 3, 5, 13, 22, 95–107, 118, Plates 17–20
  baseball hat 105
  fez 24, 32, 70–1, 73, 105
  headscarf (*hijab*) 25
  nashira (raised cap) 98
  qalansuwa (cap under turban) 99
  skullcap/*kippah* 98, 100
healing 3, 12–13, 50, 127, 129, 130–41, 197
  authority 139
  practices 50, 129, 130, 134
  spiritual 13
heaven 62, 72, 76, 95, 98–9, 107, 115, 122–3, 125, 191
hijab see headcovering
Hindu 6, 104, 105, 127, 128, 129, 133, 138, 141

Ibn 'Arabi 1, 10, 62, 64, 211 n.4
Ibn 'Asakir 49, 50, 54
icon 31, 35, 37, 38, 43, 48, 48, 93, 113
iconoclasm 53
idolatry (*shirk*) 12, 91, 129, 133, 141, 169

immigration 19, 25, 69
India (Delhi, Hyderabad) 3, 95–6, 98, 100–2, 104–5, 113, 127, 138, 169
Iran (Persia) 31, 32–8, 43–8, 96, 101, 169

jewelry 25–6, 72, 190
  necklace 75, 131
  see also lapel pin
jihad 86–7, 144
jinn 87, 90, 127, 134, 152
jurisprudence 155

Ka'ba 46, 195–6, 200

lamp/(*čerāḡ)* 2, 5, 6, 111–25
lapel pin 2, 5, 13, 21, 23, 68–79
law/sharia or fiqh 13, 61, 100, 117–18, 120, 123, 190–1, 197, 199

Malcolm X (El Hajj Malik El Shabazz) 18, 27, 74
Maqqari, Ahmad ibn Muhammad al- 50, 54–61, 63, Plates 10–1
Masons *see* Freemasonry
material agency 9, 93, 187
material religion 2, 8, 10, 12–13, 19, 20, 50, 190, 192–4, 196, 198, 200, 202–3
Mecca 9, 19, 67–8, 70, 76, 86, 102
Moorish Science Temple 19–21, 70
  see also Noble Drew Ali
Morocco 86, 143–4, 147, 149–50, 155, 157
mosque 12, 18, 22, 27–8, 43, 53–4, 74, 90–1, 94, 100, 103, 150, 151–4, 175, 180, 182–4, 196
  Mosque No. 7 74
Muhammad, Elijah 5, 17, 18, 21–4, 27–8, 67, 72, 74, 210 n.2
  see also Nation of Islam
Muhammad, Fard 19–21, 67–9, 74, 210 n.2
  see also Nation of Islam
Mujahid, Ali b. Dawud al- 163–4, 170–1, 216 n.14
mysticism *see* Sufi Islam

Nasir al-Din Shah 34–5, 37, 43–4, 46, 209 n.1
Nation of Islam 2, 5, 17–29, 79, 67–9 72, 74, 79, 105
Nizam al-Din Awliya 97–8, 100, 102, 105–6, 213 n.8

orientalism 7, 32, 172
Ottoman (Empire or period) 34, 40–3, 47, 55, 105

pen (*qalam*) 131, 152–4
photography 32, 35
piety (*taqwa*) 5, 7, 64 93, 102 161
pilgrimage *see* Hajj, *'umrah*
pilgrims 54, 86, 155, 195, 196–9
prayer 7, 12, 55, 90, 91, 99, 103, 105, 114, 129, 130, 133, 147, 151–3, 181
  daily (*namaz* or *salah*) 82–4, 147, 152–3
  congregational (*ju'mah*) 90, 163
  orientation 102
  prayer beads *see tasbih*
  rug 117
Prophet Muhammad 4, 13, 32–4, 37–47, 64, 67, 84, 86, 95, 97–100, 102, 105, 116, 122, 128, 139, 145, 149, 166, 184, 191, 195, 197, 200, Plates 2–9
  appearance 32, 34
  beard 31–2, 38
  images and depictions 32, 34–5, 39, 41, 43, 47, 64
  sandal 13, 49–64
  sword 32, 53
  tomb 55
  turban 99
  vision 55, 102

Qajar
  period 32–5, 209 n.3
  rulers 34, 36–8, 43, 46–7
Qur'an 1, 4, 10, 19, 33, 43, 52, 54, 62, 69, 83–4, 115–17, 119, 127, 163, 169, 172, 174, 175, 189–93, 195, 199, 201–3, 209 n.2, 215 n.14, 216 n.23, 217 n.25, 218 n.5

as healing 127, 129–31, 135–6, 138–41
images 116
learning 7, 13, 143, 145–6, 149, 152–3, 155, 157–8
memorizer *see hafiz*
recitation 83, 130–1, 151, 153, 155
as revelation 4, 35, 62, 139, 154
school 143, 151, 155–8
tablet (*lawh*) 2, 7, 143–58, Plates 24–6

race 19, 21, 27, 29, 67, 146
religio-racial 20
Rasulid 2–3, 161–72, 215 n.6, 216 n.15, 216 n.19, 216 n. 21, Plate 27
relics 49–64, 113
access to 54, 70, 75
acquisition 53
copies of 51, 54
life of 64
portable 52
sandal tracing 50, 52–64, Plates 10–13
veneration 52–4
ritual 6, 13, 50, 94, 114, 124, 203
initiation 76, 79, 97, 100, 152–3
pilgrimage 189, 195–9
purity 84, 140
Rumi, Maulana Jalaluddin 97

Sa'di 102–3
saint/wali; saints ('awliya) 52, 107, 113, 120, 123–4, 129, 172
intercession 172
Salafi Islam 12, 82–3, 90–1, 94
Saudi Arabia 10, 10, 82, 91, 166, 196, 197, 198
Sawadogo, Shaykh Boubacar 85–90, 93–4
senses 5–6, 144, 184
sensory experience 9, 11
sensory perception 114
shahadah (profession of faith) 87
Shar'iah Law *see* law
Sharrieff, Ethel Muhammad 2, 13, 16–18, 24–9
Shi'i Islam 34–5, 38, 47, 113, 116–17, 120, 166
Ahl al-bayt (people of the book) 34, 37, 46
Karbala 33
Shriner movement 70–2
Black Shriners 70–3
White Shriners 70, 73
see also Freemasons
Sikka 163, 167, 172, 215 n.10
see also currency
slavery 72, 145
freed slaves 149, 151
slave ancestry 145–7, 151
transatlantic slave trade 19–21
sovereignty 3, 73, 162, 163, 166, 167
divine 4, 172
earthly 163
political 166
sultanic 167
Spain (Granada) 2, 9, 55, 173–88
Sufism 83, 95, 97, 120
audition (*sama'* or *qawwali*) 106, 130, Plates 18–20
clothing *see* clothing; headcovering
shrine (*dargah*, *khanqah*, *zawiya*) 100, 105–7, 129, 141, 150, 152, Plates 18–21
Sufi Orders/tariqa/silsila 10, 76, 82, 86, 88, 94, 97, 103, 107
Akhi 118
Bektashi 2, 5, 6, 111–25; *see also* Bektashi, Haji Bektash
Chishti 3, 5, 95–108, Plates 17–21
Derkawa 147
Mevlevi 10
Nasiriyya 147
Qadiriyya 87
Shadhili 217 n.25
Tijani 2, 82–94, 147, Plates 15–16; Hamawi-Tijani 88–9, 93–4, Plate 16
sunnah 69, 195, 199
see also hadith
Supreme Wisdom Lessons 67, 68, 72–4, 76, 78–9, 210 nn.1–2
symbols 6, 27, 45, 71, 84–5, 89, 92, 96, 100–3, 105, 146, 170–1, 189, 190–4, 202

crescent moon 21, 34, 45, 73, 77–8
emblem 73, 75
light as 115

Tabari, al- 52, 200
talisman 90, 189
Tall, Umar 87, 89
tasbih (prayer beads/rosary) 2, 12, 13, 81–94, 147, 153, 175, Plates 14–16
taviz see amulet
tawhid (oneness of God) 4–5, 166
textile 36, 39, 96, 171
see also cloth; clothing
tomb 12, 104, 107
Turkey (Istanbul) 97, 105

Umayyad period 54, 217 n.7
'Umrah 195, 197

UNIA (United Negro Improvement Association) 20, 25, 71

Wahhabi Islam 90, 94
water
access to 173, 199
distribution 181, 196, 198, Plates 30–3
stairway 174
tribunal 182
Zamzam 2, 9–10, 189–203, Plate 33104,
well 181–5, 188, 189, 192, 195–201
white supremacy 20, 29, 71
wudu' see ablutions

Yemen 161–3, 166–72

Zamzam see water

PLATE 1 *Ultrasuede and feather outfit (center) designed by Carmen Muhammad in 2017 on display from the Contemporary Muslim Fashions exhibit at the Cooper Hewitt Smithsonian Design Museum, New York City (photo by the author).*

PLATE 2 *Iranian postcard of the "Young Muhammad," purchased in Tehran by author in 2001.*

PLATE 3 *The Prophet Muhammad in his youth, oil painting on canvas* (parda), *Iran,* c.*1900–1950. Private collection, Flint, Michigan.*

PLATE 4 *"Great Men" Carpet, Kirman, 1900–1930. World Cultures Museum, Amsterdam, 6407–1.*

PLATE 5 *"Great Men" Carpet, Kirman, 1918. Private collection, Michigan.*

PLATE 6 *Detail of Plate 5 showing the Prophet Muhammad labeled with the number 18, "Great Men" Carpet, Kirman, 1918. Private collection, Michigan.*

PLATE 7 *"Great Men" Carpet, Kirman,* c.1900–1920, *workshop of Milani Kirmani. From Sakhai 1997, 78.*

PLATE 8 *"Tableau des Principaux Grands Hommes," printed by Maison Basset, Paris, c.1850–80. Musée National de l'Education, Rouen, France.*

PLATE 9 *Detail of "Tableau des Principaux Grands Hommes," printed by Maison Basset, Paris, c.1850–80. Musée National de l'Education, Rouen, France.*

PLATE 10 *Tracing of the Prophet's Sandal from* Hadhihi sifa timthal na'l al-Nabi *copied by Ahmad ibn Muhammad al-Qadiri. The National Library of Israel (Ms. Yah. Ar. 353).*

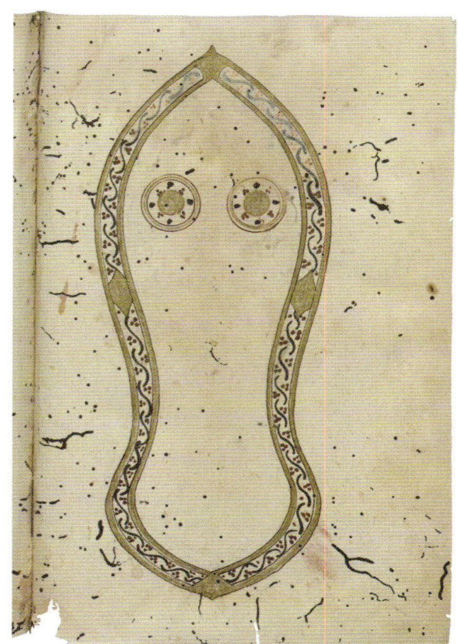

PLATE 11 *Tracing of the Prophet's Sandal from al-Maqqari,* Fath al-Muta'al. *Staatsbibliothek zu Berlin -Preußischer Kulturbesitz (Hs. Or. 10653).*

PLATE 12 *Tracing of the Prophet's Sandal from al-Maqqari,* Fath al-Muta'al. *Al-Azhar University Library, manuscripts section (Al-Maghariba, raqam khass 6299).*

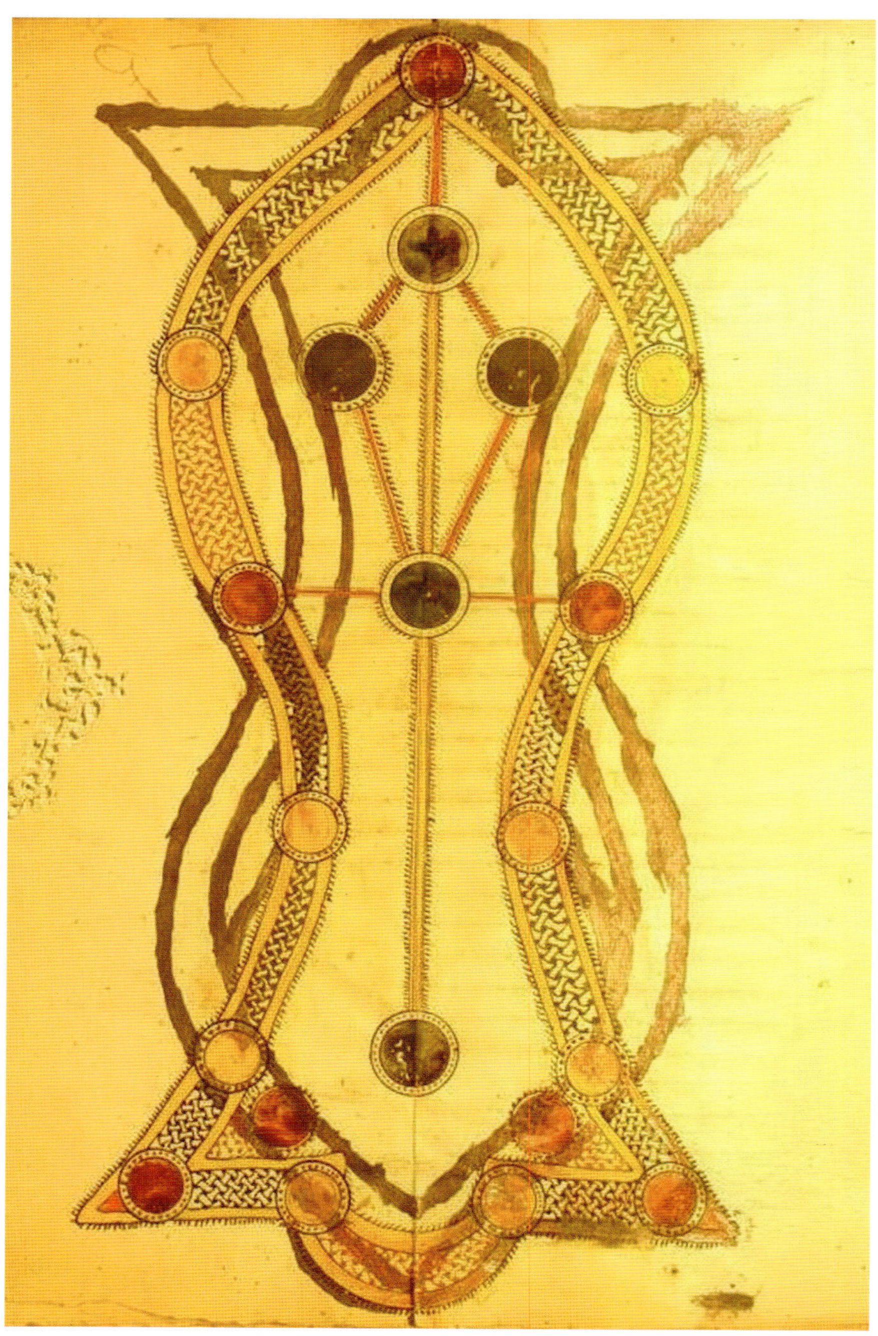

PLATE 13 *Tracing of the Prophet's Sandal from al-Maqqari,* Fath al-Muta'al. *Al-Azhar University Library, manuscripts section (Al-Maghariba,* raqam khass *6299).*

PLATE 14 *A sample of* tasbih (misbah) *(photo by C. Ryan Perkins).*

PLATE 15 A tasbih *showing the extra bead added to deceive the French (photo by C. Ryan Perkins).*

PLATE 16 *Followers of Shaykh Abdullai Maikano wearing their* tasbih. *This style of wear is comparable to the Hamawi followers of Shaykh Boubacar, although there is no connection between the two Tijaniyya groups (photo by author).*

PLATE 17 *Chishti cap given to the author at initiation in Hyderabad (photo by author).*

PLATE 18 *An elder Khadim (hereditary custodian) of the Dargah of Nizam al-Din Awliya in Delhi, wearing a white* kulah *cap wound with an ochre orange turban cloth, presides over the Qawwali performance at the Urs of Amir Khusro in 2018 (photo by Isaac Foster Mirza).*

PLATE 19 *Members of the Chishti Order, followers of the prominent modern Sufi leader, Khwaja Hasan Sani Nizami (died 2015), wear a rounded* kulah *of marigold yellow, as they listen to Qawwali at the Khanqah of Nizam al-Din Awliya, located behind the tomb of Mughal Emperor Humayun, where Bahadur Shah Zafar sought refuge from British conquest (photo by Isaac Foster Mirza).*

PLATE 20 *Young men listening to Qawwali during the Urs of Amir Khusro in Delhi sport a variety of caps that are sewn, embroidered or crocheted, including one (front center) with 786 written with sequins and one (back center) with a handkerchief tied as a cap (photo by Isaac Foster Mirza).*

PLATE 21 *Men walk in procession to the major Chishti Dargah in the Deccan, that of Banda Nawaz Gisu Daraz at Gulbarga, carrying baskets of flowers on their heads. (photo by author).*

PLATE 22 *Amma blessing patient with* dua *(prayer), 1991 (photo by author).*

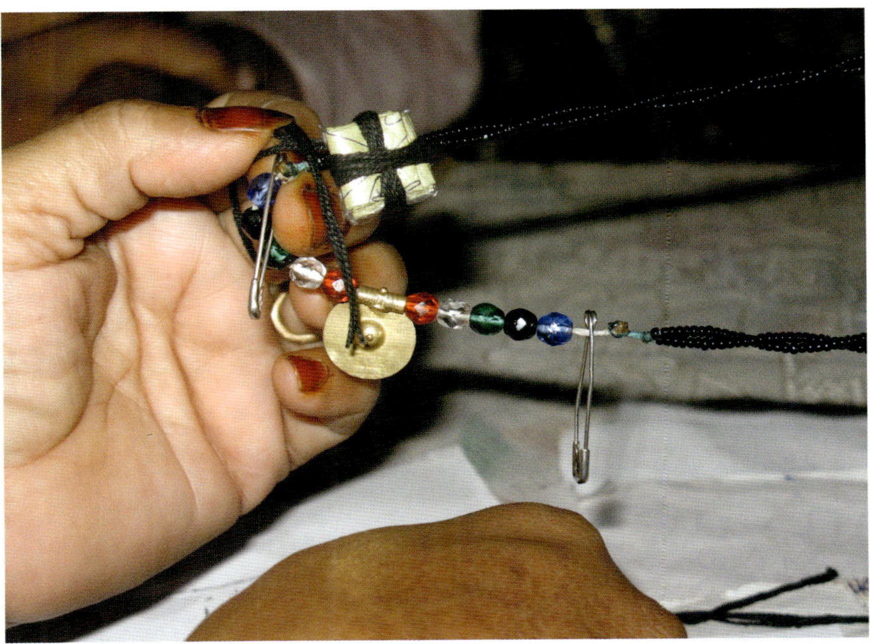

PLATE 23 Taviz *tied to Hindu woman's wedding pendant* (tali) *(photo by author).*

PLATE 24 *Qur'anic tablet exhibited at Abdellah Guennoun Cultural Building in Casablanca in July 2019 (photo courtesy of Nouria Riyadi).*

PLATE 25 *Quranic school of al-Baraka village (photo by author).*

PLATE 26 *A collection of unused tablets in Akka (photo by author).*

PLATE 27 *Tray depicting full zodiac, made in Mamluk Egypt for the Rasulid sultan al-Mu'ayyad Da'ūd b. Yūsuf (696AH/1296CE–721AH/1321CE. New York, Metropolitan Museum of Art, 91.1.605.*

PLATE 28 *The Patio de la Acequia, Generalife Palace, Granada (photo by author).*

PLATE 29 *The Alhambra and Generalife, with snow-capped mountains in the distance (photo by author).*

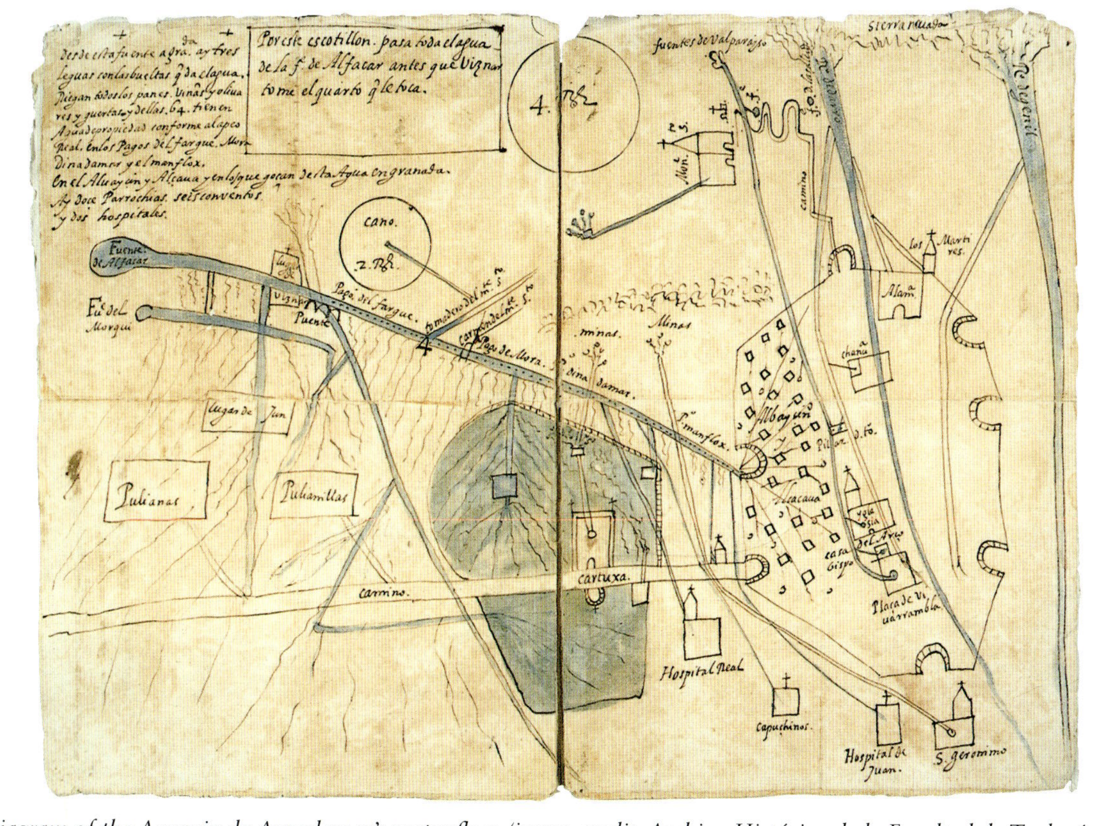

PLATE 30 *Diagram of the Acequia de Aynadamar's water flow (image credit: Archivo Histórico de la Facultad de Teología).*

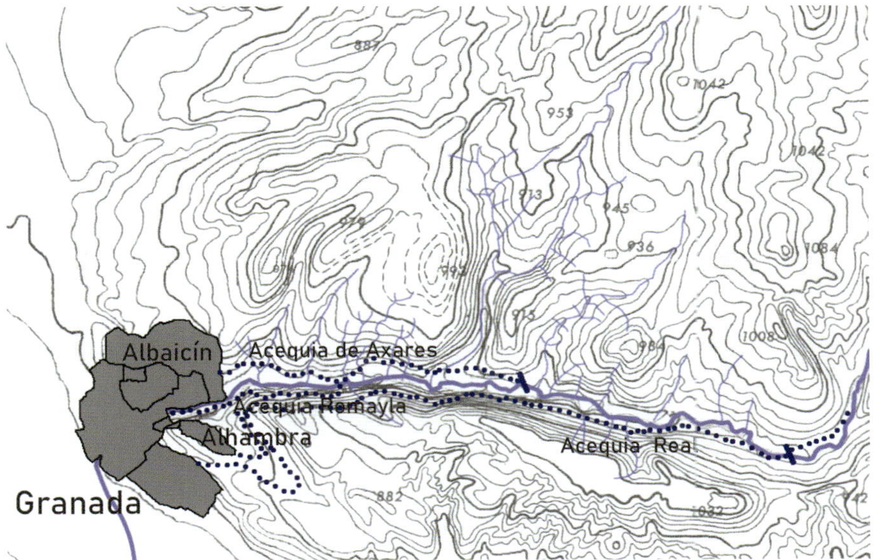

PLATE 31 *Map showing the route and source of the Acequia de Axares, Acequia Romayla, and Acequia Real (image credit: Dennis & Ruggles, after Garcia-Pulido).*

PLATE 32 *Water diverter in Timimun oasis, Algeria (photo credit: Godong/ Bridgeman Images).*

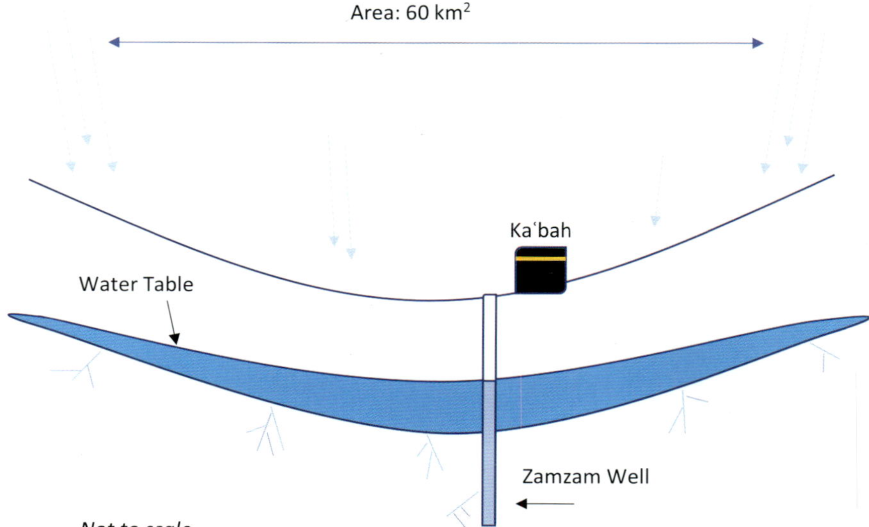

PLATE 33 *Elevation schematic of Meccan aquifer (image by author with acknowledgment to Dongeng Geologi).*